Bridge
FOR
DUMMIES®
3RD EDITION

Bridge
FOR
DUMMIES®
3RD EDITION

by Eddie Kantar

WILEY

John Wiley & Sons, Inc.

Bridge For Dummies®, 3rd Edition

Published by
John Wiley & Sons, Inc.
111 River St.
Hoboken, NJ 07030-5774
www.wiley.com

For general information on our other products and services, please contact our Customer Care Department within the U.S. at 877-762-2974, outside the U.S. at 317-572-3993, or fax 317-572-4002.

For technical support, please visit www.wiley.com/techsupport.

Wiley publishes in a variety of print and electronic formats and by print-on-demand. Some material included with standard print versions of this book may not be included in e-books or in print-on-demand. If this book refers to media such as a CD or DVD that is not included in the version you purchased, you may download this material at http://booksupport.wiley.com. For more information about Wiley products, visit www.wiley.com.

Library of Congress Control Number: 2012935792

ISBN 978-1-118-20574-7 (pbk); ISBN 978-1-118-22858-6 (ebk); ISBN 978-1-118-24083-0 (ebk); ISBN 978-1-118-26571-0 (ebk)

Manufactured in the United States of America

10 9 8 7 6

WILEY

About the Author

Eddie Kantar, a transplanted Californian, is one of the best-known bridge writers in the world. He has more than 30 bridge books in print, some translated into eight languages, and is a regular contributor to the *Bulletin, The Bridge World, Bridge Today,* and many other bridge publications.

Eddie, a two-time World Champion, is highly regarded as a player and known as one of bridge's great ambassadors.

Eddie learned to play bridge at age 11. By the time he was 17, he was teaching the game to his friends. Eddie was so enthusiastic about bridge that he often took his bridge books to school, hiding them behind his textbooks so that the teachers couldn't see him reading about bridge during class. At the University of Minnesota, where Eddie studied foreign languages, he taught bridge to pay his tuition.

Eddie gained stature as a player by winning 2 World Championship titles and 11 North American Championships. His North American titles include wins in the Spingold Knockout Teams, the Reisinger Board-a-Match Teams, the Vanderbilt Knockout Teams, and the Grand National Teams. Eddie is a Grand Master in World Bridge Federation rankings and an ACBL Grand Life Master.

Today Eddie is best known as a writer, and many of his books are considered classics. When not playing bridge or writing about the subject, he can be found playing table tennis, paddle tennis (an offshoot of tennis), or bridge at the paddle tennis courts at Venice Beach (come and join the fun in either game). By the way, Eddie is the only person ever to have played in both a World Bridge Championship and a World Table Tennis Championship (he did better at bridge).

Eddie was inducted into the Bridge Hall of Fame in 1996, the same year he was inducted into the Minnesota State Table Tennis Hall of Fame.

Dedication

I'd like to dedicate this book to my mom and dad, who stuck with me even when all the relatives were telling them that I'd come to no good end being a card player and asking why I didn't find a "regular" job like everybody else. Thanks for hanging in there with me.

Author's Acknowledgments

First, I would like to thank Elizabeth Rea, my project editor. Elizabeth is an absolute dream to work with. She couldn't have been more supportive, and her ideas, suggestions, and corrections were spot on each time. You made my life much easier.

I also had a great copy editor, Caitie Copple, and an equally wonderful technical reviewer, Dennis Cohen. What a great team!

But every team needs a coach and I had the best: my wife, Yvonne. Her patience and understanding of just how far to go in this book saved me headaches and heartaches, not to mention extra work. Just as with the first edition, there would have been no second or third edition without Yvonne. I kid you not.

Publisher's Acknowledgments

We're proud of this book; please send us your comments at http://dummies.custhelp.com. For other comments, please contact our Customer Care Department within the U.S. at 877-762-2974, outside the U.S. at 317-572-3993, or fax 317-572-4002.

Some of the people who helped bring this book to market include the following:

Acquisitions, Editorial, and Vertical Websites

Project Editor: Elizabeth Rea

(Previous Edition: Georgette Beatty)

Acquisitions Editor: Stacy Kennedy

Copy Editor: Caitlin Copple

(Previous Edition: Krista Hansing)

Assistant Editor: David Lutton

Editorial Program Coordinator: Joe Niesen

Technical Editor: Dennis Cohen

Editorial Manager: Michelle Hacker

Editorial Assistant: Alexa Koschier

Cover Photos: © iStockphoto.com/olada

Cartoons: Rich Tennant
(www.the5thwave.com)

Composition Services

Project Coordinator: Katie Crocker

Layout and Graphics: Carl Byers, Cheryl Grubbs, Corrie Niehaus

Proofreaders: Rebecca Denoncour, Betty Kish, Dwight Ramsey

Indexer: Infodex Indexing Services, Inc.

Publishing and Editorial for Consumer Dummies

    Kathleen Nebenhaus, Vice President and Executive Publisher

    Kristin Ferguson-Wagstaffe, Product Development Director

    Ensley Eikenburg, Associate Publisher, Travel

    Kelly Regan, Editorial Director, Travel

Publishing for Technology Dummies

    Andy Cummings, Vice President and Publisher

Composition Services

    Debbie Stailey, Director of Composition Services

Contents at a Glance

Table of Contents

Part V: Playing a Strong Defense and Keeping Score... 279

Chapter 17: Defending against Notrump Contracts 281

Chapter 18: Defending against Trump Contracts 299

Introduction

Bridge, quite simply, is the best card game ever. No other game even comes close. Of course, I may be a little biased. I've been playing since I was 11 years old, when my best friend's father asked our gambling group, "Why don't you guys find a good game to play?" What I found was a great game, and I've never looked back.

What exactly is it about bridge that fascinates countless millions, has fascinated countless millions, and will continue to fascinate countless millions? Let me count the ways:

✔ **Bridge is a social game:** You play with a partner and two opponents. Right off the bat, you have four people together. Inevitably, you meet a host of new friends with a strong common bond, the game of bridge. Bridge is not an "I" game — bridge is a "we" game.

✔ **Bridge is a challenging game:** Each hand is an adventure; each hand presents a unique set of conditions that you react to and solve. You have to do a little thinking. Studies have proven that playing bridge keeps the brain cells active, which is helpful when you get a bit older.

✔ **Bridge is a game of psychology:** If you fancy yourself a keen observer of human behavior, look no further. You have found your niche. Players aren't supposed to show any emotion during the play, but the dam always has a few leaks.

✔ **Bridge is fun:** Hours become minutes! Playing bridge can mean endless hours of pleasure, a host of new friends, and many laughs.

About This Book

If you're an absolute beginner, this is the book for you. I take you on a hand-held tour explaining the fundamentals in terms you can understand. I walk you through the different aspects of the game, showing you real-life examples, so you can feel comfortable with the basics before you start to play.

If you have played (or tried to play) bridge before, this book still has much to offer you. I condense my years of experience with the game into tips and hints that can make you a better player. And you don't have to read the book from start to finish if you don't want to; just flip it open and find the chapter or part on the topic that you want to know more about.

If you're a bridge novice, eventually you'll have to play a few hands to feel like a real bridge player. This book offers an easy-to-follow path that will increase your comfort zone when you actually have to play on your own!

As an update to this new edition, I've added an appendix that covers the bidding system most commonly used in the United Kingdom, called *Acol*. This appendix is a big help to up-and-coming players throughout the U.K. The play of the hand sections are standard fare throughout the world, and the section on defensive carding is also played by the majority of players worldwide as well.

Conventions Used in This Book

No, not bridge "conventions" yet! The conventions in this section are the ones I use to help you navigate this book with maximum ease.

For example, I use a few symbols when referring to cards and bids. In a deck of cards, you have four suits: spades (♠), hearts (♥), diamonds (♦), and clubs (♣). When I refer to a particular card, I use abbreviations. For example, the six of spades becomes ♠6, and the jack of hearts transforms into ♥J. However, when discussing the final contract, I use 6♠, not ♠6.

I talk a lot about cards in this book. Sometimes I want to show you all the cards in your hand, and sometimes I want to show you the cards in every player's hand (that's 52 cards!). Instead of listing those cards in the text, I set them aside in figures so you can more easily see who has which cards. The cards in a hand are separated by suit, making it even easier to see each player's holdings.

In these figures, you may notice that I assign a direction to each of the four players: You see a North, a South, an East, and a West. Again, I use directions to make it easier for you to follow the play as it goes around the table. For most of the book, you are South. If I want you to see something from a different perspective, I tell you where you're seated.

When I talk about bidding (especially in Parts III and IV), I use a table like the following to show you how a bidding sequence progresses.

South	West	North	East
1♣	1NT	Pass	Pass
Pass			

Don't worry about what this bidding means. For now, I just want you to understand that you read these tables starting at the upper-left corner, continuing to the right until the fourth player, and then going back to the second line and the first player. For example, for the preceding sequence, the bidding starts with the first player, South (who bids 1♣) and continues to the right until the fourth player, East (who passes). Then the sequence goes back to South, the first player, who passes.

To top it off, I use a few other general conventions:

- *Italics* highlight defined terms.
- **Boldface** text highlights key words in bulleted lists and the action part of numbered steps.
- `Monofont` is used for Web addresses.

At times, you may think I overrun you with rules, but I'm just giving you guidelines, something to get you started. When you begin to play, you'll see occasional exceptions to these guidelines. In bridge, "always" and "never" don't apply. Just remember that bridge is based most of all on common sense. After reading this book, you'll have a good idea of what to do when you encounter new situations.

What You're Not to Read

When I wrote this book, it wasn't with the intention of telling you what not to read! But if you can live without some items, they're the sidebars (those shaded gray boxes featured throughout the chapters). Actually, some of them are pretty funny, but if you don't read them, you won't lose any of what you're supposed to be finding out.

Foolish Assumptions

I'm assuming that you're not going to understand everything you read the first time around. Nobody does. Think of bridge as a foreign language. Patience, patience, patience.

I'm also assuming that you will go out and find three other people in your shoes who want to play bridge so you can practice. This is the "living end" for a beginner.

And I'm assuming that some of you want to understand the basics of bridge, while others may be seasoned players who want to pick up a few new techniques. I'm foolishly assuming that I can help both groups.

How This Book Is Organized

This book is divided into seven parts, each focusing on a different aspect of the game.

Part I: Beginning with Basic Notrump Play

Chapter 1 starts at ground zero and describes the mechanics of the game, giving you a bird's-eye view of bridge. The rest of the part discusses various techniques for taking tricks in a notrump contract.

Part II: Playing the Hand in a Trump Contract

In this part, you discover the special know-how you need so you can bring home the tricks when you end up in a trump contract.

Part III: Bidding for Fun and Profit

This part also covers the fundamentals of bidding — when to bid, how high to bid, and how to shut up your partner!

Part IV: Forging Ahead with Advanced Bidding Techniques

This part deals with defensive bidding, doubles, and redoubles. I also introduce slam bidding.

Part V: Playing a Strong Defense and Keeping Score

You just can't let your opponents walk all over you! In this part, you discover how to stick out your foot and really trip up your opponents with stellar defense. You also find out all about bridge scoring.

Part VI: Feeding Your Addiction to Bridge

You will come to love this game and want more of it. In this part, you can read up on finding the best software, playing in clubs and tournaments, and playing on the Internet.

Part VII: The Part of Tens

In this part, you can read about the most important factor in any hand — your partner. This part also offers a list of some really great bridge resources that you can use after you put this book back on the shelf. (But of course, you can always take this book off the shelf and use it over and over again!)

Icons Used in This Book

The icons used in this book highlight important topics and help you pick out what you want to know.

Bridge has a language all its own, and I point you to a few key terms in this new language.

If you can't remember everything you read in this book, don't worry, you're not alone — but do try to keep these items in mind.

I pack this book full of helpful hints that make you a smarter player, faster.

Watch out! You could lose many tricks or something equally disastrous if you ignore items marked with this icon.

Where to Go from Here

If you are completely new to bridge, head straight to Chapter 1 so you can get a feel for the game. If you're an old bridge pro, you can start anywhere you like and read the chapters in any order.

I describe many plays and sample hands throughout this book. To get a real feel for the game, try reading the book with a deck of cards nearby. In fact, you can save yourself weeks or months of time if you lay out the cards that you see in the example diagrams and play the cards as I suggest.

Better yet, try to find three other players who want to play this exciting game. You can read the book together and actually practice playing the hands as you read. Experience is the best teacher, and if you're not ready for a real hand, you can use the material in this book as a kind of dry run.

If, during the course of reading this book, you feel like you just have to get in on the action, feel free to jump into any game you can find. Play as often as you can. It's the best way to learn. You can find information about bridge clubs and tournaments in Chapter 21.

Finally, log on to the Net for more bridge info or even online play! Yes, you can play online! Check out Chapter 22 for more on this topic.

Part I

Beginning with Basic Notrump Play

The 5th Wave · By Rich Tennant

"I'm happy to be the 'dummy', but I prefer the term 'marionette.'"

In this part . . .

Don't get scared off by the title of the first chapter — "Going to Bridge Boot Camp." I promise, I won't ask you to drop and give me 20 sit-ups. But you can consider this chapter a kind of induction into the world of bridge; I cover all the fundamentals you need to get a quick start with the game.

In the rest of the part, I go over the various elements of playing a hand at a notrump contract, in which the highest card in the suit wins the shootin' match (the trick). I show you how to count and take sure tricks, use winning techniques, and outsmart your opponents.

Chapter 1

Going to Bridge Boot Camp

In This Chapter

▶ Gathering what you need to play bridge

▶ Taking a quick look at the basic points of the game

▶ Building your bridge skills with available resources

*Y*ou made a good choice, a very good choice, about learning to play bridge. Perhaps I'm biased, but bridge is the best card game ever. You can play bridge all over the world, and wherever you go, you can make new friends automatically by starting up a game of bridge. Bridge can be more than a game — it can be a common bond.

In this chapter, I talk about some basic concepts that you need to have under your belt to get started playing bridge. Consider this chapter your first step into the game. If you read this whole chapter, you'll graduate from Bridge Boot Camp. Sorry — you don't get a diploma. But you do get the thrill of knowing what you need to know to start playing bridge.

Starting a Game with the Right Stuff

Before you can begin to play bridge, you need to outfit yourself with some basic supplies. Actually, you may already have some of these items around the house, just begging for you to use them in your bridge game. What do you need? Here's your bottom-line list:

✔ Four warm bodies, including yours. Just find three friends who are interested in playing. Don't worry that no one knows what they're doing. Everyone begins knowing nothing; some of us even end up that way.

✔ A table — a square one is best. In a pinch, you can play on a blanket, on a bed, indoors, outdoors, or even on a computer if you can't find a game.

✔ One deck of playing cards (remove the jokers).

✔ A pencil and a piece of paper to keep score on. You can use any old piece of paper — a legal pad, the back of a grocery list, or even an ancient piece of papyrus will do.

I've been playing bridge for a long time now, so let me offer you a few hints on how you can make getting started with the game a little easier:

✔ Watch a real bridge game to observe the mechanics of the game.

✔ Follow the sample hands in this book by laying out the cards to correspond with the cards in the figures. Doing so gives you a feel for the cards and makes the explanations easier to follow.

Ranking the Cards

A deck has 52 cards divided into four suits: spades (♠), hearts (♥), diamonds (♦), and clubs (♣).

Each suit has 13 cards: the AKQJ10 (which are called the *honor cards*) and the 98765432 (the *spot cards*).

The 13 cards in a suit all have a rank — that is, they have a pecking order. The ace is the highest-ranking card, followed by the king, the queen, the jack, and the 10, on down to the lowly 2 (also called the *deuce*).

Because each card has a ranking, the more high-ranking cards you have in your hand, the better. The more honor cards you have, the stronger your hand. You can never have too many honor cards.

Knowing Your Directions

In bridge, the players are nameless souls — they are known by directions. When you sit down at a table with three pals to play bridge, imagine that the table is a compass. You're sitting at due South, your partner sits across from you in the North seat, and your opponents sit East and West.

In Parts I and II of this book, you're South for every hand, and your partner is North. Just as in the opera, where the tenor always gets the girl, in a bridge diagram, you're represented as South — you are called the *declarer,* and you always get to play the hand. Your partner, North, is always the *dummy* (no slur intended!). Don't worry about what these terms mean just yet — the idea is that you play every hand from the South position. Keep in mind that in real life, South doesn't play every hand — just in this book, every newspaper column, and most bridge books!

Figure 1-1 diagrams the playing table. Get acquainted with this diagram: You see some form of it throughout this book, not to mention in newspaper columns and magazines. For me, this diagram was a blessing in disguise — I never could get my directions straight until I started playing bridge.

Figure 1-1:
You're
South, your
partner is
North, and
your oppo-
nents are
East and
West.

North (Your Partner)

West   East

South (You)

Playing the Game in Phases

First and foremost, bridge is a partnership game — you swim together and you sink together. Your opponents are in the same boat. In bridge, you don't score points individually — you score points as a team. (I cover scoring in Chapter 20, and I suggest you just ignore keeping score until you have a handle on the ins and outs of the game.)

Each hand of bridge is divided into four phases, which occur in the same order:

1. Dealing

2. Bidding

3. Playing

4. Scoring

Phase 1: Dealing

The game starts with each player seated facing his or her partner. The cards are shuffled and placed on the table face down. Each player selects a card, and who-ever picks the highest card deals the first hand. The four cards on the table are returned to the deck, the deck is reshuffled, and the player to the dealer's right cuts the cards and returns them to the dealer. (After each hand, the deal rotates to the left so one person doesn't get stuck doing all the dealing.)

The cards are dealt one at a time, starting with the player to the dealer's left and moving in a clockwise rotation until each player has 13 cards.

Wait until the dealer distributes all the cards before you pick up your hand. That's bridge etiquette lesson number one. When each player has 13 cards, pick up and sort your hand using the following tips:

- ✔ You can sort the cards in any number of ways, but I recommend sorting your cards into the four suits.

- ✔ Alternate your black suits (clubs and spades) with your red suits (diamonds and hearts) so you don't confuse a black card for another black card or a red card for another red card. It's a bit disconcerting to think you're playing a heart, only to see a diamond come floating out of your hand.

- ✔ Hold your cards back, way back, so only you can see them. Think vertically. Winning at bridge is difficult when your opponents can see your hand.

Phase 2: Bidding for tricks

Bidding in bridge can be compared to an auction. The auctioneer tells you what the minimum bid is, and the first bid starts from that point or higher. Each successive bid must be higher than the last, until someone bids so high that everyone else wants out. When you want out of the bidding in bridge, you say "Pass." After three consecutive players say "Pass," the bidding is over. However, if you pass and someone else makes a bid, just as at an auction, you can reenter the bidding. If nobody makes an opening bid and all four players pass consecutively, the bidding is over, the hand is reshuffled and redealt, and a new auction begins.

In real-life auctions, people often bid for silly things, such as John F. Kennedy's golf clubs or Andy Warhol's cookie jars. In bridge, you bid for something really valuable — tricks. The whole game revolves around *tricks*.

Some of you may remember the card game of War from when you were a kid. (If you don't remember, just pretend that you do and follow along.) In War, two players divide the deck between them. Each player takes a turn placing a card face up on the table. The player with the higher card takes the *trick*.

In bridge, four people each place a card face up on the table, and the highest card in the suit that has been led takes the trick. The player who takes the trick collects the four cards, puts them face down in a neat pile, and leads to the next trick. Because each player has 13 cards, 13 tricks are fought over and won or lost on each hand.

Think of bidding as an estimation of how many of those 13 tricks your side (or their side) thinks it can take. The bidding starts with the dealer and moves to his left in a clockwise rotation. Each player gets a chance to bid, and a player can either bid or pass when his turn rolls around. The least you can bid is for seven tricks, and the maximum you can bid is for all 13. The bidding goes around and around the table, with each player either bidding or passing until three players in a row say "Pass."

The last bid (the one followed by three passes) is called the *final contract*. No, that's not something the Mafia puts out on you. It's simply the number of tricks that the bidding team must take to score points (see Parts III and IV for more about bidding and Chapter 20 for more about scoring).

Phase 3: Playing the hand

After the bidding for tricks is over, the play begins. Either your team or the other team makes the final bid. Because you are the star of this book, assume that your team makes the final bid for nine tricks. Therefore, your goal is to win at least nine of the 13 possible tricks.

If you take nine (or more) tricks, your team scores points. If you take fewer than nine tricks, you're penalized, and your opponents score points. In the following sections, I describe a few important aspects of playing a hand of bridge.

The opening lead and the dummy

After the bidding determines who the *declarer* is (the one who plays the hand), that person's partner becomes the *dummy*. The players to the declarer's left and right are considered the *defenders*. The West player (assuming that you're South) *leads*, or puts down the first card face up in the middle of the table. That first card is called the *opening lead*, and it can be any card of West's choosing.

When the opening lead lands on the table, the game really begins to roll. The next person to play is the dummy — but instead of playing a card, the dummy puts her 13 cards face up on the table in four neat vertical rows starting with the highest card, one row for each suit, and then bows out of the action entirely. After she puts down her cards (also called the *dummy*), she says and does nothing, leaving the other three people to play the rest of the hand. The dummy always puts down the dummy. What a game!

Because the dummy is no longer involved in the action, each time it's the dummy's turn to play, you, the declarer, must physically take a card from the dummy and put it in the middle of the table. In addition, you must play a card from your own hand when it's your turn.

The fact that the declarer gets stuck with playing all the team's cards while the dummy is off munching on snacks may seem a bit unfair. But you do have an advantage over the defenders: You get to see your partner's cards before you play, which allows you to plan a strategy of how to win those nine tricks (or however many tricks you need to make the final contract).

Following suit

The opening lead determines which suit the other three players must play. Each of the players must *follow suit,* meaning that they must play a card in the suit that was led if they have one. For example, pretend that the opening lead from West is a heart. Down comes the dummy, and you (and everyone else at the table) can see the dummy's hearts as well as your own hearts. Because you must play the same suit that is led if you have a card in that suit, you have to play a heart, any heart that you want, from the dummy. You place the heart of your choice face up on the table and wait for your right-hand opponent (East, assuming that the dummy is North) to play a heart. After she plays a heart, you play a heart from your hand. Voilà: Four hearts now sit on the table. The first trick of the game! Whoever has played the highest heart takes the trick. One trick down and only 12 to go — you're on a roll!

What if a player doesn't have a card in the suit that has been led? Then, and only then, can a player choose a card, any card, from another suit and play it. This move is called a *discard.* When you discard, you're literally throwing away a card from another suit. A discard can never win a trick.

In general, you discard worthless cards that can't take tricks, saving good-looking cards that may take tricks later. Sometimes, however, the bidding designates a *trump suit* (think wild cards). In that case, when a suit is led and you don't have it, you can discard from another suit or take the trick with a card from the trump suit. For more info, see "Understanding Notrump and Trump Play" later in this chapter.

If you can follow suit, you must. If you have a card in the suit that's been led but you play a card in another suit by mistake, you *revoke.* Not good. If you're detected, penalties may be involved. Don't worry, though — everybody revokes once in a while. I once lost a National Championship by revoking on the last hand of the tournament.

Playing defense

Approximately 25 percent of the time, you'll be the declarer; 25 percent of the time, you'll be the dummy; and the remaining 50 percent of the time, you'll be on defense! You need to have a good idea of which card to lead to the first trick and how to continue after you see the dummy. You want to be able to take all the tricks your side has coming to defeat the contract. For example, if your opponents bid for nine tricks, you need at least five tricks to defeat the contract. Think of taking five tricks as your goal. Remember, defenders can't see each other's hands, so they have to use signals (legal ones) to tell their partner what they have. They do this by making informative leads and discards that announce to the partner (and the declarer) what they have in the suit they are playing.

I show you winning defensive techniques in Part V.

Winning and stacking tricks

The player who plays the highest card in the suit that has been led wins the trick. That player sweeps up the four cards and puts them in a neat stack, face down, a little off to the side. The declarer "keeps house" for his team by stacking tricks into piles so everyone can see how many tricks that team has won. The defender (your opponent) who wins the first trick does the same for his or her side.

The player who takes the first trick *leads first,* or plays the first card, to the second trick. That person can lead any card in any suit desired, and the other three players must follow suit if they can.

The play continues until all 13 tricks have been played. After you play to the last trick, each team counts up the number of tricks it has won.

Phase 4: Scoring, and then continuing

After the smoke clears and the tricks are counted, you know soon enough whether the declarer's team made its contract (that is, took at least the number of tricks they have contracted for). The score is then registered — see Chapter 20 for more about scoring.

After the hand has been scored, the deal moves one player to the left. So if South dealt the first hand, West is now the dealer. Then North deals the next hand, then East, and then the deal reverts back to South.

Understanding Notrump and Trump Play

Have you ever played a card game that has wild cards? When you play with wild cards, playing a wild card automatically wins the trick for you. Sometimes wild cards can be jokers, deuces, or aces. It doesn't matter what the card is; if you have one, you know that you have a sure winner. In bridge, you have wild cards, too, called *trump cards*. However, in bridge, the trump cards are *really* wild, because they change from hand to hand, depending on the bidding.

The bidding determines whether a hand will be played with trump cards or in a *notrump contract* (a hand with no trump cards). If the final bid happens to end in some suit as opposed to notrump, that suit becomes the trump suit for the hand. For example, suppose that the final bid is 4♠. This bid determines that spades are trump (or wild) for the entire hand. For more about playing a hand at a trump contract, see Part II.

More contracts are played at notrump than in any of the four suits. When the final bid ends in notrump, the highest card played in the suit that has been led wins the trick. All the hands that you play in Part I are played at notrump.

Building Your Skills with Clubs, Tournaments, and the Internet

You know, you're not in this bridge thing alone. You'll find help around every corner. You won't believe how much is available for interested beginners.

- ✔ **Clubs:** Most bridge clubs offer beginning bridge lessons and/or supervised play. They also hold games that are restricted to novices, not just open games.

- ✔ **Tournaments:** Many tournaments offer free lectures for novice players as well as novice tournament events and supervised play. Watching experts (or anyone else) play is free.

- ✔ **The Internet:** After you get the knack, you can play bridge 24 hours a day online . . . free! The Internet is also an excellent venue to watch people play and learn the mechanics and techniques of the game (both what to do and what not to do!).

To find out more about expanding your bridge experiences, head for Part VI.

So what's the fascination with bridge?

You may have met a few unfortunates who are totally hooked on playing bridge. They just can't get enough of it. Being a charter member of that club, I can offer a few words on why people can get so wrapped up in the game.

✔ One fascination is the bidding. Bidding involves a lot of partner-to-partner communication skills, and cleverly exchanging information between you and your partner in the special language of the game is a great challenge. Your opponents also pass information back and forth during the bidding, so figuring out what they're telling each other is another challenge. However, no secrets! They are entitled to know what your bids mean and vice versa. Bidding is such an art that some bridge books deal entirely with bidding. (I cover bidding in Parts III and IV.)

✔ Another hook for the game is taking tricks. You get to root out all kinds of devious ways to take tricks, both as a declarer and as a defender.

✔ And don't forget the human element. Bridge is much more than a game of putting down and picking up cards. Emotions enter into the picture — sooner or later, every emotion or personality trait that you see in life emerges at the bridge table.

Chapter 2

Counting and Taking Sure Tricks

. . . .

In This Chapter

▶ Identifying sure tricks in your hand and the dummy's hand

▶ Adding sure tricks to your trick pile

. . . .

*I*f you're sitting at a blackjack table in Las Vegas, you're a goner if someone catches you counting cards. However, if you're at a bridge table and you don't count cards, you're also a goner, but in a different way.

When you play a bridge hand, you need to count several things — most importantly, you need to count your tricks. The game of bridge revolves around tricks. You bid for tricks, you take as many tricks as you can in the play of the hand, and your opponents try to take as many tricks as they can on defense. Tricks, tricks, tricks.

In this chapter, I show you how to spot a sure trick in its natural habitat — in your hand or in the dummy. I also show you how to take those sure tricks to your best advantage. (See Chapter 1 for an introduction to tricks and the dummy.)

Before the play of the hand begins, the bidding determines the final contract. However, I have purposely omitted the bidding process in this discussion. For the purpose of this chapter, just pretend the bidding is over and the dummy has come down. In Parts I and II, I want you to concentrate on how to count and take tricks to your best advantage. After you discover the trick-taking capabilities of honor cards and long suits, the bidding makes much more sense. If you can't wait, turn to Part III to discover the wonders of bidding for tricks. (I even include advanced bidding techniques in Part IV.)

Counting Sure Tricks After the Dummy Comes Down

The old phrase "You need to know where you are to know where you're going" comes to mind when playing bridge. After you know your *final contract* (how many tricks you need to take), you then need to figure out how to win all the tricks necessary to make your contract.

Depending on which cards you and your partner hold, your side may hold some sure winners, called *sure tricks* — tricks you can take at any time right from the get-go. You should be very happy to see sure tricks in either your hand or in the dummy. You can never have too many sure tricks.

Sure tricks depend on whether you have the ace in a particular suit (either in your hand or in the dummy). Because you get to see the dummy after the opening lead, you can see quite clearly if any aces are lurking in the dummy. If you notice an ace, the highest ranking card in the suit, why not get greedy and look for a king, the second-highest ranking card in the same suit? Two sure tricks are better than one!

Counting sure tricks boils down to the following points:

- ✔ If you or the dummy has the ace in a suit (but no king), count one sure trick.
- ✔ If you have both the ace and the king in the same suit (between the two hands), count two sure tricks.
- ✔ If you have the ace, king, and queen in the same suit (between the two hands), count three sure tricks. Happiness!

In Figure 2-1, your final contract is for nine tricks. After you settle on the final contract, the play begins. West makes the opening lead and decides to lead the ♠Q. Down comes the dummy, and you swing into action, but first you need to do a little planning. You need to count your sure tricks. What follows in this section is a sample hand and diagrams where I demonstrate how to count sure tricks.

North (Dummy)
♠ 7 6 5
♥ J 10 9
♦ A 2
♣ J 10 9 6 5

```
      N
  W       E
      S
```

Figure 2-1:
Looking for
nine sure
tricks is
your goal.

South (You)
♠ A K 8
♥ A K Q
♦ K Q J 5
♣ 4 3 2

Mind your manners: Being a dummy with class

The dummy doesn't do much to help you count and take sure tricks except lay down her cards. After her cards are on the table, the dummy shouldn't contribute anything else to the hand — except good dummy etiquette.

As the play progresses, the dummy isn't supposed to make faces, utter strange noises, or make disjointed body movements, such as jerks or twitches. Sometimes such restraint takes superhuman willpower, particularly when her partner, the declarer, screws up big time. A good dummy learns to control herself. If you end up as the dummy and get fidgety, you can always leave the table.

Eyeballing your sure tricks in each suit

You count your sure tricks one suit at a time. After you know how many tricks you have, you can make further plans about how to win additional tricks. I walk you through each suit in the following sections, showing you how to count sure tricks.

Recognizing the two highest spades

When the dummy comes down, you can see that your partner has three small spades (♠7, ♠6, and ♠5) and you have the ♠A and ♠K, as you see in Figure 2-2.

Because the ♠A and the ♠K are the two highest spades in the suit, you can count two sure spade tricks. (If you or the dummy also held the ♠Q, you could count three sure spade tricks.)

When you have sure tricks in a suit, you don't have to play them right away. You can take sure tricks at any point during the play of the hand.

North (Dummy)
♠ 7 6 5

Figure 2-2:
Digging up
sure spade
tricks.

```
    N
 W     E
    S
```

South (You)
♠ A K 8

Counting up equally divided hearts

Figure 2-3 shows the hearts that you hold in this hand. Notice that you and the dummy have the five highest hearts in the deck: the ♥AKQJ10 (the five cards known as *honor cards*).

North (Dummy)
♥ J 10 9

Figure 2-3:
Your hearts
are heavy
with honor
cards.

```
    N
W       E
    S
```

South (You)
♥ A K Q

Your wonderful array of hearts is worth only three sure tricks because both hands have the same number of cards. When you play a heart from one hand, you must play a heart from the other hand. As a result, after you play the ♥AKQ, the dummy won't have any more hearts left and neither will you. You wind up with only three heart tricks because the suit is *equally divided* (you have the same number of cards in both hands).

When you have an equal number of cards in a suit on each side, you can never take more tricks than the number of cards in each hand. For example, if you both hold four hearts, it doesn't matter how many high hearts you have between your hand and the dummy — you can never take more than four heart tricks. Take a look at Figure 2-4 to see how the tragic story of an equally divided suit unfolds.

In Figure 2-4, you have only one heart in each hand: the ♥A and the ♥K. All you can take is one lousy heart trick. If you lead the ♥A, you have to play the ♥K from the dummy. If the dummy leads the ♥K first, you have to "overtake" it with your ♥A. This is the only time you can have the ace and king of the same suit between your hand and dummy and take only one trick. It's too sad for words.

Figure 2-4:
An honor
collision
causes
some honor
cards to
become
worthless.

North (Dummy)
♥ K

```
    N
W       E
    S
```

South (You)
♥ A

Attacking unequally divided diamonds

In Figure 2-5, you can see that South holds four diamonds (♦K, ♦Q, ♦J, and ♦5), while North holds only two (♦A and ♦2). When one partner holds more cards in a suit, the suit is *unequally divided*.

North (Dummy)

♦ A 2

Figure 2-5:
An
unequally
divided suit
can be a
gem.

```
    N
 W     E
    S
```

South (You)

♦ K Q J 5

Strong unequally divided suits offer oodles of tricks, provided that you play the suit correctly. For example, take a look at how things play out with the cards in Figure 2-5. Suppose you begin by leading the ♦5 from your hand and play the ♦A from the dummy, which is one trick. Now the lead is in the dummy because the dummy has taken the trick. Continue by playing ♦2 and then play the ♦K from your hand. Now that the lead is back in your hand, play the ♦Q and then the ♦J. Don't look now, but you've just won tricks with each of your honor cards — four in all. Notice if you had played the king first and then the ♦5 over to dummy's ace, dummy would have no more diamonds and there you would be with the good queen and jack of diamonds in your hand, perhaps marooned forever!

Lean a little closer to hear a five-star tip: If you want to live a long and happy life with unequally divided suits that contain a number of *equal* honors (also called *touching* honors, such as a king and queen or queen and jack), play the high honor cards from the short side first. What does *short side* mean? In an unequally divided suit, the hand with fewer cards is called the short side. In Figure 2-5, the dummy has two diamonds to your four diamonds, making the dummy hand the short side. When you play the high honor from the short side first, you end up by playing the high honors from the *long side,* the hand that starts with more cards in the suit, last. (In this example, you have the longer diamonds.) This technique allows you to take the maximum number of tricks possible. And now you know why you started by leading the ♦5 over to the ♦A. You wanted to play the high honor from the short side first. You are getting to be a player!

Finding no sure tricks in a suit with no aces: The clubs

When the dummy comes down, you may see that neither you nor the dummy has the ace in a particular suit, such as the club suit in Figure 2-6. You have ♣4, ♣3, and ♣2; the dummy has ♣J, ♣10, ♣9, ♣6, and ♣5.

Figure 2-6:
Forget about counting sure tricks in a suit that doesn't have the ace in either your hand or the dummy.

North (Dummy)
♣ J 10 9 6 5

South (You)
♣ 4 3 2

Not all that pretty is it? The opponents have the ♣A, ♣K, and ♣Q. You have no sure tricks in clubs because you don't have the ♣A. If neither your hand nor the dummy has the ace in a particular suit, you can't count any sure tricks in that suit.

Adding up your sure tricks

After you assess how many sure tricks you have in each suit, you can do some reckoning. You need to add up all your sure tricks and see if you have enough to make your final contract.

Just to get some practice at adding up tricks, go ahead and add up your sure tricks from the hand shown in Figure 2-1. Remember to look at what's in the dummy's hand as well as your own cards. The total number of tricks is what's important, and you have the following:

- ✔ **Spades:** Two sure tricks: ♠A and ♠K.

- ✔ **Hearts:** Three sure tricks: ♥AKQ.

- ✔ **Diamonds:** Four sure tricks: ♦AKQJ.

- ✔ **Clubs:** No sure tricks because you have no ace. Bad break, buddy.

You're in luck — you have the nine tricks that you need to make your final contract. Now all you have to do is take them. You can do it.

More often than not, you won't have enough sure tricks to make your contract. You can see what will become of you in Chapter 3, which deals with various techniques of notrump play designed to teach you how to develop extra tricks when you don't have all the top cards in a suit.

Taking Sure Tricks

Having sure tricks is only half the battle; taking those sure tricks is the other half. In the following sections, I show you how to do it.

Starting with the strongest suit

When you have enough sure tricks between the two hands to make your contract, you *don't* have to take the tricks in any particular order. However, a reliable guideline to get you off on the right foot is to start by first playing winning cards in your strongest suit (the suit that offers you the most tricks). In the case of the hand shown in Figure 2-1, start by playing diamonds.

Recall that West's opening lead was the ♠Q. Suppose you take the trick with the ♠A, and now the lead is in your hand. You then take your four diamond tricks (♦AKQJ), and then you can take three more heart tricks by playing the ♥AKQ. Finally, you take your ninth trick with the ♠K. Your opponents take the last four tricks. No big deal — you've taken nine tricks and made your contract.

Taking sure tricks in unequally divided suits

The cards in Figure 2-7 show another example of the advantage of starting with the short-side honor cards.

Figure 2-7: Serving up sure tricks, starting with the short-side honor cards.

North (Dummy)
♠ Q J 4 3

```
  N
W   E
  S
```

South (You)
♠ A K 2

In the example shown in Figure 2-7, you decide to play spades, an unequally divided suit. You also (smartly) decide to play the high honors from the short side (your hand is the short side because you have three cards to dummy's four cards). Play the ♠A and then the ♠K. You remain with the ♠2, and the dummy has two winning tricks, the ♠Q and ♠J. Lead your ♠2 and take the trick with the dummy's ♠J. The lead is now in the dummy, and you can take a fourth spade trick with the ♠Q. You have just added four tricks to your trick pile. They can't stop you now!

Chapter 3

Using Winning Trick Techniques at Notrump Play

In This Chapter

▶ Getting the most out of your lower honor cards

▶ Squeezing extra tricks from your small cards

Winning at bridge is a breeze if you always have enough sure tricks to make your contract. The sad news is that you seldom have enough. You must come up with other ways of taking tricks, ways that may mean temporarily surrendering the lead (the right to put down the first card) to your opponents. In this chapter, I show you clever techniques to win those extra tricks that you may need to make your contract in notrump play. Specifically, I explain how to establish tricks with lower honor cards and take tricks with small cards. (Chapter 4 explains how to outsmart your opponents by side-stepping their high honor cards and cutting their lines of communication.)

Throughout this chapter, you may notice that many figures show cards in only one suit. Sometimes I want you to focus on one suit at a time, so in the following figures, you see suits that are ideal for creating extra tricks you need. Don't forget: I always put you in the hot seat by making you South, where the action is! (Your partner is North, and your opponents are West and East. See Chapter 1 for more details about positions in bridge.)

Establishing Tricks with Lower Honor Cards

When you don't have the ace in a suit, you're in bad shape as far as sure tricks are concerned (see Chapter 2 for more about sure tricks). Not to worry. Your new friend, *establishing tricks,* can see you through the tough times and help you win extra tricks you may need to make your contract. Check out the following sections for surefire techniques on establishing tricks.

Establishing tricks is about sacrificing one of your honor cards to drive out one of your opponents' higher honor cards. You can then swoop in with your remaining honor cards and take a bundle of tricks.

In case you're wondering, your opponents don't just sit around and admire your dazzling technique of establishing tricks. Oh, no — they're busy trying to establish tricks of their own. In bridge, turnabout is fair play. Whatever you can do, your opponents can also do. Many a hand turns into a race for tricks. To win the race, you must establish your tricks earlier rather than later. Remembering this rule will keep you focused and help you edge out your opponents.

Driving the opponents' ace out of its hole

The all-powerful ace wins a trick for you every time. But no matter how hard you pray for aces, sometimes you just don't get any, and you can't count any sure tricks in a suit with no aces. Sometimes you get tons of honor cards but no ace, and you still can't count even one sure trick in that suit. Ah, the inhumanity!

Cheer up — you can still create winning tricks in such a suit. When you have a number of equal honors in a suit but not the ace, you can *attack* that suit early and *drive out the ace* from your opponent's hand. Here's what you do:

1. **Lead the highest honor card in the suit in which you're missing the ace.**

   To get rid of the ace when you have a number of equal honors, lead the highest honor. So if you have the KQJ6, lead the king to drive out the ace. If they don't take the trick with the ace, play the queen. One way or another you must take two tricks with the KQJ. If you lead a low card, like the 6, 7, or 8, your opponents won't have to play the ace to take the trick. They can simply take the trick with a lower card, such as the 9 or 10, and they still have the ace! Not good.

   When you have equal honors in your hand (where they can't be seen), such as the KQJ, and wish to lead one, use the higher or highest equal to do your dirty work. It is more deceptive. Trust me.

   If the equal honors are in the dummy where everyone can see them, you have the option of which one to play. It doesn't matter, but to be uniform in this book, I have you play the lower or lowest equal.

2. **Continue playing the suit until your opponents play the ace and take the trick.**

3. **After that ace is out of the way, you can count your remaining equal honor cards as sure tricks.**

Driving out the ace is a great way of setting up extra tricks. The cards in Figure 3-1 provide an example of a suit you can attack to drive out the ace.

North (Dummy)
♠ K Q J 10

Figure 3-1:
You can
drive out an
ace to cre-
ate winning
tricks.

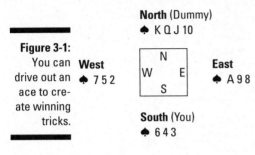

West
♠ 7 5 2

East
♠ A 9 8

South (You)
♠ 6 4 3

In Figure 3-1, you can't count a single sure spade trick because your opponent (East) has the ♠A. Yet the four spades in the dummy — ♠KQJ10 —
are extremely powerful. (Any suit that contains four honor cards is
considered powerful.)

Suppose that the lead is in your hand from the preceding trick, and you lead
a low spade (the lowest spade you have — in this case, the ♠3). West, seeing
the dummy has very strong spades, plays her lowest card, the ♠2; you play
the ♠10 from the dummy; and East decides to win the trick with the ♠A. You
may have lost the lead, but you have also driven out the ♠A. The dummy
remains with the ♠KQJ, all winning tricks. You have *established* three sure
spade tricks where none existed.

Suits with three or more equal honor cards in one hand are ideal for suit
establishment. When you see the KQJ or the QJ10 in either your hand or the
dummy, sure tricks in those suits can eventually be developed if you attack
them early!

Surrendering the lead twice to the ace and the king

When you're missing just the ace, you can establish the suit easily by just
leading one equal honor after another until an opponent takes the ace.
However, if you're missing both the ace and the king, you will have to give up
the lead twice to take later tricks.

Bridge is a game of giving up the lead to get tricks back. Don't fear giving up
the lead. Your high honor cards in the other suits protect you by allowing you
to eventually regain the lead and pursue your goal of establishing tricks.

Figure 3-2 shows a suit where you have to swallow your pride twice before
you can establish your lower honor cards.

North (Dummy)
♠ Q J 10 9

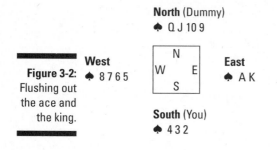

West
♠ 8 7 6 5

East
♠ A K

Figure 3-2:
Flushing out
the ace and
the king.

South (You)
♠ 4 3 2

Notice that the dummy in Figure 3-2 has a sequence of cards headed by three *equal* honors — the ♠QJ10. The ♠9, though not considered an honor card, is equal to the ♠QJ10 and has the same value. When you have a sequence of equals, all the cards have equal power to take tricks — or to drive out opposing honor cards. For example, you can use the ♠9 or the ♠Q to drive out your opponent's ♠K or ♠A.

In Figure 3-2, your opponents hold the ♠AK. To compensate, you have the ♠QJ109, four equals headed by three honors — a very good sign. You lead a low spade, the ♠2; West plays the ♠5; you play the ♠9 from the dummy; and East takes the trick with the ♠K. You've driven out one spade honor. One more to go. Your spades still aren't established, but you're halfway home! The next time you have the lead, lead a low spade, the ♠3, and then play the ♠10 from the dummy, driving out the ♠A. Guess what? You started with zero sure spade tricks, but now you have two: the ♠Q and ♠J.

Playing the short-side honors first

Never forget this simple and ever-so-important rule: When attacking an unequally divided suit, where either your hand or the dummy holds more cards than the other in that suit, play the high equal honors from the shorter side first (see Figure 3-3). Doing so enables you to end up with the lead on the long side (the dummy), where the remainder of the winning spades are. If you remember to play your equal honors from the short side first, your partner will kneel down and declare you Ruler of the Universe.

Liberation time! As you see in Figure 3-3, the short hand (your hand) has two equal honor cards, the ♠KQ. Start by playing the ♠K, the higher honor on the short side, and a low spade from the dummy, the ♠5. As it happens, East must take the trick with the ♠A because she doesn't have any other spades.

Figure 3-3:
The partner
with fewer
honor cards
should lead
the highest
(or equal)
honor card.

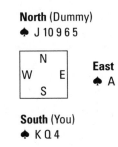

North (Dummy)
♠ J 10 9 6 5

West
♠ 8 7 3 2

East
♠ A

South (You)
♠ K Q 4

You've established your spades because the ♠A is gone, but you still need to remember the five-star tip of playing the high remaining equal honor from the short side next. When you or dummy next regains the lead in another suit, play the ♠Q, which takes the trick, and then lead the ♠4. The dummy remains with the ♠J109, all winning tricks. You have established four spade tricks by playing the high card from the short side twice.

Using length to your advantage with no high honor in sight

In this section, you hit the jackpot — I show you how to establish tricks in a suit where you have the J1098 but you're missing the ace, king, and queen!

If you don't have any of the three top dogs but you have four or more cards in the suit, you can still scrape a trick or two out of the suit. When you have *length* (usually four or more cards of the same suit), you know that even after your opponents win tricks with the ace, king, and queen, you still hold smaller cards in that suit, which become — voilà! — winners.

Perhaps you're wondering why you'd ever want to squeeze some juice out of a suit in which you lack the ace, king, and queen? The answer: You may need tricks from an anemic suit like this to make your contract. Sometimes you just get the raw end of the deal, and you need to pick up tricks wherever you can eke them out.

When you look at the dummy and see a suit such as the one in Figure 3-4, try not to shriek in horror.

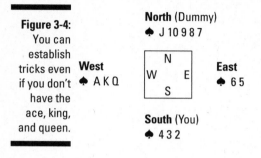

Figure 3-4:
You can establish tricks even if you don't have the ace, king, and queen.

North (Dummy)
♠ J 10 9 8 7

West
♠ A K Q

East
♠ 6 5

South (You)
♠ 4 3 2

True, the spades in Figure 3-4 don't look like the most appetizing suit you'll ever have to deal with, but don't judge a book by its cover. You can get some tricks out of this suit because you have the advantage of length: You have a total of eight spades between the two hands. The strength you get from numbers helps you after you drive out the ace, king, and queen.

Suppose you need to develop two tricks from this hopeless-looking, forsaken suit. You start with a low spade, the ♠2, which is taken by West's ♠Q (the dummy and East each play their lowest spade, the ♠7 and ♠5, respectively). After you regain the lead in some other suit, lead another low spade, the ♠3, which is taken by West's ♠K (the dummy plays the ♠8, and East plays her last spade, the ♠6). After you gain the lead again in another suit, lead your last spade, the ♠4, which loses to West's ♠A (the dummy plays the ♠9). You have lost the lead again, but you have accomplished your ultimate goal: The dummy now holds two winning spades — the ♠J10. Nobody at the table holds any more spades; if the dummy can win a trick in another suit, you can go right ahead and cash those two spade tricks. You had to work, but you did it!

Practicing establishment

Practice makes perfect, they say, so I want you to practice making your contract by establishing tricks. In this section, you hold the entire hand shown in Figure 3-5. Your final contract is for 12 tricks. West leads the ♠J. Now you need to do your thing and establish some tricks.

Before you even think of playing a card from the dummy, count your sure tricks (see Chapter 2 if you need some help counting sure tricks):

- ✔ **Spades:** You have three sure tricks — ♠AKQ.

- ✔ **Hearts:** You have another three sure tricks — ♥AKQ. (Don't count the ♥J; you have three hearts in each hand, so you can't take more than three tricks.)

- ✔ **Diamonds:** No ace = no sure tricks. Sad.

- ✔ **Clubs:** You have three sure tricks — ♣AKQ.

North (Dummy)
♠ K Q 6
♥ A Q J
♦ K Q J 10
♣ A 4 3

Figure 3-5:
Establish
the three
extra tricks
you need
from that
powerful
diamond
suit.

West
♠ J

```
      N
  W       E
      S
```

East

South (You)
♠ A 3 2
♥ K 9 8
♦ 6 5 4 2
♣ K Q 7

You have nine sure tricks, but you need 12 tricks to make your contract. You must establish three more tricks. Look no further than the dummy's magnificent diamond suit. If you drive out the ♦A, you can establish three diamond tricks and have 12 just like that. Piece of cake.

When you need to establish extra tricks, pick the suit you plan to work with and start establishing immediately. *Do not* take your sure tricks in other suits until you establish your extra needed tricks. Then take all your tricks in one giant cascade.

First you need to deal with West's opening lead, the ♠J. You have a choice: You can win the trick in either your hand with the ♠A or in the dummy with the ♠Q. In general, with equal length on both sides, you want to leave a high spade in each hand. Leaving the king in the dummy and the ace in your hand gives you an easier time going back and forth if necessary. However, on this hand it really doesn't matter where you win the trick; you have three spade tricks regardless. But to keep in practice, say you take it with the queen.

Remember, your objective is to establish tricks in your target suit: diamonds. Following your game plan, you lead the ♦K from the dummy. West takes the trick with the ♦A and then leads the ♠10. Presto — your three remaining diamonds in the dummy, ♦QJ10, have just become three sure tricks because you successfully drove out the ace. Your sure-trick count has just ballooned to 12. Don't look now, but you have the rest of the tricks and have just made your contract.

Next comes the best part: the mop-up, taking your winning tricks. You capture West's return of the ♠10 with the ♠K. Then you take your three established diamonds, your three winning hearts, your three winning clubs, and finally your ♠A. You now have 12 tricks, three in each suit. Ah, the thrill of victory.

Steering clear of taking tricks before establishing tricks

Establishing extra needed tricks is all about giving up the lead. Sometimes you need to drive out an ace, a king, or an ace *and* a king. Giving up the lead to establish tricks can be painful for a beginner, but you must steel yourself to do it.

You may hate to give up the lead for fear that something terrible may happen. And you're right. Something terrible is going to happen — if you're afraid to give up the lead to establish a suit. Most of the time, beginners fail to make their contracts because they don't establish extra tricks soon enough. Very often, beginners fall into the trap of taking their sure tricks before establishing tricks.

I know that you'd never commit such a grievous error as taking sure tricks before you establish other needed tricks. But just for the fun of it, take a look at Figure 3-6 to see what happens when you make this mistake. This isn't going to be pretty, so clear out the children.

In this hand (showing all the cards from the hand in Figure 3-5), the opening lead is the ♠J, and you need to take 12 tricks. Suppose you take the first three spade tricks with the ♠AKQ, and then the next three heart tricks with the ♥AKQ, and finally the next three club tricks with the ♣AKQ. Figure 3-7 shows what's left after you take the first nine tricks. (Remember: You need to take 12 tricks.)

You lead a low diamond. But guess what — West takes the trick with the ♦A. The hairs standing up on the back of your neck may tell you what I'm going to say next: West has all the rest of the tricks! West remains with a winning spade, a winning heart, and a winning club. Nobody else at the table has any of those suits, so all the other players are forced to discard. West's three cards are all winning tricks, and those great diamonds in the dummy are nothing but dead weight, totally worthless.

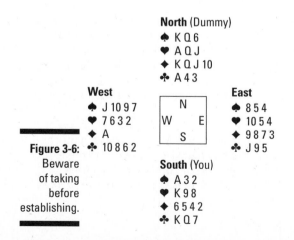

North (Dummy)
- ♠ K Q 6
- ♥ A Q J
- ♦ K Q J 10
- ♣ A 4 3

West
- ♠ J 10 9 7
- ♥ 7 6 3 2
- ♦ A
- ♣ 10 8 6 2

	N	
W		E
	S	

East
- ♠ 8 5 4
- ♥ 10 5 4
- ♦ 9 8 7 3
- ♣ J 9 5

South (You)
- ♠ A 3 2
- ♥ K 9 8
- ♦ 6 5 4 2
- ♣ K Q 7

Figure 3-6: Beware of taking before establishing.

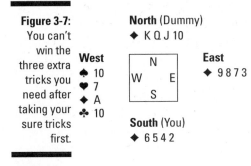

Figure 3-7:
You can't win the three extra tricks you need after taking your sure tricks first.

North (Dummy)
♦ K Q J 10

West
♠ 10
♥ 7
♦ A
♣ 10

East
♦ 9 8 7 3

South (You)
♦ 6 5 4 2

A word to the wise: Nothing good can happen to you if you take sure tricks before establishing extra needed tricks.

Taking Tricks with Small Cards

Grab a man off the street, and he can take tricks with aces and kings. But can that same man take tricks with 2s and 3s? Probably not, but you can!

Only very rarely do you get a hand dripping with all the honor cards you need to make your contract. Therefore, you must know how to take tricks with the smaller cards. *Small cards* are cards that are lower than honor cards. They are also called *low cards* or *spot cards.* You seldom have enough firepower (aces and kings) to make your contract without these little fellows.

Small cards frequently take tricks when attached to *long suits* (four or more cards in the suit). Eventually, after all the high honors in a suit have been played, the little guys start making appearances. They may be bit actors when the play begins, but before the final curtain is drawn, they're out there taking the final bows — and taking tricks.

In the following sections, I give you the scoop on using small cards to your great advantage.

Turning small cards into winning tricks: The joy of length

Deuces (and other small cards for that matter) can take tricks for you when you have seven cards or more in a suit between the two hands. You may then have the length to outlast all your opponents' cards in the suit. Figure 3-8 shows a hand where this incredible feat of staying power takes place.

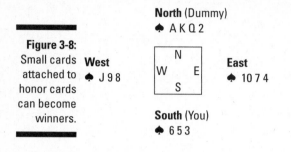

Figure 3-8:
Small cards
attached to
honor cards
can become
winners.

North (Dummy)
♠ A K Q 2

West
♠ J 9 8

East
♠ 10 7 4

South (You)
♠ 6 5 3

You choose to attack spades in the hand in Figure 3-8. Because the ♠AKQ in the dummy are all equals, the suit can be started from either your hand or the dummy. Pretend that the lead is in your hand. You begin by leading a low spade, the ♠3, to the ♠Q in the dummy, and both opponents follow suit. With the lead in the dummy, continue by leading the ♠K and then the ♠A from the dummy. The opponents both started with three spades, meaning that neither opponent has any more spades. That tiny ♠2 in the dummy is a winning trick. It has the power of an ace! The frog has turned into a prince.

Whenever you have four cards in a suit in one hand and three in the other, good things can happen. If your opponents' six cards are divided three in each hand and you lead the suit three times, leaving each opponent *without* any cards in that suit, you're destined to take a trick with any small card attached to the four-card suit.

Don't expect that fourth card to turn into a trick every time, though. Your opponents' six cards may not be divided 3-3 after all. They may be divided a more likely 4-2, as you see in Figure 3-9.

When you play the ♠AKQ as you do in Figure 3-9, East turns up with four spades, so your ♠2 won't be a trick. After you play the ♠AKQ, East remains with the ♠J, a higher spade than your ♠2. Live with it.

Figure 3-9:
You may not
be able to
use small
cards to
your advan-
tage when
your oppo-
nents' cards
are split 4-2.

North (Dummy)
♠ A K Q 2

West
♠ 10 9

East
♠ J 8 7 6

South (You)
♠ 5 4 3

Subtracting your way to success

Happiness is having small cards that turn into winning tricks. Misery is having small cards that are winning tricks and not knowing it. Total misery is thinking your small cards are winning tricks only to find out they aren't.

To know when your small cards are winners, you must become familiar with the dreaded "c" word, *counting.* If you count the cards in the suit you're playing, you can tell whether your little guys have a chance. You have to do a little simple subtraction as well, but I can assure you it's well worth the effort.

A neat way of counting the suit you're attacking is with the *subtraction-by-two method.* Follow these steps for successful counting every time:

1. Count how many cards you and the dummy have in the suit.

2. Subtract the number of cards you and dummy have from 13 (the number of cards in a suit) to get the total number of cards your opponents have in that suit.

3. Each time you lead the suit and both opponents follow suit, subtract two from the number of cards your opponents have left.

4. When your opponents have no cards left, all your remaining small cards are winning tricks.

With this method, the numbers get smaller and become easier to work with. Some people think doing stuff like this is fun — with any luck, you're one of these people.

You may discover an easier way of counting, but for most people the subtraction-by-two method works just fine. If you just have to be different, here are a couple of other methods:

✔ **The digital (fingers and toes) method:** This method requires playing with sandals so you can see your digits clearly.

✔ **The faking-a-count method:** You look intently at the cards that have been played as if you're counting them. Then you look up at the ceiling as if you can see the count up there, and finally, you nod sagely even though you don't have the vaguest idea of how many cards your opponents have left.

Bridge is a game of strategy and luck. When it comes to taking tricks with small cards, you just have to hope that the cards that they hold divide evenly (3-3 instead of 4-2, for example).

Turning low cards into winners by driving out high honors

Sometimes you have to drive out an opponent's high honor card (could be an ace, a king, or a queen) before you can turn your frogs into princes (or turn your deuces into tricks). Figure 3-10 shows you how (with a little luck) you can turn a deuce into a winner.

Figure 3-10:
Drive out
your oppo-
nents' high
cards to use
your low
cards
successfully.

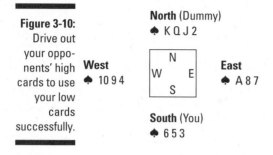

North (Dummy)
♠ K Q J 2

West
♠ 10 9 4

East
♠ A 8 7

South (You)
♠ 6 5 3

With the cards shown in Figure 3-10, your plan is to develop (or establish) as many spade tricks as possible, keeping a wary eye on turning that ♠2 in the dummy into a winner. Suppose you begin by leading a low spade, the ♠3, and West follows with a low spade, the ♠4. You play the ♠J from the dummy, which loses to East's ♠A. At this point, you note the following points:

- The ♠KQ in the dummy are now both winning tricks because your opponents' ♠A is gone.

- Your opponents started with six spades. By counting cards (see the nearby sidebar, "Subtracting your way to success"), you know that your opponents now have only four spades left. Four is your new key number.

After regaining the lead by winning a trick in another suit, lead another low spade, the ♠5, to the ♠Q in the dummy (with both opponents following suit). Your opponents now have two spades left between them. When you continue with the ♠K, both opponents follow suit again. They now have zero spades left — triumph! The ♠2 in the dummy is now a sure trick. Deuces love to take tricks — doing so makes them feel wanted.

Make sure that you count the cards in the suit you're attacking. You're in a pretty sad state if you have to leave a low card in your hand or the dummy untouched because you don't know (or aren't sure) whether it's a winner.

Losing a trick early by making a ducking play

Suits that have seven or eight cards between your hand and the dummy, including the ace and the king, lend themselves to taking extra tricks with lower cards, even though you have to lose a trick in the suit. Why do you have to lose a trick in the suit? Because the opponents have the queen, the jack, and the 10 between them. After you play the ace and the king, the opponent with the queen is looking at a winning trick.

When you know you have to lose at least one trick in a suit that includes the ace and king, face the inevitable and lose that trick early by playing low cards from both your hand and the dummy. Taking this dive early on is called *ducking a trick.* It only hurts for a little while.

Ducking a trick is a necessary evil when playing bridge. A ducking play in a suit that has an inevitable loser allows you to keep your controlling cards (the ace and the king) so you can use them in a late rush of tricks.

When you duck a trick and then play the ace and king, you wind up in the hand where the small cards are — just where you want to be. In the following sections, I present two situations in which you can duck a trick successfully.

When you have seven cards between the two hands

The cards in Figure 3-11 show how successful ducking a trick can be. You have seven cards between the two hands with ♠AK in the dummy — a perfect setup for ducking a trick. You can only hope that your opponents' six cards are divided 3-3 so that they'll run out of spades before you do. To find out, you have to play the suit *three* times.

Figure 3-11:
Ducking a
trick leaves
you in
control of
the suit.

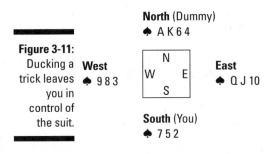

North (Dummy)
♠ A K 6 4

West
♠ 9 8 3

East
♠ Q J 10

South (You)
♠ 7 5 2

You know you have to lose at least one spade trick because your opponents hold ♠QJ10 between them. Because you have to lose at least one spade trick, your best bet is to lose the trick right away, keeping control (the high cards) of the suit for later.

Play a low spade from both hands! No, you aren't giving out presents; actually, you're making a very clever ducking play by letting your opponents have a trick they're entitled to anyway.

After you concede the trick with the ♠2 from your hand and the ♠4 from the dummy, you can come roaring back with your big guns, the ♠K and the ♠A, when you regain the lead. Notice that because your opponents' spades are divided 3-3, that little ♠6 in the dummy takes a third trick in the suit — neither opponent has any more spades.

When you have eight cards between the two hands

If the dummy has a five-card suit headed by the ace and the king facing three small cards, you can usually take two extra tricks with a ducking play. See Figure 3-12, where you make a ducking play, and then watch the tricks come rolling in.

Figure 3-12:
Set up an avalanche of tricks via a ducking play.

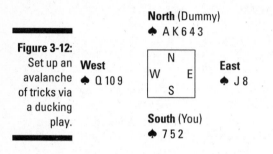

North (Dummy)
♠ A K 6 4 3

West
♠ Q 10 9

N
W   E
S

East
♠ J 8

South (You)
♠ 7 5 2

In Figure 3-12, the opponents have five spades between the two hands, including ♠QJ. You have to lose a spade trick no matter what, so lose it right away by making one of your patented ducking plays. Lead the ♠2. West plays the ♠9, you play the ♠3 from the dummy, and East plays the ♠8. West wins the trick. Not to worry — you'll soon show them who's boss!

The next time either you or the dummy regains the lead, play the ♠K and ♠A, removing all of your opponents' remaining spades. You have the lead in the dummy, and the dummy remains with ♠64, both winning tricks.

When you have five cards in one hand and three in the other, including the ace and the king, you have a chance to take four tricks by playing a low card from both hands at your first opportunity. This ducking play allows you to save the highest cards in the suit, intending to come swooping in later to take the remaining tricks.

Finding heaven with seven small cards

Having any seven cards between the two hands may mean an extra trick for you — if your opponents' cards are divided 3-3. The hand in Figure 3-13 shows you how any small card(s) can morph into a winner when your opponents' cards are split evenly. You have seven cards between your hand and the dummy, the signal that something good may happen for your small cards. Of course, you'd be a little happier if you had some higher cards in the suit (such as an honor or two), but beggars can't be choosers.

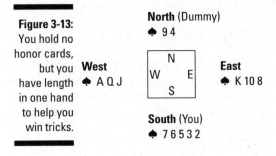

Figure 3-13:
You hold no honor cards, but you have length in one hand to help you win tricks.

North (Dummy)
♠ 9 4

West
♠ A Q J

East
♠ K 10 8

South (You)
♠ 7 6 5 3 2

Remember Cinderella and how her stepsisters dressed her up to look ugly even though she was beautiful? Well, those five cards in South are like Cinderella — you just have to cast off the rags to see the beauty underneath.

Suppose you lead the ♠2, and West takes the trick with the ♠J. Later, you lead the ♠3, and West takes that trick with the ♠Q. You've played spades twice, and because you've been counting those spades, you know that your opponents have two spades left. (See the earlier sidebar, "Subtracting your way to success," for details on counting.)

After you regain the lead, you again lead a *rag* (low card) — in this case, the ♠5. Crash, bang! West plays the ♠A, and East plays the ♠K. Now they have no more spades, and the two remaining spades in your hand, the ♠7 and ♠6, are winning tricks. You conceded three spade tricks (tricks they had coming anyway) but established two tricks of your own by sheer persistence.

Avoiding the risk of blocking a suit

Even when length is on your side, you need to play the high honor cards from the short side first. Doing so ensures that the lead ends up in the hand with the length — and therefore the winning tricks. If you don't play the high honor(s) from the short side first, you run the risk of *blocking a suit*. You block a suit when you have winning cards stranded in one hand and no way to enter that hand in order to play those winning cards. It hurts to even talk about it.

Figure 3-14 shows you a suit that's blocked from the very start. It's a bridge tragedy: seeing the dummy come down with a strong suit, only to realize that it's blocked and you can't use it. You have five spade tricks but may be able to take only two. After you play ♠AK, you're fresh out of spades, and the dummy remains with ♠QJ10.

A blocked suit to end all blocked suits

Blocking your own suit brings to mind a true story that took place in a swanky London bridge club some 60-odd years ago. I call this story my own personal *Gone with the Wind,* and I share it to show you how treacherous blocking a suit can be.

In what was a high-stakes game, North was the pro playing with one of the weaker players at the club. The idea when playing with this young man wasn't to win — that was impossible — but to hold the losses to as little as possible. The day was scorchingly hot, and all the windows in the club were wide open. The pro happened to be sitting with his back to one of the windows.

The pro tried to arrange the bidding never to let his partner play a hand if he could help it. The way the young man played a hand was just too painful to watch. Then came the ill-fated hand to end all hands, shown in the figure. Going against his better judgment, the pro allowed his partner to play the hand. The final contract, 3NT, was for nine tricks (a staggering total for the young gentleman).

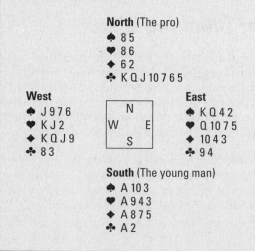

North (The pro)
♠ 8 5
♥ 8 6
♦ 6 2
♣ K Q J 10 7 6 5

West
♠ J 9 7 6
♥ K J 2
♦ K Q J 9
♣ 8 3

East
♠ K Q 4 2
♥ Q 10 7 5
♦ 10 4 3
♣ 9 4

South (The young man)
♠ A 10 3
♥ A 9 4 3
♦ A 8 7 5
♣ A 2

The opening lead was the ♦ K. After the pro put down the dummy, he went to get a drink but couldn't resist walking behind his partner to peek at what he had. When he saw what the young man had, the pro was ecstatic. His partner was actually going to take ten tricks: seven clubs (by playing the ♣A from the short side, and then a low club to the dummy's ♣10, followed by five more winning clubs) plus three other aces. The pro was going to win a bundle. Unheard of! He returned to his seat to enjoy the hand and also to figure out how many pounds (the game was in England, remember) he was about to win.

The young gentleman took the first trick with the ♦ A and immediately led the ♣ 2. Instead of playing the high card from the short side (the ♣ A), he played the low card from the short side. By this one stroke, the young man had *blocked* the club suit and seven club tricks suddenly became two club tricks!

Here's what happened: After playing the ♣ 2 and winning the trick in the dummy with the ♣ 10, the young man led a low club from the dummy back to the ♣ A in his hand. Unfortunately, the dummy now held five — count 'em, five — winning clubs. Poor South had no more clubs in his hand and no way to get to the dummy in another suit (rendering all the remaining clubs in North's hand worthless). The club suit in the dummy was dead, totally dead. The inexperienced young man had blocked the club suit and compressed seven club tricks into only two club tricks, which is something you would never do, right? Nod your head, for goodness sake.

When the pro saw the mistake the young man had made, he took his remaining ten cards and tossed them out the window. "Why are you doing that?" the young man asked. "You won't need them anymore," the pro replied.

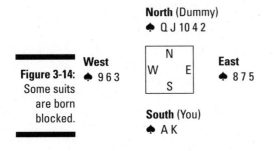

North (Dummy)
♠ Q J 10 4 2

West
♠ 9 6 3

East
♠ 8 7 5

South (You)
♠ A K

Figure 3-14:
Some suits are born blocked.

If you don't have an *entry* (a winning card) in another suit to get the lead over to the dummy (called a dummy entry), dummy's three winning spades will die on the vine. A side-suit ace is a certain dummy entry, and a side-suit king or queen may turn out to be a dummy entry.

The more poignant tragedy is when you block a suit by failing to play the high card(s) from the short side first. Then you wind up in the wrong hand, instead of winding up in the long hand where the winning tricks are. Instead, you wind up in the short hand that has no more cards in the suit. The hand may not have a side-suit entry to enter the hand with the winning tricks. It hurts.

Chapter 4

Outsmarting Your Opponents at Notrump Play

In This Chapter

▶ Trapping your opponents' honor cards with a finesse

▶ Cutting lines of communication with a hold-up play

▶ Playing two honor cards on the same trick by overtaking

---

*I*n this chapter, you discover how to establish tricks with lower honor cards as well as how to take tricks with small cards. As always, you work with long suits, count your sure tricks (guaranteed tricks, come what may), and then when you begin playing this long suit, you play the high honors from the short side. But now you're going to add some new trick-taking techniques to your repertoire: taking a finesse, making a hold-up play, and dealing with the danger hand. Don't go away!

Throughout this chapter, as in Chapter 3, many figures show cards in only one suit. I leave out the other suits because I want you to focus on just the one suit. In the following figures, you see suits ideal for creating the extra tricks you may need. And again, I always make you South. (Your partner is North, and your opponents are West and East. See Chapter 1 for details about positions in bridge.)

Slipping Lower Honors Past Higher Honors: The Finesse

In this section I discuss other techniques for establishing tricks (see Chapter 3 for the basics on establishing tricks). This technique requires you to start by leading the suit from the correct hand.

When you have the ace in a suit, you can just take the trick any time you want (it's a sure trick). But what if you have a king in a suit but no ace? If you lead the king, the opponent with the ace will zap it. In cases such as these, you need to *lead toward* the king, meaning that you need to lead the suit from the side opposite the king. For example, if the king is in the dummy, start by leading the suit from your hand; if the king is in your hand, start by leading the suit from the dummy.

Welcome to the world of the *finesse,* a technique for taking tricks with lower honor cards (jacks, queens, and kings) when your opponents have higher honor cards (queens, kings, and aces). Think of your opponents' higher honors as big bullies that you have to sidestep. Finesses are a 50-50 proposition. Because you can't see your opponents' cards, you can never be sure that your finesse will work. Each time you take a finesse, you may think to yourself, "Will this finesse work, or will it be a bad day at the office?" Sometimes your only chance for needed tricks is to attempt a finesse and hope that it works. After all, a 50-50 chance is better than no chance.

When you want to take tricks with lower honor cards, such as the king, queen, or jack, you need to lead from the side opposite the honor card you want to take a trick with. Think of leading from weakness toward strength. The following sections show you a few examples of finesses so you can get acquainted with this new kid on the block.

Sneaking a king by an ace

Figure 4-1 shows a classic finesse position. You have the ♠K in the dummy; your opponents have the ♠A. You want to take a trick with the ♠K. Lead a low spade from your hand, the ♠3, from weakness toward strength.

West happens to have the ♠A. If West plays the ♠A, your ♠K becomes a later sure trick because the king is now the highest-ranking remaining card in the spade suit. If West plays a low spade, the ♠8, you play the king and take a trick immediately with the ♠K. Your finesse works. No matter what West does, you take either an immediate or an eventual trick with the ♠K.

Figure 4-1:
You can give your opponents' ace the slip with a king in the dummy.

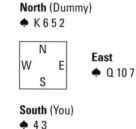

North (Dummy)
♠ K 6 5 2

West
♠ A J 9 8

```
    N
  W   E
    S
```

East
♠ Q 10 7

South (You)
♠ 4 3

Now check out Figure 4-2, which presents a scenario just as likely as the one in Figure 4-1.

When you lead a low spade, the ♠3, and then play the ♠K in the dummy, East (the last to play to the trick) takes your ♠K with the ♠A. Your ♠K doesn't take a trick. Your finesse has lost. Don't grieve — remember, a finesse loses about half the time. Everyone thinks that their finesses always lose while the opponents' finesses always win. It's just a temporary pain. Successful finesses even out over the long haul. Except mine! Just kidding.

Figure 4-2:
Finesses fail when the fourth hand holds the important missing honor.

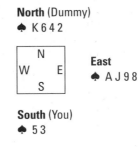

North (Dummy)
♠ K 6 4 2

West
♠ Q 10 7

East
♠ A J 9 8

South (You)
♠ 5 3

Sliding a queen past the king

Queens are akin to kings. If you want to take a trick with a queen, do her a favor and lead toward her; she may be able to escape the clutches of the king. Figure 4-3 shows you how the queen can elude the king.

You want to take a trick with your ♠Q, but you don't know who has the ♠K. You can see the ♠K in East's hand in the figure, but if you were playing for real, you couldn't see that ♠K unless you were Superman.

North (Dummy)
♠ 8 6 3 2

Figure 4-3:
The queen can get past the king in this layout.

West
♠ J 9 7

East
♠ K 10 5 4

South (You)
♠ A Q

Suppose you lead a low spade from the dummy, the ♠2 — again, weakness toward strength. East, second to play after the lead, usually plays his lowest card, the ♠4, so as not to give away any information about his hand. You, South, play the ♠Q, which wins the trick. Your finesse works. If West (last to play to the trick) had the ♠K, your finesse would have lost.

Figure 4-4 shows another very common finesse involving the queen. This time, the ♠Q is in the dummy separated from her guardian, the ♠A. Begin by leading a low spade, the ♠6, from your hand, the hand opposite the ♠Q. You're hoping that West, the second hand, has the missing honor, the ♠K. In this case, West does have the ♠K. Am I good to you or what?

If West plays a low spade, the ♠2, you take the trick with the ♠Q; if West takes the trick with the ♠K, your ♠Q becomes a later trick. Of course, if East, fourth hand, has the ♠K, he gobbles up your ♠Q, and your finesse loses. *C'est la vie.*

North (Dummy)
♠ Q 5 4

Figure 4-4:
A very common finesse involves the queen and the ace.

West
♠ K 10 3 2

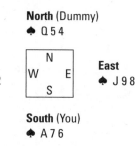

East
♠ J 9 8

South (You)
♠ A 7 6

Combining length with a finesse

When you take finesses in suits that have seven or more cards between your hand and the dummy, meaning your side has more cards in that suit than your opponents (known as *length*), you always have a chance of developing an extra trick with small cards even if the finesse loses, as Figure 4-5 shows.

North (Dummy)
♠ 5 4 3

Figure 4-5:
The best of two worlds: Finessing in a long suit.

West
♠ 10 9 7

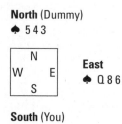

East
♠ Q 8 6

South (You)
♠ A K J 2

You have the ♠A and ♠K between the two hands, but you want more than two tricks. You also want to take a trick with your ♠J. You even want to take a trick with your ♠2. You may as well think big when you have seven or more cards in the same suit between your hand and the dummy.

You lead a low spade, the ♠3, from the dummy (from weakness toward strength), East plays low, the ♠6, and you play the ♠J. West doesn't have the ♠Q, so the ♠J wins! Now you can play the ♠A and ♠K, which both win tricks. Guess what? You're the only person left at the table with any spades. So once again, that lowly ♠2 takes a trick for you. You've managed to take four spade tricks because you combined a finesse with the power of length. Of course, you knew that ♠2 was high because you counted the spades. Right?

TIP

If West has the ♠Q, your finesse doesn't work, but don't give up! You're still slated to take a trick with that ♠2. After West takes the ♠Q, the next time you have the lead, play the ace and then the king of spades and then the deuce, a good trick! The tip here is to keep your cool when a finesse fails. You may still be able to develop extra tricks with small cards in that suit.

REMEMBER

Don't let the risk involved with finesses scare you away from trying them, especially if you're finessing in a long suit. A finesse in a longer suit has the advantage of setting up small cards in the suit, even if the finesse doesn't work.

The story of Too-Tall Tex

Once upon a time, there lived a bridge player called Too-Tall Tex. Tex was so tall that he could easily look down into his opponents' hands and see all their cards. It didn't take Tex long to figure out that he played much better when he knew where all the missing honor cards were before he started to play. Too-Tall Tex never lost a finesse!

In one particular hand, Too-Tall Tex (sitting South) knew from his partner's bidding that his team should try for either 12 or 13 tricks. Tex was afraid that if his partner, North, didn't have the ♠K he would need a finesse to take all 13 tricks. Too-Tall Tex didn't want to bid for 13 tricks until he took a "surveillance." So Too-Tall Tex went out on a scouting mission looking for the ♠K.

West knew all about Too-Tall. While Tex went out on his scouting mission, West, who had the ♠K9, tucked his ♠9 in with his clubs, making Too-Tall Tex believe that West's ♠K was a *singleton,* or the only card he had in the suit.

When Tex saw that the ♠K was a singleton, he thought he had all the tricks in the bag, and so he quickly bid for 13 tricks. The opening lead from West was the ♣Q, which Tex won in the dummy with the ♣K. At trick two, Tex led a spade to his ♠A, expecting to snag West's ♠K (if West had only the ♠K, he would have had to play it in order to follow suit). When West produced the ♠9 instead, Too-Tall Tex stormed away from the table, shouting, "I can't play in a game with cheaters!"

Some finesses bear repeating

Sometimes the honor cards that you hold dictate that you lead from weakness toward strength *twice*. The only thing better than taking one finesse in a suit is taking two finesses in the same suit. This move sounds tricky, but I assure you it can be done: Just remember to lead from weakness toward strength, and watch yourself slide right by your opponents' honor cards. I show you two different card combinations illustrating taking two finesses in the same suit.

Finessing with the king and the queen

I want to show you one particular situation that has a romantic pairing: the king and the queen. The cards in Figure 4-6 illustrate a hand where you can pull off this stunt.

In Figure 4-6, the ♠K and the ♠Q in the dummy make an item. Bridge nuts try to clean everything up, so some call this coupling a *marriage,* which is actually a pinochle term.

Forgetting the social aspects of the suit, you need to take as many spade tricks as you can. Start by leading a low spade, the ♠3, from your hand, weakness to strength. West can simplify your life by playing the ♠A right away, a friendly play that immediately makes both the ♠K and the ♠Q in the dummy winning tricks for later use. But West thinks better of such a gift and plays the ♠2, allowing you to take the trick with the ♠Q.

You took a trick with the ♠Q by leading toward it, and you must repeat the process if you want to take a trick with the ♠K. Return to your hand (South) in another suit and lead another low spade, the ♠7. If West takes the trick with this ♠A, your ♠K becomes a later trick; if West plays low again, ♠4, you take the trick with the ♠K. You prevail because West, second to play, has the missing honor. You wouldn't be so lucky if East had the ♠A.

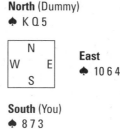

Figure 4-6:
The king and the queen in the dummy have double the finessing power.

North (Dummy)
♠ K Q 5

West
♠ A J 4 2

N
W   E
S

East
♠ 10 6 4

South (You)
♠ 8 7 3

Finessing with a hole in your honor cards

Figure 4-7 shows you another suit where you can repeat your finesse to great success. This particular finesse has "holy" overtones. You have three honor cards in your hand (♠AQJ), but they aren't all equal honors. Do you see that hole (missing honor) between the ♠A and the ♠Q? A "holy" suit is a finessable suit.

Lead a low spade, the ♠3, from the dummy (from weakness toward strength), and when East plays low, the ♠5, play the ♠Q to win the trick. You remain with the ♠AJ in your hand, and if you want to take a trick with the ♠J, you need to return to the dummy in another suit and lead another low spade, the ♠6. When East plays low again with the ♠9, you play the ♠J and take the trick. Nor does playing the ♠K do East any good — you just zap it with your ♠A. You just took three tricks in the suit.

When you have equal honors in your hand, such as the ♠QJ, play the higher equal first. It makes it much harder for the defenders to know which honor you're concealing. However, when you have equal honors in the dummy, the hand that both your opponents can see, the honor you play first doesn't matter (but in this book you play the lower or lowest just to be consistent).

North (Dummy)
♠ 7 6 3

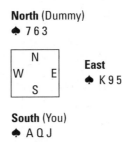

Figure 4-7:
The ace, queen, and jack trap the king.

West
♠ 10 8 4 2

East
♠ K 9 5

South (You)
♠ A Q J

Finessing against split honors

Sometimes your opponents have two important honors in the suit that you want to attack. You should assume that those honors are split and that each opponent has one honor. When you make this assumption and plan your play accordingly, you're *playing for split honors*.

You have a chance to play for split honors with the cards shown in Figure 4-8, a hand where you can take two finesses. (See the previous section for the basics on finessing twice in a suit.)

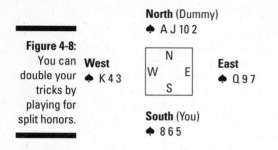

North (Dummy)
♠ A J 10 2

West
♠ K 4 3

East
♠ Q 9 7

South (You)
♠ 8 6 5

Figure 4-8:
You can double your tricks by playing for split honors.

In Figure 4-8, you have a powerful three-card honor combination in the dummy: the ♠AJ10. You normally attack suits with powerful honor combinations early, particularly when the suit has seven or more cards. When you're missing both the ♠K and the ♠Q, two important honors, assume that the honors are split between the two opposing hands.

Start by leading a low spade from your hand, the ♠5, weakness to strength. West, second to play, sees that the dummy has a higher spade, the ♠A, than West has with the ♠K, so West properly plays low, the ♠3. You insert the ♠10 from the dummy, and East wins the trick with the ♠Q, as expected (split honors, remember?). Hang on, though; it ain't over 'til it's over.

After you regain the lead in another suit, you persist by leading another low spade from your hand, the ♠6. Once again, West properly plays low, the ♠4, and this time you insert the ♠J from the dummy. Success! Your second finesse has worked. The missing spade honors were split after all (the ♠K in one hand and the ♠Q in the other). (Of course they were split; I set them up that way!)

You have a little bonus in store for you, to boot. After your ♠J wins the trick, you take the next trick by playing the ♠A. After both opponents follow, that little ♠2 in the dummy also morphs into a trick because nobody has any more spades. Of course, you were counting cards, so you already knew that. (See Chapter 3 for tips on how to count cards.)

Taking a surefire finesse when an opponent shows out

Finessing is a risky business. On a good day, all finesses work, but on a bad day, don't ask. However, you can take some of the risk out of finessing by watching the cards your opponents play.

Finesses work best when you know who has the missing honors. However, at times you can be smart without peeking over your opponents' shoulders. Say that you lead a suit, and one of your opponents *shows out* (discards a card from another suit because she has no cards left in the suit that you're playing). Now you can be sure that your other opponent has all the missing cards in that suit, including any vital honor cards that you may be missing.

Figure 4-9 shows a suit where you can take a surefire finesse after your opponent shows out.

In this hand, you begin by playing the ♠A and then the ♠K, the high honors from the short side (the side with fewer cards — see Chapter 3 for details on playing from the short side first). On the second lead of spades, East, who has no more spades, makes a discard (shows out).

"Aha!" you say to yourself. If East has no more spades, West must have all the missing spades, including the ♠J. When you lead the ♠4 and West plays a low spade (in this case, pretty much any card below the ♠J), you can rest 100 percent assured that you can play the ♠10 from the dummy and take the trick. After the ♠10 wins, you can take a fourth trick with the dummy's ♠Q.

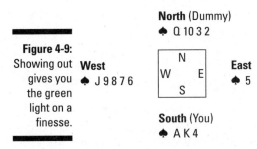

North (Dummy)
♠ Q 10 3 2

West
♠ J 9 8 7 6

East
♠ 5

South (You)
♠ A K 4

Figure 4-9: Showing out gives you the green light on a finesse.

Corralling a missing king

The more honor cards you have in a suit between your hand and the dummy, the better your chances of taking all the tricks in the suit via a finesse. Sometimes you strike gold and have a suit with four of the top honors, including the ace, but you're missing the king.

To corral the king, start the suit by leading an honor card from the side opposite the ace. Then hopefully watch your left-hand opponent squirm. Figure 4-10 gives you a chance to make West very uneasy. In this suit, you're missing the ♠K.

The telltale signs of a finesseaholic

Some players become addicted to taking every finesse in sight. If you think you or your partner is one of these people, check by looking for these giveaway signs:

✔ Prowling around looking for every opportunity to finesse.

✔ Taking practice finesses — finesses you don't need just to see whether they work

✔ Taking finesses for the sheer joy of it

If you or your partner exhibits one or more of these tendencies, one or both you may need help.

But seriously, the idea when playing a hand is to avoid finesses in short suits, aiming instead to take finesses in long suits. The reason is that even if the long-suit finesse loses, you frequently can establish enough sure tricks with small cards after the suit has been played several times that you may not need to take any other risky finesse.

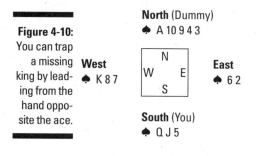

Figure 4-10:
You can trap a missing king by leading from the hand opposite the ace.

North (Dummy)
♠ A 10 9 4 3

West
♠ K 8 7

East
♠ 6 2

South (You)
♠ Q J 5

If West doesn't play the ♠K when you lead the ♠Q, play low from the dummy and take the trick. Next, play the ♠J (again, the high card from the short side). West is caught in the same pickle. If West plays the ♠K, you zap it with dummy's ♠A. If West plays low, the ♠J takes the trick. West can kiss that ♠K so long, auf Wiedersehen, good-bye.

You can corral a missing king if you have the rest of the honor cards. Always start the suit by leading from the side opposite the ace. Hopefully, you have an honor card to lead. If not, and the dummy has them all, lead a low card, intending to take a finesse. This story will have a happy ending if the second hand has the king.

Cutting Communications:
The Hold-Up Play

When you play a notrump contract, the highest of the four cards played to the trick takes the trick. In a notrump contract, you typically establish tricks by driving out an opponent's ace when you have the lower honor cards between your hand and the dummy (see Chapter 3 for more details on this technique).

Driving out the ace is great strategy, but don't forget your opponents. They have the opening lead and are also trying to set up tricks — perhaps by driving out one of your aces. The *nerve!* After they get rid of the ace in the suit they're attacking, they remain with winning tricks in that suit. Not good.

Can you do anything about it? Yes, you do have countermeasures. Enter the *hold-up play,* a technique that may stop your opponents dead in their tracks. No, the hold-up play doesn't involve robbing a bank. The successful hold-up play allows you to cut the lifeline between your opponents' hands.

The typical hold-up play involves taking a trick with the ace on the third round in the suit your opponents have led. The idea behind the hold-up play is to try to void one opponent in this suit. Later, if the opponent who is void gets the lead, he won't have any cards left in the suit to lead over to his partner, who is sitting over there champing at the bit with winning tricks.

A hold-up play usually follows this sequence:

1. **Your opponents attack your weakest suit, in which you have the ace but no other significant honor cards.** Perhaps you have the ace with two little cards and dummy has two little cards.

2. **You see from what the dummy has that you have to drive out an ace in another suit to establish enough tricks in that suit to make your contract.** In other words, you're going to have to surrender the lead.

3. **To neutralize the suit that your opponents lead, you allow your opponents to win the first two tricks, and then you take the third trick with your ace — your hold-up play in action.** This move drives out the opposing honor to establish your extra needed tricks.

4. **You pray that the opponent who wins the trick doesn't have any more cards in the suit that was led originally, the reason for the hold-up play.**

Figure 4-11 shows a hand where you can commit the perfect crime — a successful hold-up play.

In the hand shown in Figure 4-11, you need to take nine tricks. West leads the ♠K with the intention of driving out your ♠A and then making the rest of his spades into winning tricks. After the lead, the dummy comes down, and it's your turn to enter center stage by counting your sure tricks suit by suit (Chapter 2 has more details on counting sure tricks):

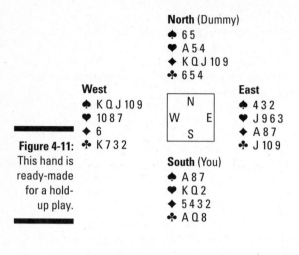

North (Dummy)
♠ 6 5
♥ A 5 4
♦ K Q J 10 9
♣ 6 5 4

West
♠ K Q J 10 9
♥ 10 8 7
♦ 6
♣ K 7 3 2

East
♠ 4 3 2
♥ J 9 6 3
♦ A 8 7
♣ J 10 9

South (You)
♠ A 8 7
♥ K Q 2
♦ 5 4 3 2
♣ A Q 8

Figure 4-11: This hand is ready-made for a hold-up play.

> ✔ **Spades:** One sure trick — the ♠A
>
> ✔ **Hearts:** Three sure tricks — the ♥AKQ
>
> ✔ **Diamonds:** No sure tricks — no ace
>
> ✔ **Clubs:** One sure trick — the ♣A

You have five sure tricks; you need nine, and those super strong diamonds in the dummy offer your only chance of making your contract. If you can drive out the ♦A, you get four diamond tricks just like that. But life isn't quite that easy. You have that little matter of the ♠K lead to deal with.

In the following sections, I go over the hand in Figure 4-11 at length, walking you through the hold-up play you use in this scenario to make your contract. I explain two crucial concepts in using the hold-up play: paying attention to your opponents' opening lead and dealing with the danger hand. Hang in there with me and I'll have you stopping your opponents dead in their tracks while scooping up all the tricks you need to make your contract.

Opening your eyes to the opening lead

When you play a hand, the opening lead is a very important card because it tells you a lot about what your opponents are up to. Make sure to take a good look at the opening lead. Speaking from experience, the opening lead can come back to haunt you if you don't pay attention to it.

In the case of the cards in Figure 4-11, the lead of an honor card by West, the ♠K, sends a special message around the table. It says, "Partner, my spades are very strong, and I am leading my highest of three or four equal honors." In other words, West is saying loud and clear that he has the ♠KQJ or perhaps the ♠KQ10. (For more information on the opening lead, see Chapter 18.)

Even though West holds ominous spades, you don't have to just sit there and take it. You should at least try to plot a countermeasure. Take a look at those spades again, which you can see in Figure 4-12.

The two key suits in this hand are spades and diamonds. Spades is the suit your opponents are trying to establish, and diamonds is the suit you want to establish. Because your opponents have the opening lead, they're ahead in the race.

More contracts are lost at trick one than at all the other tricks combined! Keeping that terrifying statistic in mind, take yet another look at those spades in Figure 4-12. Notice that East has the ♦A, the card you must drive out to develop those four extra tricks you need, and three spades.

The good news is that your spade stopper is the ♠A (a *stopper* is a card that at least temporarily keeps your opponents from taking their winning tricks). The bad news is that your opponents have attacked a suit in which you have only that one stopper. If you win the first trick with your ♠A, West remains with four winning spades and East remains with two spades. If you win the second spade, West remains with three winning spades and East with one spade. And if you win the third spade, West remains with two winning spades, and East has no more spades. West has been able to set up (establish) his spades before you can even begin to set up your diamonds. There's trouble, right here in River City.

At least your spade stopper is the ♠A. The ♠A is a *flexible stopper,* the best kind. A flexible stopper is one you can take whenever you want to. You can take that ♠A at trick one, trick two, or trick three. Does it matter when you take the trick? It matters big time.

Suppose you win the ♠A at the first trick, and you then lead a low diamond from your hand, the ♦2, and play the ♦9 from the dummy. East takes the trick with the ♦A and leads a spade over to those lovely spades in West. West has the ♠QJ109, all winning tricks, which she takes one by one as you watch in silent agony. You wind up losing four spade tricks plus the ♦A. After you lose these five tricks, you can't take the nine tricks you need to make your contract. Your partner isn't happy, but your opponents are. What went wrong? Plenty.

Figure 4-12:
You can neutralize West's spades by making a hold-up play.

North (Dummy)
♠ 6 5

West
♠ K Q J 10 9

```
  N
W   E
  S
```

East
♠ 4 3 2
♦ A

South (You)
♠ A 8 7

Return to the scene of the crime (the first trick) and gaze once again at those spades. This time, you're going to let the bad guys have the first two spade tricks, and you're going to win the third round of the suit with the ♠A. By holding up the ace until the third round, you isolate the two remaining winning spades with West. East has none. Now you can turn your attention to diamonds, arriving at the position you see in Figure 4-13.

The moment East wins the trick with his ♦A, your sure trick count increases from five to nine because you established four winning diamond tricks in the dummy: the ♦KQJ10. Wait, I have even more good news: East doesn't have any more spades, while West is sitting over there with two winning spades. By winning the third round of spades, you cut the spade lifeline between East and West, forcing East to lead another suit upon winning the ♦A. East does best to shift to the ♣J.

After you drive out the ♦A and survive the spade onslaught, you have enough sure tricks to make your contract, so take them! Win the ♣A and take four diamonds, three hearts, and two black aces for nine big ones.

Don't even think of risking your contract by trying to finesse clubs by playing the ♣Q. The finesse goes smack into West, the guy with the two winning spades. Only a finesseaholic makes such a play.

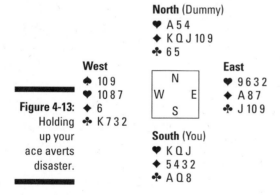

North (Dummy)
♥ A 5 4
♦ K Q J 10 9
♣ 6 5

West
♠ 10 9
♥ 10 8 7
♦ 6
♣ K 7 3 2

East
♥ 9 6 3 2
♦ A 8 7
♣ J 10 9

Figure 4-13:
Holding up your ace averts disaster.

South (You)
♥ K Q J
♦ 5 4 3 2
♣ A Q 8

Dealing with the danger hand

In bridge, when a particular opponent has winning tricks and can hurt you by gaining the lead, you call that opponent the *danger hand*. For example, in Figure 4-13, after you win the third round of spades, West is the danger hand because West has two winning spades. Stay clear of West. East has no more spades, so East is the *nondanger hand.* You can hang out with East because East can't hurt you even if East gets the lead in another suit.

In the following sections, I provide advice on dealing with the danger hand.

Voiding one opponent to isolate the danger hand

When you make a hold-up play, your intent is to void one opponent in the suit that was led. Usually you're trying to void the partner of the opening leader — usually, but not always, as you can see in Figure 4-14.

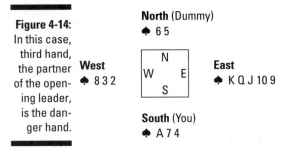

Figure 4-14:
In this case, third hand, the partner of the opening leader, is the danger hand.

North (Dummy)
♠ 6 5

West
♠ 8 3 2

East
♠ K Q J 10 9

South (You)
♠ A 7 4

In the hand in Figure 4-14, East bids spades, and West leads a low spade, the ♠2. You win the third round of spades with your ♠A, a flexible stopper. In this case, East is the danger hand because he has two winning spades and West has none. If you have to lose a trick, you hope that West wins that trick because West has no more spades to lead.

Using a flexible stopper to your advantage

A *flexible stopper* is the highest remaining card in a suit that can take a trick whenever you wish. Aces are always flexible stoppers, but a king can be a flexible stopper if the ace has already been played. Figure 4-15 shows a hand where the king gets upgraded to flexible-stopper status.

In this hand, West leads the ♠5, and East plays the ♠A. After taking the trick, East returns the ♠7. Your ♠K is the highest outstanding spade and is a flexible stopper. You don't have to take the trick just yet. You can play the ♠10 and allow West to take the trick with the ♠J. Say that West plays a third spade, the ♠Q, which you must take with your ♠K. Fine. Because of your hold-up play, you have cut your opponents' spade lifeline. If East gets the lead later in the hand, East can't hurt you by playing a spade, because he doesn't have any!

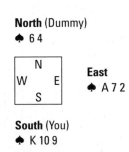

Figure 4-15:
A king is a flexible stopper after the ace is played.

North (Dummy)
♠ 6 4

West
♠ Q J 8 5 3

East
♠ A 7 2

South (You)
♠ K 10 9

Avoiding a hold-up when you don't have a flexible stopper

When your stopper isn't flexible, grab the trick while you can. Figure 4-16 shows you when not to hold up.

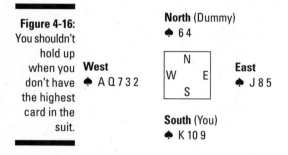

Figure 4-16:
You shouldn't hold up when you don't have the highest card in the suit.

North (Dummy)
♠ 6 4

West
♠ A Q 7 3 2

N
W   E
S

East
♠ J 8 5

South (You)
♠ K 10 9

West leads the ♠3, and East plays the ♠J. Grab the ♠K! Your ♠K isn't the highest outstanding spade. The ♠A is still out there roaming around. If you don't take your ♠K, East's ♠J will take the trick. Now East returns a spade, and your ♠K is mincemeat. You remain with the ♠K10. If you play the ♠10, West wastes no time or effort snatching it up with the ♠Q. If you play the ♠K, West then tramples all over it with the ♠A. East-West will take five spade tricks, and you won't take any!

You can make a hold-up play only when you have the highest card or the highest remaining card in the suit. If you don't have the highest card in the suit, just take the trick.

If you have enough tricks to make your contract, take them. Whatever you do, try to avoid taking any finesses into the danger hand.

Overtaking One Honor with Another

When you're taking tricks, sometimes you can't afford to be miserly with your honor cards. With equal honors between the two hands, you may have to play two honors on the same trick (*overtaking* one with another) to wind up in the hand with the greater length. It only hurts for a little while. Figure 4-17 shows you what you have to do.

At notrump, your goal is to take three spade tricks. Lead the ♠K from your own hand, overtake with the ♠A in the dummy, and then play the ♠Q and ♠J from the dummy on the next two tricks. If you don't overtake the ♠K with the ♠A, you may not be able to reach the dummy in another suit to take the other two spade tricks. Greed and miserliness will beat you.

Figure 4-18 is another example of where stinginess strikes out.

Figure 4-17:
Overtake
the king
with the ace
to land in
the dummy
and be able
to take the
queen and
jack.

North (Dummy)
♠ A Q J

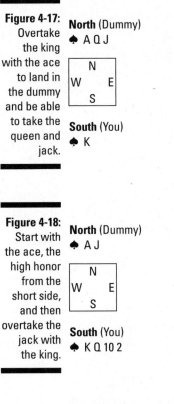

South (You)
♠ K

Figure 4-18:
Start with
the ace, the
high honor
from the
short side,
and then
overtake the
jack with
the king.

North (Dummy)
♠ A J

South (You)
♠ K Q 10 2

At notrump, you want to take four spade tricks. Begin with the ♠A (the high card from the short side, which is the dummy in this case) and play the ♠2 from your own hand. Continue with the ♠J from the dummy. Your hand remains with the ♠KQ10, all equal to the jack. Overtake the ♠J with the ♠K, the higher of equals from the closed hand for deceptive purposes, and take two more winning spades.

If you play the ♠10 under your jack (ugly!), you're stuck in the dummy and may not be able to reenter your hand in another suit to take your remaining spade winners.

When all your honor cards (or even spot cards) are equals, you may have to overtake one with another in order to continue playing the suit. Just do it!

Part II
Playing the Hand in a Trump Contract

The 5th Wave   By Rich Tennant

"No, it's not my ex-husband. Worse — my ex-bridge partner."

In this part . . .

Yٰou've come to the right part of the book if you want to discover the beauty and glory of playing in a trump contract. The addition of wild (trump) cards can wreak havoc on your opponents. Unfortunately, it can backfire and wreak havoc on *you* if you're not careful in the play of the hand. In this part, I show you how to get the most out of a hand when a trump suit is involved. Among other topics, I cover trump suits, counting losers, using extra winners to discard losers, and long-suit establishment.

Chapter 5

Introducing Trump Suits

In This Chapter

▶ Discovering the pros and cons of playing in a trump suit

▶ Disarming your opponents by drawing trumps

▶ Searching for eight-card or longer trump fits

▶ Keeping track of losers and extra winners

The previous chapters focus on notrump play because the basics of taking tricks are easier to understand without the complicating factor of trump suits. But this chapter introduces you to an exciting new aspect of the game. Trump suits are an unavoidable (and intriguing) part of bridge.

In this chapter, you discover how to use your trump suit to your best advantage. I show you how to knock the wind out of your opponents' sails by preventing them from taking scads of tricks in their strong suits. I also show you the proper sequence of plays, which allows you to take your winning tricks safely. In short, this chapter gives you your first taste of the wonderful powers of the trump suit.

Understanding the Basics of Trump Suits

In bridge, the bidding often designates a suit as the *trump suit*. If the final contract has a suit associated with it: 4♠, 3♥, 2♦, or even 1♣, for example, that suit becomes the trump suit for the entire hand. (See Chapter 9 for a primer on bidding; Parts III and IV are full of great bidding techniques.)

Often, in bridge books such as this one, a single card like the four of spades is written *S4* because it saves space. Similarly, a bid made by any player, such as four spades, is written *4S* (notice the difference). A final contract is written the same way as a bid, so a contract of three diamonds usually appears as *3D*.

When a suit becomes the trump suit, any card in that trump suit potentially has special powers; any card in the trump suit can win a trick over any card of another suit. For example, suppose that spades is the trump suit and West leads with the ♥A. You can still win the trick with the ♠2 (if you have no hearts in your hand and can't follow suit).

Because trump suits have so much power, naturally everyone at the table wants to have a say in determining the trump suit. Because bridge is a partnership game, your partnership determines which suit is the best trump suit for your side or whether there shouldn't be a trump suit at all.

In the following sections, I show you the glory (and potential danger) of trump suits.

Finding out when trumping saves the day

You can easily see the advantage of playing with a trump suit. When the bidding designates a trump suit, you may well be in a position to neutralize your opponents' long, strong suits quite easily. After either you or your partner is *void* (has no cards left) in the suit that your opponents lead, you can play any of your cards in the trump suit and take the trick. This little maneuver is called *trumping* your opponents' trick (which your opponents really hate).

In contrast, if you play a hand at a *notrump contract,* the highest card played in the suit led always takes the trick (see Chapters 3 and 4 for more information on playing at notrump). If an opponent with the lead has a suit headed by all winning cards, that opponent can wind up killing you by playing all her winning cards — be it four, five, six, or seven — taking one trick after another as you watch helplessly. Such is the beauty and the horror of playing a hand at notrump. You see the beauty when your side is peeling off the tricks; you experience the horror when your opponents start peeling them off one by one — sometimes slowly, to torture you.

The hand in Figure 5-1 shows you the power of playing in a trump suit.

North (Dummy)
♠ 9 8 5 3
♥ 7 6 3
♦ A K Q
♣ A 7 6

West
♠ 10 6
♥ A K Q J 2
♦ 8
♣ 10 9 5 3 2

	N	
W		E
	S	

East
♠ 7 4
♥ 10 9 5
♦ J 10 7 5 4 3
♣ J 8

Figure 5-1:
Your
trump suit
stops the
bleeding.

South (You)
♠ A K Q J 2
♥ 8 4
♦ 9 6 2
♣ K Q 4

A quick history lesson on bridge terms

Trumping is also called *ruffing*. The words *trump* and *ruff* have a very interesting history. Trump derives from *Triomphe*, a French game, which may have something in common with *Trionfi*, an Italian word used to describe tarot cards in the 15th century. *Ruff* derives from a variation of whist (the predecessor of bridge), which was known as *Ruff and Honors* for reasons lost in the mists of time.

On this hand, suppose that you need nine tricks to make your contract of 3NT (*NT* stands for *notrump*). Between your hand and the dummy, you can count 11 sure tricks: five spades (after the ♠AK are played and both opponents follow, the opponents have no more spades, so ♠QJ2 are all sure tricks), three diamonds, and three clubs. (Chapter 2 has details on how to count sure tricks.)

If you play the hand shown in Figure 5-1 in notrump, all your sure tricks won't help you if your opponents have the lead and can race off winning tricks in a suit where you're weak in both hands, such as hearts. Playing in notrump, West can use the opening lead to win the first five heart tricks by leading the ♥AKQJ2, in that order. To put it mildly, this start isn't healthy. You need to take nine tricks, meaning you can only afford to lose four, and you've already lost the first five.

On this hand, you and your partner need to communicate accurately in the bidding to discover which suit (hearts, in this case) is woefully weak in both hands. When you both are weak in the same suit, you need to end the bidding in a trump suit so you can stop the bleeding by eventually trumping if the opponents stubbornly persist in leading your weak suit.

In Figure 5-1, assume that during the bidding, spades becomes the trump suit and you need ten tricks to fulfill your contract. When West begins with ♥AKQ, you can trump the third heart with your ♠2 and take the trick. (You must follow suit if you can, so you can't trump either of your opponents' first two hearts.) Instead of losing five heart tricks, you lose only two.

Seeing how trumping can ruin your day

Bear in mind that your opponents can also use their trump cards effectively; if they hold no cards in the suit that you or your partner lead, they can trump one of your tricks. Misery.

After you have the lead, you want to prevent your opponents from trumping your winning tricks. You don't want your opponents to exercise the same strategy on you that you used on them! You need to get rid of their trumps before they can hurt you. This move is called *drawing trumps,* which I show you how to do in the following section.

Eliminating Your Opponents' Trump Cards

If you can trump your opponents' winning tricks when you don't have any cards in the suit that they're leading, it follows that your opponents can turn the tables and do the same to you. Instead of allowing your opponents to trump your sure tricks, play your higher trumps early on in the hand. Because your opponents must follow suit, you can remove their lower trumps *before* you take your sure tricks. If you can extract their trumps, you effectively remove their fangs. This extraction is called *pulling* or *drawing trumps.* Drawing trumps allows you to take your winning tricks in peace, without fear of your opponents trumping them.

The dangers of taking sure tricks before drawing trumps

Send the children out of the room and see what happens if you try to take sure tricks *before* you draw trumps. For example, in Figure 5-1 (where spades are trump), after you trump the third round of hearts, if you lead the ♦2, West has to follow suit by playing the only diamond in his hand, the ♦8. You then play the ♦Q from the dummy, East plays a low (meaning lowest) diamond, the ♦3, and you take the trick. However, if you follow up by playing the ♦A, West has no more diamonds and can trump the ace with the ♠6 because the bidding has designated spades as the trump suit for this hand.

The same misfortune befalls you if, instead of playing diamonds, you try to take three club tricks. East can trump the third round of clubs with the lowly ♠4. Imagine your discomfort when you see your opponents trump your sure tricks. They, on the other hand, are thrilled over this turn of events.

You should usually try to draw trumps as soon as possible. Get your opponents' pesky trump cards out of your hair. Then you can sit back and watch as your winning tricks come home safely to your trick pile.

The joys of drawing trumps first

To see how drawing trumps can work to your advantage, take a look at Figure 5-2, which shows only spades (the trump suit) in the hand in Figure 5-1. Remember, your goal is ten tricks.

Drawing trumps is just like playing any suit — you have to count the cards in the suit to know if you have successfully drawn all your opponents' trump cards. For more about counting cards, see Chapter 3.

In the hand shown in Figure 5-2, you and your partner start life with nine spades between you, leaving only four spades that your opponents can possibly hold. Suppose that you play the ♠A — both opponents must follow suit and play one of their spades. You win the trick, and you know that your opponents have only two spades left. Suppose that you continue with the ♠K, and both opponents follow. Now they have no spades left (no more trump cards). You have drawn trumps. See? That wasn't so bad.

Refer back to Figure 5-1 (where West begins with the ♥AKQ, and you trump the third heart with your ♠2). After you trump the third heart, you draw trumps by playing the ♠AK. You can then safely take your ♣AKQ and your ♦AKQ — you wind up losing only two heart tricks. You needed to take 10 tricks to fulfill your contract, and you in fact finished up with 11 tricks. Pretty good! Drawing trumps helped you make your contract.

Figure 5-2:
Drawing
trumps
removes
your
opponents'
fangs.

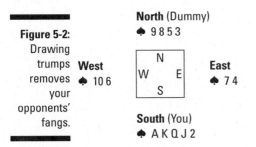

North (Dummy)
♠ 9 8 5 3

West
♠ 10 6

East
♠ 7 4

South (You)
♠ A K Q J 2

Looking at How Trump Suits Can Be Divided

In the discussions about bidding in Parts III and IV, you discover when to play a hand with a trump suit and when to play a hand without a trump suit (notrump). In this section, keep in mind that if you have eight or more cards in a suit between your hand and the dummy, particularly in a *major suit* (either hearts or spades), you try to make that suit your trump suit.

An *eight-card fit* (eight cards in a single suit between your hand and the dummy) gives you a safety net because you have many more trumps than your opponents: Your trumps outnumber theirs eight to five. Having more trumps than your opponents is always to your advantage. You may be able to survive a seven-card trump fit, but having an eight- or nine-card trump fit relieves tension. The more trumps you have, the more tricks you can generate and the less chance your opponents have of taking tricks with their trumps. You can never have too many trumps! The fewer trump cards your opponents have, the easier it is for you to get rid of their fangs — oops, I mean trumps.

In the following sections, I show you a variety of trump fits.

Scoring big with the 4-4 trump fit

During the bidding, you may discover that you have an eight-card fit divided 4-4 between the two hands. Try to make such a fit your trump suit. A 4-4 trump fit almost always produces at least one more trick in the play of the hand, as opposed to notrump.

At a notrump contract, the 4-4 fit in Figure 5-3 takes four tricks. At notrump, when each partner has four cards in the same suit, four tricks is your max.

Figure 5-3:
In this 4-4 trump fit, you can take five tricks.

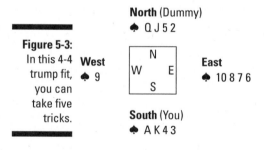

North (Dummy)
♠ Q J 5 2

West
♠ 9

East
♠ 10 8 7 6

South (You)
♠ A K 4 3

However, when spades is your trump suit, you can do better. In Figure 5-3, suppose that your opponents lead a suit that you don't have, which allows you to trump their lead with the ♠3. By drawing trumps now (see "Eliminating Your Opponents' Trump Cards" earlier in this chapter for more on drawing trumps), you can take four more spade tricks by playing the ♠A and the ♠K from your hand (high honors from the short side first) and then playing the ♠4 over to the ♠J and ♠Q from the dummy. You wind up taking a total of five spade tricks — the card you trumped plus four more high spades.

A 4-4 trump fit is primo. You can get more for your money from this trump fit. Every so often you can take six (or more) trump tricks when you have a 4-4 trump fit, so keep your eyes open for 4-4 trump fits!

Being aware of other eight-card trump fits

Eight-card trump fits can come in different guises. Consider the eight-card trump fits in Figure 5-4. The figure shows examples of a 5-3, a 6-2, and a 7-1 fit. Good bidding uncovers eight-card (or longer) fits, which makes for safe trump suits. There is joy in numbers.

Figure 5-4: Some of the many faces of an eight-card trump fit.	♠ Q 4 2 **North** (Dummy) ♠ K J 7 5 3 **South** (You) 1	♠ J 4 **North** (Dummy) ♠ Q 10 7 5 3 2 **South** (You) 2	♠ 6 **North** (Dummy) ♠ A J 9 7 4 3 2 **South** (You) 3

Counting Losers and Extra Winners

When playing a hand at a trump contract, instead of counting sure tricks (discussed in Chapter 2), your strategy is to count how many losers you have. If you have too many losers to make your contract, you need to look in the dummy for extra winners (tricks) that you can use to dispose of some of your losers.

You may find this approach a rather negative way of playing a hand. But counting losers can have a very positive impact on your play at a trump contract. Your loser count tells you how many extra winners you need, if any. Extra winners are an indispensable security blanket to make your contract — extra winners help you get rid of losers.

In the following sections, I define losers and extra winners and show you how to identify them. I also explain when to draw trumps before taking extra winners and when to take extra winners before drawing trumps.

Defining losers and extra winners

When playing a hand at a notrump contract, you count your sure tricks (as I describe in Chapter 2); however, when you play a hand at a trump contract, you count losers and extra winners. *Losers* are tricks you know you have to lose. For example, if neither you nor your partner holds the ace in a suit, you know you have to lose at least one trick in that suit unless, of course, you are void (have no cards) in the suit. *Extra winners* may allow you to get rid of some of your losers. What exactly is an extra winner? An extra winner is a winning trick in the dummy (North) on which you can discard a loser from your own hand (South).

Get ready for some good news: When counting losers, you have to count only the losers in the *long hand,* the hand that has more trumps. The declarer usually is the long trump hand, but not always.

Do me a favor and, for the time being, just accept the fact that you don't have to count losers in the dummy. Counting losers in one hand is bad enough; counting losers in the dummy is not only unnecessary but also confusing and downright depressing.

Recognizing immediate and eventual losers

Losers come in two forms: *immediate* and *eventual.* Immediate losers are losers that your opponents can take when they have the lead. These losers have a special danger signal attached to them that reads, "Danger — Unexploded Bomb!" Immediate losers spell bad news.

Of course, eventual losers aren't exactly a welcome occurrence, either. Your opponents can't take your eventual losers right away because those losers are *protected* by a winning card in the suit that you or your partner holds. In other words, with eventual losers, your opponents can't take their tricks right off the bat, which buys you time to get rid of those eventual losers. One of the best ways to get rid of eventual losers is to discard them on extra winners.

You help yourself by knowing which of your losers are eventual and which are immediate. Your game plan depends on your immediate loser count. See "Drawing trumps before taking extra winners" and "Taking extra winners before drawing trumps" later in this chapter for more about how to proceed after counting your immediate losers.

Because identifying eventual and immediate losers is so important, take a look at the spades in Figures 5-5, 5-6, and 5-7 to spot some losers. Assume in these figures that spades is a *side suit* (any suit that is not the trump suit) and hearts is your trump suit.

Figure 5-5 shows a suit with two eventual losers. In the hand in this figure, as long as you have the ♠A protecting your two other spades, your two spade losers are eventual. However, after your opponents lead a spade (which forces out your ace), your two remaining spades become immediate losers because they have no winning trick protecting them.

In Figure 5-6, you have one eventual spade loser. With the spades in Figure 5-6, the dummy's ♠AK protect two of your three spades — but your third spade is on its own as a loser after the ♠A and ♠K have been played.

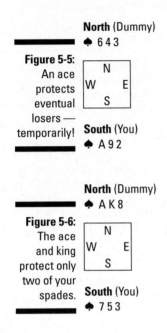

North (Dummy)
♠ 6 4 3

Figure 5-5:
An ace
protects
eventual
losers —
temporarily!

South (You)
♠ A 9 2

North (Dummy)
♠ A K 8

Figure 5-6:
The ace
and king
protect only
two of your
spades.

South (You)
♠ 7 5 3

In Figure 5-7, you have two immediate spade losers. Notice that you count two, not three, spade losers — you count losers only in the long trump hand (which presumably is your hand). You don't have to count losers in the dummy. Actually, when you are playing a 4-4 trump fit, no long hand exists, so assume the hand with the longer side suit (five or more cards) is the long hand. When neither hand has a long side suit, the hand with the stronger trumps is considered the long hand.

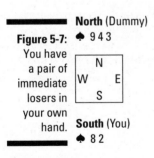

North (Dummy)
♠ 9 4 3

Figure 5-7:
You have
a pair of
immediate
losers in
your own
hand.

South (You)
♠ 8 2

Identifying extra winners

Enough with losers already — counting them is sort of a downer. You can get rid of some of your losers by using extra winners. Extra winners come into play only after you (South) are void in the suit being played. Therefore, extra winners can exist only in a suit that's unevenly divided between the two hands and is usually in the dummy. The stronger the extra winner suit (that is, the more high cards it has), the better.

Figure 5-8 shows you two extra winners in their natural habitat. The cards in this figure fill the bill for extra winners because spades is an unevenly divided suit, and the greater length is in the dummy. After you lead the ♠3 and play the ♠Q from the dummy, you're void in spades. Now you can discard two losers from your hand when you lead the ♠A and the ♠K from the dummy. Therefore, you can count two extra winners in spades.

North (Dummy)
♠ A K Q

Figure 5-8:
You find two extra winners in the dummy.

South (You)
♠ 3

By contrast, the cards in Figure 5-9 look hopeful, but unfortunately, they can't offer you any extra winners. They don't fit the mold for extra winners because you have the same number of spades in each hand. No matter how strong a suit is, if you have the same number of cards in each hand, you can't squeeze any extra winners out of the suit. You just have to follow suit each time. True, the ♠AKQ aren't chopped liver; although this hand has no spade losers, it gives you no extra winners, either. Sorry!

Figure 5-9:
You won't find any extra winners in this suit, no matter how hard you squint.

North (Dummy)
♠ A K Q

```
    N
W       E
    S
```

South (You)
♠ 8 6 4

The cards in Figure 5-10 contain no extra winners, either. The dummy's ♠AK take care of your two losing spades, but you have nothing "extra" over there — no ♠Q, for example — on which you can discard one of your losers. This spade suit has no losers and no extra winners. You need to have "extra" winners to be able to throw a loser away. In Figure 5-10, your ♠A and ♠K do an excellent job of covering your two spade losers, but no more. You can't squeeze blood out of a turnip.

North (Dummy)
♠ A K 7 6

Figure 5-10:
This hand
has losers
but no extra
winners.

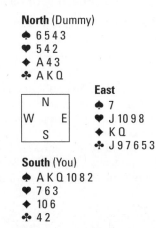

South (You)
♠ 4 2

Drawing trumps before taking extra winners

After counting your immediate losers (see "Recognizing immediate and eventual losers" earlier in this chapter), if you still have enough tricks to make your contract, go ahead and draw trumps before taking extra winners. That way, you can make sure that your opponents don't swoop down on you with a trump card and spoil your party. Figure 5-11 illustrates this point by showing you a hand where spades is your trump suit. You need to take ten tricks to make your contract. West leads the ♥A.

North (Dummy)
♠ 6 5 4 3
♥ 5 4 2
♦ A 4 3
♣ A K Q

Figure 5-11:
Be sure to
count losers
and extra
winners so
you have a
plan for the
hand.

West
♠ J 9
♥ A K Q
♦ J 9 8 7 6 5
♣ 10 8

East
♠ 7
♥ J 10 9 8
♦ K Q
♣ J 9 7 6 5 3

South (You)
♠ A K Q 10 8 2
♥ 7 6 3
♦ 10 6
♣ 4 2

Before playing a card from the dummy, count your losers one suit at a time, starting with the trump suit, the most important suit. You can't make a plan for the hand until your opponents make the opening lead because you can't see the dummy until the opening lead is made. But as soon as the dummy comes down, try to curb your understandable eagerness to play a card from the dummy and do a little loser counting in each suit instead:

- **Spades:** In your trump suit (spades), you're well heeled. You have ten spades between the two hands, including the ♠AKQ. Because your opponents have only three spades, you should have no trouble removing their spades. A suit with no losers is called a *solid suit.* You have a solid spade suit — you can never have too many solid suits.

- **Hearts:** In hearts, however, you have trouble — big trouble. In this case, your own hand has three heart losers. But before you count three losers, check to see whether the dummy has any high cards in hearts to neutralize any of your losers. In this case, your partner doesn't come through for you at all, having only three baby hearts. You have three heart losers, and they're immediate losers.

- **Diamonds:** In diamonds, you have two losers, but this time your partner does go to bat for you, with the ♦A as a winner. The ♦A negates one of your diamond losers, but you still have to count one eventual diamond loser.

- **Clubs:** In clubs, you have two losers, but in this suit your partner really does come through. Not only does your partner take care of your two losers with the ♣AK, but your partner also has an extra winner, the ♣Q. Count one extra winner in clubs.

Your mental score card for this hand reads as follows:

- **Spades:** A solid suit, no losers

- **Hearts:** Three losers (the three cards in your hand)

- **Diamonds:** One loser, because your partner covers one of your losers with the ace

- **Clubs:** One extra winner

Next, you determine how many losers you can lose and still make your contract. In this case, you need to take ten tricks, which means that you can afford to lose three tricks. (Remember, each hand has 13 tricks up for grabs.)

If you have more losers than you can afford, you need to figure out how to get rid of those pesky deadbeats. One way to get rid of losers is by using extra winners — and you just happen to have an extra winner in clubs.

Follow the play: West starts out by leading the ♥AKQ, taking the first three tricks. You can do absolutely nothing about losing these heart tricks — which is why you call them *immediate* losers (tricks that your opponents can take whenever they want). Immediate losers are the pits, especially if they lead that suit.

After taking the first three heart tricks, West decides to shift to a low diamond, which establishes an immediate winner for your opponents in diamonds and an immediate loser for you in diamonds when the ♦A is played from dummy. You may be strongly tempted to get rid of that loser immediately on the dummy's clubs — just looking at it may be making you nervous. Don't do it. Draw trump first. If you play the ♣AKQ from the dummy before you draw trump, West will trump the third club, and down you go in a contract you should make.

You need to draw trumps first and *then* play the ♣AKQ. West won't be able to trump any of your good tricks, nor will East — they won't have any trumps left. You wind up losing only three heart tricks — and making your contract!

The most favorable sequence of plays, after losing the first three heart tricks and winning the ♦A, is as follows:

1. **Play the ♠AK, removing all your opponents' trumps.**

2. **Play the ♣AKQ and throw that diamond loser away.**

3. **Sit back and take the rest of the tricks now that you have only trumps left.**

Any time you can draw trump before taking your extra winners, do it.

Taking extra winners before drawing trumps

When you have more immediate losers than you can afford to make your contract but you also have an extra winner, use that extra winner immediately before you give up the lead in the trump suit. If you don't, your opponents will mow you down by taking their tricks all at once. However, if you can draw trumps without giving up the lead, do that first and then take your extra winner as in Figure 5-11.

Figure 5-12 shows you the importance of taking your extra winners before drawing trump. In this hand, your losers are immediate — if your opponents get the lead, you can pack up and go home.

In the hand in Figure 5-12, your contract is for ten tricks, with spades as the trump suit. West leads the ♦K, trying to establish diamond tricks after the ♦A is played. After dummy's ♦A has been played, West's ♦Q and ♦J are promoted to sure winners on subsequent tricks.

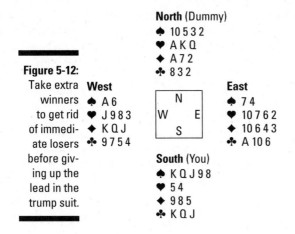

Figure 5-12:
Take extra winners to get rid of immediate losers before giving up the lead in the trump suit.

North (Dummy)
♠ 10 5 3 2
♥ A K Q
♦ A 7 2
♣ 8 3 2

West
♠ A 6
♥ J 9 8 3
♦ K Q J
♣ 9 7 5 4

East
♠ 7 4
♥ 10 7 6 2
♦ 10 6 4 3
♣ A 10 6

South (You)
♠ K Q J 9 8
♥ 5 4
♦ 9 8 5
♣ K Q J

After you count your losers, you tally up the following losers and extra winners:

✔ **Spades:** One immediate loser — the ♠A

✔ **Hearts:** One extra winner — the ♥Q

✔ **Diamonds:** Two losers, which are immediate after you play the ♦A

✔ **Clubs:** One immediate loser — the ♣A

You win the opening lead with the ♦A. Suppose that you lead a low spade from dummy at trick two and play the ♠K from your hand, intending to draw trumps, *usually* a good idea. (See "Eliminating Your Opponents' Trump Cards," earlier in this chapter, for more information on drawing trumps.)

However, West wins the trick with the ♠A and takes the ♦QJ, and East still gets a trick with the ♣A. You lose four tricks. What happened? You went down in your contract while your extra winner, the ♥Q, was still sitting over there in the dummy, gathering dust. You never got to use your extra winner in hearts because you drew trumps too quickly. When you led a spade at the second trick, you had four losers, all immediate. And sure enough, your opponents took all four of them.

If you want to make your contract on this hand, you need to play that extra heart winner *before* you draw trumps. You can't afford to give up the lead just yet. The winning play goes something like this:

1. **You take the ♦A at trick one, followed by the ♥AKQ at tricks two, three, and four.**

2. **On the third heart you can discard one of your diamond losers.** This play reduces your immediate loser count from an unwieldy four to a workable three.

3. **Now you can afford to lead a trump and give up the lead.** After all, you do want to draw trumps sooner or later.

If you play the hand properly, you wind up losing only one spade, one club, and one diamond — and you make your contract of ten tricks.

You may think that playing the ♥AKQ before you draw trumps is dangerous, but you have no choice. You have to get rid of one of your immediate diamond losers before giving up the lead if you want to make your contract. Otherwise, you're giving up the ship without a fight.

Chapter 6

Creating Extra Winners and Discarding Losers

· ·

In This Chapter

▶ Creating extra winners

▶ Taking finesses to establish extra winners

▶ Determining how to make your contract

· ·

Extra winners are a twofold blessing: They allow you to take tricks while you discard losers. When you have an extra winner in the dummy, you can play that winner and at the same time discard a loser from your hand. (See Chapter 5 for details on discarding losers on extra winners.)

On a good day, you find extra winners perched in the dummy, just waiting to take tricks for you. Unfortunately, those good days are few and far between. On most days, you need to set up your own extra winners in order to make your contract. I show you just how to establish extra winners in this chapter.

Establishing Extra Winners in the Dummy

To create extra winners, a suit should meet both the following conditions:

✔ Be unequally divided, meaning one hand holds more cards in the suit than the other

✔ Have the greater length (more cards) in the dummy

The more honor cards between your hand and the dummy, the better. (Remember that the honor cards are the ace, king, queen, jack, and 10.)

In the following sections, I show you how to create extra winners and explain when you can't establish extra winners. I also give you tips on driving out your opponents' honor cards to set up extra winners.

Recognizing a great chance for creating extra winners

Figure 6-1 shows you a suit that's just prime for developing extra winners: The suit is unevenly divided, with the greater length in the dummy. Plus, the dummy holds three honors, a running head start.

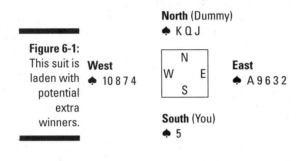

Figure 6-1: This suit is laden with potential extra winners.

North (Dummy)
♠ K Q J

West
♠ 10 8 7 4

N
W E
S

East
♠ A 9 6 3 2

South (You)
♠ 5

Start by leading the ♠5. West plays a low spade, the ♠4 (in this book, *low* means lowest), and you play the dummy's ♠J. Assume that the ♠J drives out the ♠A in East's hand. (See Chapter 3 for more information on driving out the ace.)

With the ♠A out of the way, you have created two extra winners: the ♠K and ♠Q. The ♠K and ♠Q are extra winners because they're the *boss* spades (the highest cards left in the suit), and you have no spades left. Later, when you play the ♠K and ♠Q, you can discard two losers from your hand (see Chapter 5 to find out how to count the losers in your hand).

Determining when you can't create extra winners

Unfortunately, you can't create extra winners in every suit you play. Figure 6-2 shows you the sad case of a suit that can't yield any extra winners because the cards are evenly divided (both you and the dummy hold three cards).

In Figure 6-2, suppose the lead is in the dummy from a previous trick and you lead the ♠J. (With equal honors you can just lead one of the equals without having to lead from weakness to strength; see Chapter 4 for details on leading toward a certain card.) Assuming that the ♠J drives out the ♠A in the East hand, you establish two tricks, the ♠K and ♠Q, but no extra winners (see Chapter 3 for more information on establishing tricks). You can't use either of the dummy's spades to discard a loser from your hand because both you and the dummy have the same number of spades, the death distribution for discarding losers. Live with it.

Figure 6-2: Because cards are evenly divided, this hand strikes out in extra winners.

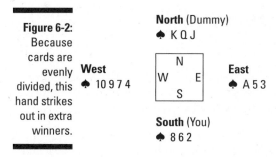

North (Dummy)
♠ K Q J

West
♠ 10 9 7 4

East
♠ A 5 3

South (You)
♠ 8 6 2

Driving out your opponents' honor cards to establish extra winners

On occasion, you have to do a little work to make those extra winners appear. You may have to drive out two honors in the same suit before you can create any extra winners in that suit. But the bottom line is that the suit you're working with must be unevenly divided, with the greater length in the dummy. You're spinning your wheels if you try to create extra winners in an evenly divided suit.

Take the cards in Figure 6-3 as an example.

Figure 6-3: Drive out two honor cards to create an extra winner.

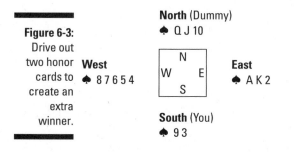

North (Dummy)
♠ Q J 10

West
♠ 8 7 6 5 4

East
♠ A K 2

South (You)
♠ 9 3

The cards in Figure 6-3 offer the opportunity to create an extra winner, but you need to drive out the ♠A and the ♠K before you can claim the extra winner. Start by leading the ♠3. West plays low, the ♠4, and you play the ♠10 from the dummy. As it happens, the ♠10 loses to East's ♠K. After you regain the lead by winning a trick in another suit, lead your remaining spade, the ♠9, West follows low again with the ♠5, and you play the ♠J. This time the ♠J loses to the ♠A, also in the East hand. You're left with the ♠Q in the dummy — an extra winner because the queen is the highest remaining spade at large and you have no more spades. After the dummy regains the lead by winning a trick in another suit, play the ♠Q and discard a loser. Phew!

Making sure you can reach your extra winners

When your suit fills the bill for creating extra winners but your equal honors are divided between the two hands, play the high honor card from the short side first. Doing so helps you reach the extra winner(s) you create.

Playing the high honor cards from the short side is a bit like unblocking a logjam; if you leave the honor in the hand with shortness, you leave the log in place and potentially create a fatal blockage. Be a beaver — unblock those honors!

In Figure 6-4, for example, you have three equal honor cards, the ♠KQJ, but the honors are divided between the two hands. Start by playing the ♠K, the high honor from the short side (South). Assume that your ♠K loses to West's ♠A. The dummy is left with the ♠QJ, and you're left with the ♠5. When you regain the lead, you can lead the ♠5 to the dummy's ♠J and then discard one of your losers on the extra winner, the ♠Q. If dummy regains the lead first in another suit, just take your two winning spade tricks. Nice unblock.

Figure 6-4:
Create extra winners by playing the high equal honor(s) from the short side first.

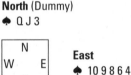

North (Dummy)
♠ Q J 3

West
♠ A 7 5 2

East
♠ 10 9 8 6 4

South (You)
♠ K 5

Finessing for Extra Winners

When playing at a trump contract, you can take a *finesse* to create extra winners, just as you do at a notrump contract (see Chapter 4 for more on finessing). You need the following setup to take a finesse and establish extra winners:

✔ An unevenly divided suit, meaning the dummy holds more cards in the suit than you do

✔ A majority of the honor cards, usually in the dummy

✔ The absence of one or more of the top four honor cards

In the following sections, I show you when to give finessing a whirl and when not to. I also show you a desperation finesse.

The good and the bad: When to try and when to avoid finessing

When you behold such a treasure as the items in the previous list, you can create extra winners in that suit by taking a finesse, leading from weakness to strength. This maneuver usually means playing a low card from your hand with the intention of playing an honor card from the dummy. But keep in mind that luck plays a role when taking a finesse. Because you don't know who has the missing honor(s), finesses work about half the time. Shed no tears if your finesse doesn't pan out. If the suit you're finessing has enough honor cards between the two hands, even if the finesse loses, you can still create at least one extra winner. Check this scenario out in Figure 6-5.

North (Dummy)
♠ A Q J

Figure 6-5:
Even when your finesse loses, you wind up with an extra winner!

South (You)
♠ 4 3

In Figure 6-5, you have the makings of an extra winner in spades because the dummy holds more cards than you, not to mention three honor cards.

You begin by leading the ♠3, from weakness to strength. West also plays a low spade, and you play the ♠J from the dummy.

Suppose East has the ♠K and takes the trick. It's not the end of the world; ♠AQ in the dummy are now the two highest remaining spades in the game — so you know you can win two tricks with those cards. When you or the dummy regain the lead by winning a trick in another suit, play the ♠A, removing your last spade, and then play the ♠Q. By the time you play the ♠Q, you won't have any more spades in your hand, so you can discard a loser. Voilà — an extra winner!

If the ♠J wins the trick, indicating that West figures to have the king, repeat the finesse (see Chapter 4 if you need help seeing the advantages of repeating a finesse). You must return to your hand with a winning trick in another suit and lead your remaining spade, the ♠4. Assuming West plays low, play the

♠Q, which should win the trick. Finally, you can discard a loser on the ♠A. In this scenario, you not only create an extra winner, but your finesse also works. Luck is on your side, and you don't lose a trick. (Note that it doesn't do West any good to play ♠K the second time the suit is led from your hand. The dummy, next to play, has the AQ and will cheerfully zap the king with the ace. Check out Chapter 19 for more information on second-hand play.)

On the other hand, in the cards in Figure 6-6, your honor strength isn't strong enough to create any extra winners. When you have only two honors in the dummy and no honors in your hand, it helps if the two honors are equals, such as the queen and the jack or the king and the queen. Because that's not the case here, this suit isn't such a hot one to attack early on. True, if the finesse wins, you have no loser, but you have no extra winner either. And if the finesse loses (if East has the ♠K), you lose one trick, and you have no extra winner to show for it.

In general, try to attack suits that have the potential for extra winners.

Figure 6-6:
Creating an extra winner is easier when the two honor cards in the dummy are equals — not the case here.

North (Dummy)
♠ A Q 7

```
    N
W       E
    S
```

South (You)
♠ 4 3

Take your best shot: Finessing when you really need extra winners

The way you attack a suit depends on the number of immediate losers you have and the number of extra winners you need. Desperate circumstances call for desperate plays!

In Figure 6-7, you have a suit with *one* extra winner simply by playing the ♠A and the ♠K. You can get that extra winner without losing a trick — an attractive prospect. But if your immediate loser count demands that you play spades for two extra winners (or three tricks), you have to take a chance on a finesse and lead a small card from your hand, from weakness toward strength. With your heart in your mouth, try playing the dummy's ♠J! If the ♠J wins, you create two extra winners; if the ♠J loses, at least you gave it your all. Bridge isn't for the faint of heart.

Figure 6-7:
Try to create two extra winners by playing the jack.

North (Dummy)
♠ A K J

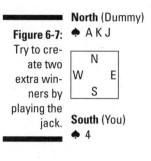

South (You)
♠ 4

In Figure 6-8, you have only one honor card in the dummy, but beggars can't be choosers. Lead low with the ♠3 from your hand toward the ♠K in the dummy. If West has the ♠A and plays it, your ♠K becomes an extra winner because you have no more spades in your hand. If West doesn't play the ♠A, you take the trick with your ♠K, and your spade loser vanishes. If East has the ♠A and takes your ♠K, don't send me a tear-stained letter bemoaning your fate; you took a risk that had a 50 percent chance of success. Sometimes it's just not your day!

Figure 6-8:
This hand gives you a 50-50 shot at creating an extra winner.

North (Dummy)
♠ K 7 6 4

```
    N
W       E
    S
```

South (You)
♠ 3

Determining How to Make Your Contract with Extra Winners

In this section, I want you to look at a hand and determine if you need to create any extra winners. In Figure 6-9, you can see both your hand and the dummy's. Count your losers in each suit and determine whether a straightforward plan of attack will do or whether you need to create extra winners to make your contract. (See Chapter 5 for more information about counting losers.)

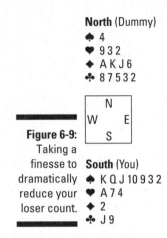

North (Dummy)
♠ 4
♥ 9 3 2
♦ A K J 6
♣ 8 7 5 3 2

Figure 6-9:
Taking a
finesse to
dramatically
reduce your
loser count.

South (You)
♠ K Q J 10 9 3 2
♥ A 7 4
♦ 2
♣ J 9

For the hand in Figure 6-9, your contract is for ten tricks and spades is the trump suit. West leads the ♥K. You count the following losers:

- **Spades:** One loser, because they're sure to take the ♠A.

- **Hearts:** Two immediate losers (after you play the ♥A): The dummy's hearts can't cover your two remaining small hearts, the ♥7 and the ♥4.

- **Diamonds:** No losers! In fact, you have one sure extra winner (the ♦A and ♦K. One covers your ♦2, and you still have an extra winner). You may have two extra winners if you want to risk a finesse by leading a low diamond to the ♦J.

- **Clubs:** Two immediate losers: The dummy doesn't have any winners that can cover the ♣9 and ♣J.

You have to take ten tricks, so you can afford only three losers. But you have five — count 'em, *five* — losers. The situation looks a little bleak, doesn't it? To make matters worse, all your losers are *immediate* after your ♥A is gone. The only resource you have is your diamond suit.

Getting rid of one heart or club loser by playing the ♦AK isn't enough. You need to get rid of *two* losers if you want to make your contract.

So what can you do? Go for a finesse! Win the first trick with the ♥A and lead a low diamond, the ♦2, to the ♦J in the dummy. If your finesse works, you can play the ♦AK, and because you have no more diamonds in your hand, you can discard two losers in either hearts or clubs. If the finesse loses (because East takes your ♦J with the ♦Q), you will lose your contract big time. However, you can console yourself knowing that you made the right play, the gutsy play that allows you to make your contract if the finesse works.

Before leaving the hand in Figure 6-9, pretend for a moment that you need to take only nine tricks, with spades still trumps and with the same opening lead (West's ♥K). In this contract, you can afford to lose four tricks, so you only have to get rid of *one* of your five losers to make the hand. Life is now a lot less challenging. Win the first trick with the ♥A and play the ♦AK from the dummy, discarding one loser from your hand on the second winning diamond, and then play a spade. No risky finesse is necessary in this contract — your loser count tells you how to play your diamond suit.

With all this finessing and creating extra winners going on, you may lose sight of your goal, which is making your final contract. Don't take any unnecessary risks, such as an unnecessary finesse, unless you need to do so to make your contract.

Chapter 7

Setting Up the Dummy's Long Suit

Most beginning bridge players rush to take aces and kings with the speed of summer lightning. But after the high of taking those few tricks is over, reality sets in. What now? The truth is that you seldom have enough aces and kings to make any contract. If you think about it, all the aces (four) and all the kings (four) add up to only eight tricks, and most contracts require you to take more than that number. And how often do you think you're going to have all the aces and kings between the two hands? Almost never, I'm afraid.

The answer to too many losers is being able to take tricks with the smaller cards attached to five- or six-card suits usually in the dummy. When your partner presents you with a five-card or six-card *side suit* (any suit that isn't the trump suit), he doesn't expect you to just sit there and admire it; he expects you to work with it so you can take extra tricks with the smaller cards in the suit. And I show you how to do exactly that in this chapter.

Laying out the cards as you read this chapter can help you see the plays more clearly. Have your deck of cards handy as you read.

Turning Small Cards into Winning Tricks

Whenever the dummy presents you with a five- or six-card side suit, you may have a chance to turn one or more of the small cards in that suit into winning tricks. Just play the suit and keep playing it, trumping one or two of those small cards in your hand, until both opponents are void in the suit (in other words, they have no cards left in the suit). Suddenly you may find yourself with an extra winner or two or *three* in the dummy! That situation is what the following sections are all about.

Knowing how to turn small cards into winners

To turn small cards in long suits into winning tricks, here's what you need:

- ✔ A five- or six-card side suit in the dummy with fewer than three cards in that suit in your hand.

- ✔ A strong five- or six-card trump suit in your hand.

- ✔ *Entries* to the dummy, which are high cards in the dummy either in the trump suit or in a side suit. (See "Ending up in the right place — the dummy" later in this chapter for more about entries.)

Squeezing tricks out of small cards in the dummy's long suit requires a bit of effort, and you may ask yourself if the tricks are really worth all the trouble. To spare yourself any unnecessary work, don't even think about messing with the dummy's long suit unless you have too many losers to make your contract or too few dummy entries to pull off this little caper.

Figure 7-1 shows a hand where the three requirements come into play, allowing you to establish the dummy's side suit. You and your partner determine during the bidding that your trump suit is hearts, and you contract for ten tricks. West leads the ♠A. If you need to take ten tricks, you can afford to lose three tricks. See whether you have more than three losers, and if you do, whether you can get rid of some of those losers.

The first rule of playing a hand is to think before you do something silly.

North (Dummy)
- ♠ 7 5 3
- ♥ A 3 2
- ♦ A K 4 3 2
- ♣ J 5

West
- ♠ A K Q
- ♥ 6 5 4
- ♦ 9 8 7
- ♣ K Q 7 6

```
  N
W   E
  S
```

East
- ♠ 10 9 4 2
- ♥ 7
- ♦ Q J 10
- ♣ 10 9 4 3 2

South (You)
- ♠ J 8 6
- ♥ K Q J 10 9 8
- ♦ 6 5
- ♣ A 8

Figure 7-1: Mine your small diamonds in this hand for winning tricks.

Take a look at your loser count for the hand in Figure 7-1 (see Chapter 5 for the basics on counting losers in your hand): You usually start counting losers in the trump suit, the most important suit. In this case, start with hearts.

- ✔ **Hearts:** No losers — hearts is a *solid suit.* You can never have too many solid suits.

- ✔ **Diamonds:** No losers and some potential to establish small cards in the suit (which is what this section is all about).

- ✔ **Clubs:** One loser, which is eventual rather than immediate. The loser is eventual because the ♣A allows you to control the suit, but your ♣8 is still a loser.

- ✔ **Spades:** Three relatively small spades in your hand add up to three immediate losers because your partner also has three small spades — the kiss of death. (Yes, the ♠J is an honor card, but because the opponents have the ♠AKQ, it has the value of a small card.)

You need to win ten tricks, but you have a total of four losers in your hand — that's one too many to make your contract. The potential answer to your club loser is that five-card diamond suit staring you in the face — your salvation. You need to turn one of those little diamonds into a winning trick and then use that established diamond to discard your losing ♣8. This maneuver sounds simple when I say it like that, doesn't it? Well, read on; the answer may not be as simple as ABC, but I think you'll agree it's not rocket science either.

Playing the long suit to the bitter end

In the hand in Figure 7-1, West begins by taking the first three spade tricks with the ♠AKQ and then switches (smartly) to the ♣K, driving out your ♣A and turning your ♣8 into an immediate loser. Fortunately, you have the lead *and* a five-card diamond suit to work with. You want to establish the dummy's long suit (make at least one of the small cards there into a winner), so you have to play the suit and keep playing it until both of your opponents run out of diamonds.

Start by leading a low diamond to the ♦K in the dummy; both of your opponents play low. Next, play the ♦A; both of your opponents play low again. You remain with three little diamonds in the dummy; the opponents have two diamonds left. The next step is to lead a low diamond from the dummy and trump it with the ♥8. Do you see what happens? Your opponents have both played their last diamond, and suddenly both remaining diamonds in the dummy are winning tricks! You've just set up a suit. But wait — you still have one more hurdle to clear.

Do you see those little hearts (four to be exact) in the West and East hands? Until you remove all those hearts, your winning diamonds in the dummy are worthless. If you try to play one, one of your opponents will trump your winning trick!

Banishing your opponents' trump cards

After you establish your small cards, you can't use them until you *draw all your opponents' trumps.* If you leave your opponents with trump cards, they'll trump the dummy's established small-card tricks. Figure 7-2 shows only the trump suit (the hearts) from Figure 7-1 after you've trumped a diamond. You desperately need to draw trumps to protect the small diamonds you've established as winners.

Figure 7-2: Draw trumps to protect your established winners.

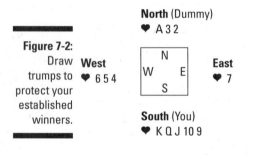

North (Dummy)
♥ A 3 2

West
♥ 6 5 4

East
♥ 7

South (You)
♥ K Q J 10 9

Your opponents have four hearts between their two hands. Those four hearts are tiny, but until you get rid of them, they can pester you to death — or at least to the death of your contract. Your plan of attack is to lead hearts three times, removing each and every heart from your opponents' hands. Now nothing can rain on your parade.

Ending up in the right place — the dummy

When drawing trumps to protect established winning tricks in the dummy, some players draw trumps helter-skelter, ending up in one hand or the other without focusing on a game plan of where they need to end up. These players run the risk of ending up with the lead in the wrong hand.

The dummy's established small-card tricks are of absolutely no use until you draw trumps, ending up in the dummy.

Keep a high card in the dummy either in the trump suit or in a side suit so you can reach your established tricks after you've drawn trumps. You have only the ♥A as a way to reach those beautiful diamonds, so for heaven's sake, don't play the ♥A until the last possible moment.

In the case of the cards in Figure 7-1, you have two winning diamonds in the dummy, and you want to use one of them to get rid of your losing club, the ♣8. The only way to use one of those diamonds is by *entering* the dummy with the ♥A (leading a small heart from your hand to the ♥A in the dummy). The ♥A is called a *dummy entry*. When the only entry to your established tricks is in the trump suit, you have to draw trumps, *ending* in the dummy.

In Figure 7-2, you want to draw trumps, ending in the dummy. You play the ♥K, West plays the ♥4, the dummy contributes the ♥2, and East plays her only trump card, the ♥7. You take the trick and then continue by playing the ♥Q. West follows with the ♥5, you play the dummy's ♥3, and East discards a club. You take this trick as well. West still has one heart left. No problem; you lead the ♥9, West plays the ♥6, the dummy plays the ♥A, and East discards another club.

Congratulations! You've drawn trumps, ending in the dummy, where two established diamonds are waiting to take tricks for you. Teacher is proud.

Setting Up a Long Suit with a Finesse

When you're missing a critical high card in the dummy's long suit, usually a king, you may have to rely on a finesse. A finesse involves leading from weakness to strength, trying to win a trick with a lower honor card. To pull off this move, the player who plays second to the trick must hold the honor card you're missing. (I cover finesses in more detail in Chapter 4.)

Some five-card suits require a finesse before you can set them up. No problem; take the finesse! Win or lose, continue playing the suit at your next opportunity. Then, when you trump the suit later, you create extra winners that provide a home for some (or all) of your losers.

Don't forget about entries to the dummy when setting up suits. After you set up a suit by trumping the small cards, you need to reach the dummy, where the established tricks reside, to enjoy the fruits of your labor. If you don't have enough dummy entries to set up a long suit, forget it. You're spinning your wheels.

Finessing in a side suit requires the following basic steps:

1. **Decide which suit you want to work with and notice which of the high honor cards you're missing.**

2. **Determine how many cards your opponents have in that suit.**

3. **Lead from weakness to strength, hoping that the opponent who plays** *second* **to the trick has the missing honor.**

4. **Establish the suit by trumping the dummy's small cards until your opponents are out of the suit.**

5. **Draw trumps, ending up in the dummy.**

   If you can't end up in the dummy, draw trumps ending up in your hand and then enter the dummy in another suit.

   Most important when setting up a long suit is the ability to enter the dummy after the opponents' trumps have been removed so you can take your winning tricks. Without that last dummy entry, you're history.

6. **Sit back and collect the tricks you've established.**

Figure 7-3 shows a suit where finessing can establish an extra trick for you.

In Figure 7-3 you need to take *three* diamond tricks. Suppose spades are trump and you have high spades coming out of your ears in both your hand and the dummy. You want to take the finesse in diamonds, and you're missing the critical ♦K. You hope that West, who plays second to the trick, has it.

North (Dummy)
♦ A Q 7 3 2

Figure 7-3:
This suit is
ready and
waiting to
be finessed.

West
♦ K 10 9 4

East
♦ J 5

South (You)
♦ 8 6

Before you set up tricks by finessing in the diamond suit, ask yourself how many diamonds your opponents have. Otherwise, how will you know when both of your opponents are void in that suit? In Figure 7-3, because you have seven diamonds, you know that they have six diamonds. Being able to count to 13 goes a long way in this game.

Start by leading a low diamond, the ♦6, from your hand toward the ♦Q in the dummy (weakness to strength). When West plays low, you play the ♦Q and take a finesse, which is a 50-50 proposition. Good news: The ♦Q wins the trick because West has the ♦K. Your finesse worked! Your opponents now have four diamonds left.

When you continue by playing the ♦A from the dummy, both opponents follow low, and you play your remaining diamond. Your opponents now have two diamonds left. Flushed with success, you lead a low diamond from the dummy. Alas, East discards, meaning that West has both remaining diamonds. The nerve! Never mind. You trump this diamond in your hand with a spade, leaving the cards that you see in Figure 7-4.

Figure 7-4:
You still need two dummy entries to set up one of the dummy's diamonds.

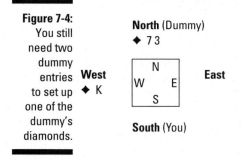

North (Dummy)
♦ 7 3

West
♦ K

East

South (You)

You can still succeed, but you need two more dummy entries. Do you see why? For openers, you have to get to the dummy to trump a diamond. After you do that, the dummy's remaining diamond is a winner because neither East nor West has any more diamonds. If you can get to the dummy one more time, while removing any remaining spades they may have, you can play your established diamond and discard a loser. Phew!

Taking matters into your own hands

I once played bridge with a woman who had established a long suit in the dummy, but she didn't have an entry to the dummy to play her established cards. She was very frustrated — she'd worked so hard to set up the suit, but she had no entry, or path, to the cards in the dummy.

The next time her turn came to play, she solved the problem by leaving her seat, walking over to the dummy, and taking the established tricks. She fixed the problem of how to get to the cards in the dummy by taking matters into her own hands; she became the entry to the dummy!

Paying Attention to Long Suits in the Dummy

Trump cards can prove invaluable when establishing the dummy's long side suit. Tiny trumps can conquer your opponents' aces, kings, and queens in the suit you're establishing. In the following sections, I provide several scenarios in which you can use your trumps to set up winners in the dummy's long suit.

Winning tricks in long suits without honor cards

You may not believe it, but you can set up tricks in long suits even if you don't hold a single honor card (the ace, king, queen, jack, or ten). All you need is a five-card (or longer) suit in the dummy, entries to the dummy, and persistence.

When attempting to coax a trick or two out of such a scrawny five- or six-card suit, your strategy is to play the suit and keep playing it at every opportunity until your opponents finally run out of cards in the suit. Eventually they will.

In Figure 7-5, I spring a really pathetic five-card suit on you — this is five-card suit appreciation time. Pretend that spades are trump and that this side suit greets you. This is a side suit? Yes, it is. You really can set up even a puny five-card side suit such as this one.

Figure 7-5:
You can squeeze some tricks out of this suit despite your lack of honor cards.

North (Dummy)
♦ 8 7 4 3 2

West
♦ K 10 9

```
    N
  W   E
    S
```

East
♦ A Q J

South (You)
♦ 6 5

Start by leading a low diamond, the ♦5 (one of your two kamikaze pilots about to sacrifice themselves for the greater good). West plays the ♦9, you play low from the dummy, ♦2 (what else?), and East takes the trick with the ♦J. Suppose East leads some other suit, but you recapture the lead and obstinately play your second diamond, West plays the ♦10, the dummy plays low, ♦3 (surprise), and East takes the trick with the ♦Q. West remains with the ♦K, East remains with the ♦A, and you're void in diamonds. The dummy has three diamonds left.

Because East has the lead, he can lead another suit. But you won't be denied. Enter the dummy in another suit by leading a low card from your hand to a winning card in the dummy. Now trump a diamond with one of your spades. East has to play the ◆A, and West has to play the ◆K. Presto, your opponents have no more diamonds, and you have two diamond winners in the dummy.

Of course, you still have to draw trumps, ending in the dummy. If you can't draw trumps ending in the dummy, you will need a side-suit entry to the dummy to enjoy your diamond winners. You can do it!

Taking tricks in long suits with honor cards

Take a look at the five-card suit in Figure 7-6, which has a little more beef to it than the one shown in Figure 7-5 because it features honor cards in the dummy. Say that spades is your trump suit.

Start by leading a low diamond, the ◆7, to the ◆Q in the dummy (from weakness to strength). West plays low, the ◆5, and East captures the dummy's ◆Q with the ◆A. Are you counting the diamonds? Big Brother is watching. Your opponents started with six diamonds, and now they have four left.

Figure 7-6:
With honor cards in the dummy, this suit has a little more meat in it.

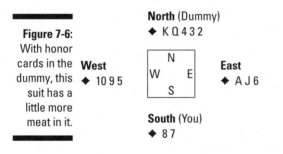

North (Dummy)
◆ K Q 4 3 2

West
◆ 10 9 5

East
◆ A J 6

South (You)
◆ 8 7

When you regain the lead in another suit, play a second diamond from your hand and play the ◆K from the dummy. Both opponents follow with low diamonds (West plays the ◆9; East plays the ◆6). Now they have two diamonds left. When you continue by leading a low diamond from the dummy, the ◆2, East plays the ◆J. Because you have no more diamonds, you can trump the ◆J with a spade; West follows with the ◆10. Neither East nor West has any more diamonds, so both of the dummy's low diamonds have turned into winning tricks — after you draw trumps! You're setting up suits like a veteran player. People are noticing.

Understanding the dangers of setting up a side suit

Setting up a side suit by trumping small cards from the dummy entails certain risks. When you set up the small cards in a long suit, you often can't draw trumps first because you may need trump entries to the dummy to reach your winners after you establish the suit. If the only entries to the dummy are in the trump suit, you can't put the cart before the horse; you have to use the trump entries to help you set up the side suit. Hence, drawing all your opponents' trumps has to wait.

The dangers of trumping a side suit increase when the opponents still have trumps. When you trump a card, the player who plays after you may also be void in that suit and may be able to play a higher trump card and take the trick, called *overtrumping*. Overtrumping can be a major pain in the you-know-where.

In addition, you may have entry problems. What if you set up a long suit and then can't get back to the dummy to use it? Well, I'm trying to work up a little sympathy for you, but if you don't have the entries, why bother trying to set up the suit? It can't work!

You also need enough trumps in your hand to trump a card or two in the suit you're establishing *and* still have enough trumps left to remove all your opponents' trump cards. Sometimes you're not dealt such riches in the trump suit.

Don't despair. I mention the downside to establishing a suit just to let you know that it doesn't always work out. Nevertheless, with a strong trump suit, dummy entries, and losers in other suits, consider establishing a five- or six-card side suit even though it may be so puny that you can't bear to look at it.

Making a Grand Slam with Long-Suit Establishment

Does establishing a suit seem like a ton of work? Sometimes it can be. But the rewards can be great.

You can achieve greatness by setting up a long suit. In Figure 7-7, you score up a *grand slam* (taking all 13 tricks) by establishing a side suit. Making a grand slam is even exciting for expert players who've seen it all (see Chapter 16 for the glorious details on slams). The risks when bidding for all 13 tricks are high, but they sure pay off if you make your contract.

Fasten your seat belt and take a look at the cards in Figure 7-7. Your contract for this hand is for all 13 tricks; hearts is your trump suit, and don't forget what this chapter is all about! West leads the ♠Q.

Whether you have to take 7 or 13 tricks, you still go through the same steps, counting your losers and looking for extra winners.

> ✔ **Hearts:** No losers, a solid suit
>
> ✔ **Spades:** No losers (the ♠AK take care of your two baby spades)
>
> ✔ **Diamonds:** No losers and a five-card suit (hint, hint, hint)
>
> ✔ **Clubs:** One eventual loser

You have one loser in clubs, the fly in the ointment. You must try to get rid of that club on one of the dummy's diamonds, but first you have to set up those diamonds. Are you ready? You've been groomed for this!

Win the opening lead with the dummy's ♠K and then lead a low diamond, the ♦2, from the dummy to the ♦A in your hand (following the general principle of unblocking the logjam by playing the high card from the short side). Both opponents play a low diamond at trick two, so they have four diamonds left. Then lead the ♦7, from your hand to the ♦K in the dummy; again, both opponents play low so they have two diamonds left.

When you play a third diamond from the dummy, the ♦3, East follows with the ♦J, you trump with the ♥8, and West discards a worthless spade because he can't overtrump the ♥8.

The two diamonds in the dummy still aren't winners, because East has the ♦Q. Hang in there. Enter the dummy by leading the ♥9 to the ♥Q (using your trump entry before your side-suit entry), and then trump the ♦4 from the dummy in your hand, flushing out the last obstacle to your happiness: East's ♦Q.

North (Dummy)
♠ A K 3
♥ Q 2
♦ K 5 4 3 2
♣ 6 4 2

West
♠ Q J 10 8 4
♥ 6 5
♦ 10 9
♣ 10 7 5 3

```
    N
W       E
    S
```

East
♠ 9 6 5
♥ 7 4 3
♦ Q J 8 6
♣ Q J 9

Figure 7-7:
You can take all the tricks in this hand by setting up a long suit.

South (You)
♠ 7 2
♥ A K J 10 9 8
♦ A 7
♣ A K 8

Don't look now, but the ♦5 in the dummy is an established trick. But wait, you can't use it until you draw trumps! Play the ♥AK, drawing your opponents' remaining trumps, and then enter the dummy by leading your remaining spade, the ♠7, to the dummy's ♠A (dummy entry number two). Finally, you can triumphantly play your ♦5, discarding your losing club.

You've just bid and made a grand slam by winning all 13 tricks, but you needed the dummy's ♦5 to do it. How does it feel?

Chapter 8

Getting Rid of Losers by Using the Dummy's Trump Cards

In This Chapter

▶ Looking for a short side suit in the dummy

▶ Using trumps in the dummy to take extra tricks

▶ Preparing for your opponents' trump leads

▶ Avoiding trumping losers in the long hand

*Y*ou find a bad apple in every barrel. In bridge, you also come across some rotten apples — your losers, those losing cards that keep you from making your contract.

Just as you can throw out a rotten apple, you can get rid of your losers. This chapter presents a fun and easy technique for ridding your hand of unwanted losers by putting the dummy's trump cards to good use. For other methods of chucking your losers, check out Chapters 5, 6, and 7.

Using the Dummy's Trumps to Your Advantage

Playing a hand at a trump contract is all about getting rid of your side-suit losers (a *side suit* is any suit that isn't the trump suit). One of the easiest ways to get rid of your losers is to put the dummy's trump cards to work. Exactly how do you do that?

Look for a side suit in the dummy that has *shortness* — zero, one, or two cards (a void, singleton, or doubleton) — and then check to see whether you have more cards in that suit than the dummy. When you find such an unequally divided suit, you're in business.

Figure 8-1 shows how you can open up shop. Assume that hearts is your trump suit and that the spade suit in Figure 8-1 is a side suit. Pretend that the dummy has three hearts.

Figure 8-1:
Look for a short suit in the dummy so you can trump your losers.

North (Dummy)
♠ 7 3

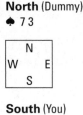

South (You)
♠ 6 5 4

The spades in Figure 8-1 meet the criteria; you see two spades in the dummy and longer spades in your hand, an unequally divided suit. As it stands, you have three losing spades in your hand (see Chapter 5 for details on counting losers). However, if you lead spades twice and concede two spade tricks, the dummy won't have any more spades. When the dummy is void in spades, you can trump your remaining spade loser from your hand in the dummy. After all, losing two spade tricks is better than losing three spade tricks.

Knowing When to Trump in the Short Hand

When you trump your loser(s) in the dummy, you're usually trumping in the hand that has fewer trumps. For that reason, the dummy is called the *short hand*. Here's a little secret: Each time you trump a loser in the short hand, you gain a trick.

As you see in "Steering Clear of Trumping Losers in the Long Hand" later in this chapter, you seldom gain a trick when you trump one of the dummy's losers in the long trump hand. Your primary goal is to trump losers in the short hand.

Figure 8-2 presents a best-case scenario of trumping losers in the short hand. You hit the jackpot. The dummy starts out void in spades, so you plan to start trumping your spade losers as fast as you can.

Figure 8-2:
Finding a
side-suit
void in the
dummy is an
ideal setup
for trumping
losers.

North (Dummy)
♠ (None)

South (You)
♠ 9 5 4 2

In the following sections, I show you a surefire way to trump losers in the short hand and explain the importance of postponing the drawing of trumps until you do.

Getting a grip on the basic method

The basic technique for trumping losers in the short hand, usually the dummy, works like this:

1. **Identify a side suit in which your hand has more cards than the dummy and the dummy has zero, one, or two cards in the suit.**

2. **Lead the suit until the dummy is void.**

3. **When the dummy is void, trump your remaining losers in that suit.**

The cards in Figure 8-3 show you how the miracle of trumping losers in the short hand plays out in a sample hand.

Figure 8-3:
Count your
losers
before you
decide to
trump in the
short hand.

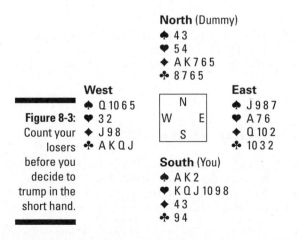

North (Dummy)
♠ 4 3
♥ 5 4
♦ A K 7 6 5
♣ 8 7 6 5

West
♠ Q 10 6 5
♥ 3 2
♦ J 9 8
♣ A K Q J

East
♠ J 9 8 7
♥ A 7 6
♦ Q 10 2
♣ 10 3 2

South (You)
♠ A K 2
♥ K Q J 10 9 8
♦ 4 3
♣ 9 4

In Figure 8-3, you have the following losers (see Chapter 5 for help counting losers):

- ✔ **Hearts:** One immediate loser because you don't have the ♥A
- ✔ **Spades:** One eventual loser, the ♠2, unless you can find some way to cover it
- ✔ **Diamonds:** No losers because the dummy's ♦AK cover your two little ones (♦43)
- ✔ **Clubs:** Two immediate losers, the ♣94; the dummy is no help at all

On this hand, your contract is for ten tricks and hearts is the trump suit. West leads the ♣AKQ. When West plays the ♣Q, you've run out of clubs, so you trump the ♣Q with a low heart, the ♥8, and it's your lead.

You've lost two tricks, you have a certain loser in hearts, and you also have the little matter of the ♠2 to deal with. You must find a way to get rid of that spade loser, or you're doomed. Remember: You need to win ten tricks to make your contract, so you can afford only three losers. At this point, you've lost two clubs and are sure to lose a trick to the ♥A.

Sometimes losers can be discarded on the dummy's long suit (diamonds, in this case) using the technique I share in Chapter 7, but not this time. Even if you could set up the diamonds by playing the ♦AK and then trumping one, you would have no entry to get back to the dummy to take the winning diamonds. Scratch diamonds; this suit has no losers, but it can't help you get rid of any losers from your hand. Try plan B: Search your hand for a suit in which you have more cards than the dummy.

Take a closer look at that spade suit in Figure 8-3. You have three spades and the dummy has two spades, the signal that you may be able to trump your losing ♠2.

Play the ♠AK, voiding the dummy of spades, and then lead the ♠2, trumping it with the lowly ♥4 in the dummy. Don't look now, but you just got rid of that losing spade. Your only remaining loser is the ♥A, a trick that even a great player like you will have to lose.

Postponing the drawing of trump

Clearly, you need to keep as many trumps in the dummy as you have losers to trump. If you plan to trump one or more losers from your hand in the dummy, well then, keep that many trumps in the dummy. You may have to defer *drawing trump* (extracting your opponents' trumps — see Chapter 5 for details) until after you trump those losers.

In Figure 8-3, you need to trump one spade before you draw the opponents' hearts. If you draw trumps early and remove the dummy's trumps, you won't be able to trump your spade loser in the dummy and you'll go down.

Frequently, you have a side suit that looks like the spades in Figure 8-4. In this side suit, you have two spade losers, the ♠7 and ♠3, but if you play the ♠A and void the dummy in spades, you can eventually trump your two remaining spades. Instead of two spade losers, you have no spade losers. Of course, you need two trumps in the dummy to pull off this little caper.

Figure 8-4:
Keep your
trump cards
available
for use in a
typical side
suit like
this one.

North (Dummy)
♠ 6

```
    N
 W     E
    S
```

South (You)
♠ A 7 3

Saving Enough Trumps in the Dummy When Facing a Counterattack

By the way, your opponents are also at the table. They watch you try to trump your losers in the dummy when you lead the dummy's short suit, and they don't like it. You're trumping their tricks! But for every strategy in bridge, a counterstrategy exists.

Each time you give up the lead in the dummy's short suit, expect clever opponents to return a trump. Each time they lead a trump, it's one less trump in the dummy you have to trump a loser. Of course, you can always hope that your opponents haven't read this book . . . maybe they'll lead something else, but don't count on it unless you're playing against a close friend or relative.

You may be able to take the sting out of your opponents' trump leads if you save enough trumps in the dummy to outlast their attack. Figure 8-5 depicts a hand in which you can ward off any trump leads from the opponents.

In Figure 8-5, your contract is to take ten tricks and hearts is the trump suit. West leads the ♣K.

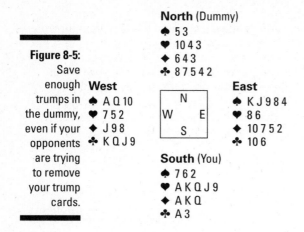

North (Dummy)
♠ 5 3
♥ 10 4 3
♦ 6 4 3
♣ 8 7 5 4 2

Figure 8-5:
Save enough trumps in the dummy, even if your opponents are trying to remove your trump cards.

West
♠ A Q 10
♥ 7 5 2
♦ J 9 8
♣ K Q J 9

East
♠ K J 9 8 4
♥ 8 6
♦ 10 7 5 2
♣ 10 6

South (You)
♠ 7 6 2
♥ A K Q J 9
♦ A K Q
♣ A 3

Before doing anything else, first take stock of your losers (as I show you in Chapter 5); you can afford to lose only three tricks:

- **Hearts:** No losers
- **Spades:** Three losers, the ♠762
- **Diamonds:** No losers
- **Clubs:** One eventual loser, the ♣3 (becomes immediate after you win the ♣A)

The nerve of your partner to present you with such a dummy! However, you do have a ray of hope. Did you notice that the dummy has two spades, one fewer spade than you have? If you play spades twice before you draw trump, you can void the dummy in spades. You can then trump your third spade with one of dummy's hearts, reducing your loser count to three.

You have to give up the lead twice in spades, but even if your opponents lead a trump each time they have the lead, you'll still have one trump left in the dummy that you can use to trump your third spade. Strike one for the forces of light. Notice that an opening trump lead by West and trump continuation each time you lead a spade defeats the contract. Not to worry, I'm here for you. West has a normal club lead, giving you time to trump a spade.

What about drawing trump first? Later, man, later. If you remove all the dummy's trumps, you won't have a trump in the dummy to care for your third spade. It's too sad for words.

Steering Clear of Trumping Losers in the Long Hand

If you can generate extra tricks by trumping your losers in the dummy, you may think that you can generate extra tricks by trumping the dummy's losers in your hand. Sorry, it doesn't work that way.

For a moment, turn things around and think about trumping a loser in your hand — the long hand. Figure 8-6 gives you a chance to put this theory into practice. Assume that hearts is your trump suit.

You want to draw trump, so you play ♥AKQ, removing all of your opponents' trump cards. You remain with ♥J2, both of which are winners. You score five heart tricks. Agreed?

Figure 8-6:
Don't attempt to trump a loser in the wrong hand — in this case, the long hand.

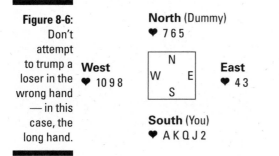

North (Dummy)
♥ 7 6 5

West
♥ 10 9 8

East
♥ 4 3

South (You)
♥ A K Q J 2

Now see what happens if your opponents lead a suit that you don't have and you trump the lead with your ♥2. You remain with the ♥AKQJ, four tricks, plus the deuce you have already used. Same five trump tricks. Trumping with the ♥2 doesn't give you an extra trick. But if you can manage to trump a loser in the dummy, you still have five winning heart tricks in your hand plus the ruff in the dummy. Six trump tricks!

Trumping in the long hand, at times unavoidable, is a break-even play at best unless you're trumping in the long hand purposely trying to establish the dummy's long suit (see Chapter 7). On the other hand, each time you trump in the short hand, you gain a trick.

Part III
Bidding for Fun and Profit

The 5th Wave   By Rich Tennant

"I don't care what kind of clowns you two are, I know a signal when I hear one! You honk that thing one more time and I'm leaving the table!"

In this part . . .

The number-one cause of bridge disasters is improper bidding. Think of the countless tricks that you could've saved (from your opponents' trick pile) if you'd had a strong foundation in bidding.

In this part, you discover when to bid and when to apply the brakes. I talk about opening, responding, and rebidding. In short, you see how to arrive at the best contract. After you read this part, you'll find fewer of your tricks falling into the perilous hands of the opponents.

Chapter 9

Starting with Bidding Basics

*B*idding for the proper number of tricks is an important part of the game of bridge. Some would say it's what the game is all about! Successful bidding can either make or break your chances of fulfilling your contract.

In this chapter, you discover some of the fundamentals of bidding. You find out how the bidding progresses around the table, the proper way to make a legal bid, and how to assess the strength of your hand (so you can make good decisions about how many tricks you and your partner can reasonably expect to take). You certainly shouldn't pass on this chapter.

Grasping the Importance of Bidding

Bidding determines the *final contract* for a hand. The pressure is on the partnership that gets (or *buys*) the final contract — whoever gets the final contract has to win the number of tricks that they contract for. If the partnership fails to win that number of tricks, penalty points are scored by the opponents. If the partnership takes at least the number of tricks it has contracted for, it then scores points. (I talk about scoring in Chapter 20.)

In addition to determining how many tricks a partnership needs to win, bidding determines the following details:

- ✔ **The declarer and the dummy for the hand:** For the partnership that buys the final contract, the bidding determines who plays the hand for the partnership (the *declarer*) and who gets to watch (the *dummy*). See "Settling Who Plays the Hand," later in this chapter, for details.

- ✔ **The number of tricks the partnership needs to take to make the final contract:** Each bid is like a stepping stone to the number of tricks that a partnership thinks it can take. The goal of the partnership that buys the final contract is to take at least the number of tricks contracted for.

- ✔ **The trump suit (if the hand has one):** Depending on the cards held by the partnership that winds up playing the hand, there may be a trump suit (or the bidding may end in a notrump contract). See Chapters 3 and 4 to find out more about playing at notrump. Part II discusses playing at a trump contract.

Proper bidding also allows the partners to exchange information about the strength (the number of high-card points) and distribution of their cards. (See "Valuing the Strength of Your Hand," later in this chapter.) Through bidding, you and your partner can tell each other which long suits you have and perhaps in which suits you have honor cards (aces, kings, queens, jacks, and tens).

Based on the information exchanged during the bidding, the partnership has to decide how many tricks it thinks it can take. The partnership with the greater combined high-card strength usually winds up playing the hand. The declarer (the one who plays the hand) tries to take the number of tricks (or more) that his side has contracted for. The opponents, on the other hand, do their darndest to prevent the declarer from winning those tricks.

Partnerships exchange vital information about the makeup of their hands through a *bidding system.* Because you can't tell your partner what you have in plain English, you have to use a bidding system. Think of it as a foreign language in which every bid you make carries some message. Although you can't say to your partner, "Hey, partner, I have seven strong hearts but only one ace and one king," an accurate bidding system can come close to describing such a hand.

The bidding (or *auction*) consists of only the permitted bids; you don't get to describe your hand by using facial expressions, kicking your partner under the table, or punching him in the nose. Your partner must also understand the conventional significance of your bids to make sense of what you're trying to communicate about your hand and to know how to respond properly. If not, it's the Tower of Babel all over again!

Of course, everyone at the table hears your bid as well as every other bid made at the table. No secrets are allowed. Your opponents are privy to the same information your bid tells your partner. Similarly, by listening to your opponents' bidding, you get a feel for the cards that your opponents have (their strength and distribution). You can then use this information to your advantage when the play of the hand begins.

Bridge authorities agree that bidding is the most important aspect of the game. Using a simple system and making clear bids is the key to getting to the proper contract and racking up the points. Bidding incorrectly (giving your partner a bum steer) leads to lousy contracts, which, in turn, lets your opponents rack up the points when you fail to make your contract. Of course, you have to know how to take the tricks you contracted for, or else even the most beautiful contracts in the world will lead nowhere. Not to worry; the play-of-the-hand techniques in Chapters 2 through 7 pull you through.

Surveying the Stages of Bidding

The bidding begins after the cards have been shuffled and dealt. The players pick up their hands and assess their strength (see "Valuing the Strength of Your Hand," later in this chapter, for details). In the following sections, I explain the different elements of the bidding process.

Assessing the strength of your hand is something I cover in more detail in Chapter 10 and beyond. In this chapter, I just want you to concentrate on the mechanics of the bidding process. I take you through this part of the game one step at a time.

Opening the bidding

The player who deals the cards has the first opportunity to either make a bid or pass. The dealer looks at her hand; if she has sufficient strength, she makes a bid that begins to describe the strength and distribution (how the cards are divided). If she doesn't have enough strength to make the first bid, called the *opening bid,* she can *pass* (not make a bid).

Being second in line

After the dealer bids or passes, the bidding continues in a clockwise rotation. The next player can take one of two actions:

- Make a bid higher than the dealer's bid (assuming that the dealer makes an opening bid)
- Pass

He can't make a bid unless he bids higher than the dealer's bid. See "Bidding suits in the proper order," later in this chapter, for more information on determining whether one bid is higher than another bid. If you've ever attended an auction, you can see why bidding is sometimes referred to as an auction — each bid must outrank the previous one.

Responding to the opening bid

After the second player makes a bid or passes, the bidding follows a clockwise rotation to the next player at the table, the dealer's partner. After someone opens the bidding, the partner of the opening bidder is called the *responder*.

If the dealer opens the bidding, the responder has a chance to make a bid, called a *response*. This bid begins to describe the strength and distribution of the responding hand. The partnership is looking for some suit in which they have eight or more cards together, called an *eight-card fit*. It may take a few bids to uncover an eight-card fit. Sometimes it doesn't exist, which is a bummer. The responder also has the option to pass her partner's opening bid, which communicates more information (albeit of a rather depressing nature) about the strength of her hand.

Buying the contract

The bidding continues clockwise around the table, with each player either making a bid higher than the last bid or passing. After a bid has been made, three successive passes ends the bidding. The partnership that makes the last bid has *bought the contract* and plays the hand, trying to take at least the number of tricks that corresponds to the final bid.

During the bidding, think of yourself as being in an "up-only" elevator that doesn't stop until three of its passengers say "Stop!" (or, in this case, "Pass") consecutively. Furthermore, this elevator has no down button! The only way you can refrain from driving the elevator up is by saying "Pass" when it's your turn to bid.

Passing the buck

Note one special case that comes up once in a while during bidding. Sometimes no one wants to make a bid, as you can see in the following bidding sequence.

West	North (Your Partner)	East	South (You)
Pass	Pass	Pass	Pass

The hand has been *passed out*. Nobody wants to get on the elevator, not even on the lowly first floor! No player has a strong enough hand to open the bidding. When a hand is passed out, the cards are reshuffled and the same person deals again.

Looking at the Structure and the Rank of a Bid

Bridge bids have a legal ranking structure all their own. Remember that each new bid any player makes must outrank the previous one.

During the bidding, players call out their bids to communicate information about their hands. Each bid you make is supposed to begin painting a picture of your strength and distribution to help the partnership arrive at the best final contract. Of course, your partner is doing the same with the same goal in mind. Bridge is a partnership game.

In the following sections, you get acquainted with the look and feel of the bids you use to describe your hand to your partner. I cover these bids in more detail in Chapters 10 through 16.

Knowing what elements make a proper bid

A bid consists of two elements:

- ✔ **The suit:** During the bidding you actually deal with five suits: spades, hearts, diamonds, clubs, and notrump. (Note this expanded meaning of a suit.)

- ✔ **The number of tricks you're bidding for in that suit:** You start with an automatic, unspoken six tricks, called a *book,* and build from there.

When you make a bid, you don't say, "I want to bid three in the spade suit." Instead you simplify it: You say "three spades," "four notrump," "two diamonds," and so on. When you see bids referred to in books (including the bids in this book), the bids are abbreviated to card number and suit symbol. For example, the written equivalent of the preceding bids looks like this: 3♠ (three spades), 4NT (four notrump), and 2♦ (two diamonds).

Each bridge hand consists of exactly 13 tricks, and the minimum opening bid must be for at least 7 of those 13 tricks. Therefore, each bid has an automatic 6 tricks built into it; thus, a 1♥ bid actually says that if the bidding ends in 1♥ you have to take 7 tricks with hearts trump, not just 1 trick. In other words, your bridge elevator starts on the *seventh* floor.

The numbers associated with a bid correspond to bidding levels. Bids of 1♠, 1♥, 1♦, and 1♣ are called *one-level bids*. A bid that starts with a 3 is a *three-level bid*. The highest level is the seven level. (Doing a little math tells you that 7NT, 7♠, 7♥, 7♦, and 7♣ are the highest bids because 7 + 6 = 13.)

Bidding suits in the proper order

During the bidding, players can't make a bid unless their bid is higher than the previous bid. In bridge, two factors determine whether your bid is legal:

- ✔ Which suit you're bidding

- ✔ How many tricks you're bidding for in that suit

During the play of a hand, the rank of the suits has no significance. The rank of the suits only matters during the bidding. The suits are ranked in the following order:

- ✔ **Notrump (NT):** Notrump isn't really a suit in the strictest sense of the word, but notrump *is* considered a suit! In fact, notrump is the highest suit you can bid. Notrump is the king of the hill when it comes to bidding — you can score the most points with notrump bids.

- ✔ **Spades (♠):** Spades is the highest-ranking suit (after notrump).

- ✔ **Hearts (♥):** Hearts ranks behind spades; hearts and spades are referred to as the *major suits* because they're worth more in the scoring (discussed in Chapter 21).

- ✔ **Diamonds (♦):** Diamonds don't carry as much weight; they outrank only clubs.

- ✔ **Clubs (♣):** Clubs are the lowest suit on the totem pole. Diamonds and clubs are called the *minor suits.*

To remember the rank of the suits (excluding notrump), look at the first letter of each suit. The *S* in *spades* is higher in the alphabet than the *H* in *hearts,* which is higher than the *D* in *diamonds,* which is higher than the *C* in *clubs.*

To see how the rank of the suits comes into play during the bidding, consider the following example. Assume that you are seated in the South position:

South (You)	West	North (Your Partner)	East
1♥	?		

Suppose that you open the bidding with 1♥ (check out opening bids in Chapter 10). Because the bidding goes clockwise, West has the next chance to bid. West doesn't have to bid if he doesn't want to; however, the most likely reason for not bidding is that West simply doesn't have a strong enough hand. West can say "Pass" (which is not considered a bid).

However, if West wants to join in the fun, he must make some bid that is *higher ranking* than 1♥. For example, West can bid 1♠ or 1NT — but not 1♣ or 1♦ — because both bids are higher ranking than a 1♥ bid.

On the other hand, if West wants to bid diamonds (a lower-ranking suit than hearts), West must bid at least 2♦ for his bid to be legal. That is, only by upping the *level* of the bid (from 1 to 2) can West make a legal bid in diamonds (a lower-ranking suit than hearts).

Making the final bid

When three consecutive passes follow a bid, the last bid is the *final contract*. The following issues are resolved when the bidding is over:

- ✔ **Whether the hand will be played in notrump or in a trump suit:** If the final bid is in notrump, the hand will have no wild cards, or *trump cards* (see Part I for more information on playing at notrump). If clubs, diamonds, spades, or hearts is named in the final bid, that suit is designated as the trump suit for the hand. For example, if the final bid is 4♥, the trump suit is hearts for that hand.

- ✔ **How many tricks need to be won:** By automatically adding six to the number of the final bid, you know how many tricks you need to take. For example, if the final contract is the popular 3NT, the partnership needs to win nine tricks to make the contract (6 + 3 = 9).

Putting it all together in a sample bidding sequence

In the following example, you can see the bids each player makes during a sample bidding sequence. You don't see the cards on which each player bases his or her bid — they aren't important for now. Just follow the bidding around the table, noting how each bid is higher than the one before it. Assume that you're in the South position.

South (You)	West	North (Your Partner)	East
1♥	Pass	2♣	2♦
3♣	3♦	4♥	Pass
Pass	Pass		

After your opening 1♥ bid, West passes and your partner (North) bids 2♣. East joins in with a bid of 2♦, a bid that is higher than 2♣. When it's your turn to bid again, you show support for your partner's clubs by bidding 3♣. Then West comes to life and supports East's diamonds by bidding 3♦. Your partner (don't forget your partner) chimes in with 4♥, a bid that silences everybody. Both East and West pass, just as they would at an auction when the bidding gets too rich for their blood.

It has been a somewhat lively auction, and your side has *bought the contract* with your partner's 4♥ bid, which means that you need to take ten tricks to make your contract. (Remember, a book — six tricks — are automatically added to the bid.) If you don't make your contract, the opponents score penalty points and you get zilch. The final contract of 4♥ also designates hearts as the trump suit.

Keep in mind the following points about the bidding sequence:

✔ Each bid made is higher ranking than the previous bid.

✔ A player can pass on the first round and bid later (as West did), or a player can bid on the first round and pass later (as East did).

✔ After a bid has been made and three players in a row pass, the bidding is over.

Settling Who Plays the Hand

If your partnership buys the final contract, the bidding determines who plays the hand (the *declarer*) and who kicks back and watches the action (the *dummy*). For example, if the final contract ends in some number of hearts, whoever bid hearts first becomes the declarer, and his partner is the dummy.

Take a look at this sample bidding sequence:

South (You)	West	North (Your Partner)	East
1♥	Pass	2♣	2♦
3♣	3♦	4♥	Pass
Pass	Pass		

The contract ends in 4♥, which is the final bid because it is followed by three passes. Both you and your partner bid hearts during the bidding. However, you bid hearts first, which makes *you* the declarer.

The player to the left of the declarer (in this case, West) makes the opening lead, and the partner of the declarer (North) is the dummy. After the opening lead, the dummy puts down her cards face up in four vertical rows, one for each suit the trump suit, hearts, to your left and dummy's right and bows out of the action.

Valuing the Strength of Your Hand

During the bidding, try to work out the strength and distribution of your partner's hand, at the same time trying to tell your partner the strength and distribution of your hand. The point of this communication is to determine the best trump suit, including notrump, and then finally to decide how many tricks to contract for. Consider two elements when valuing the strength of your hand:

- ✔ Your high-card points (see the following section for a definition)
- ✔ The distribution of your cards (how your cards are divided in the various suits)

In the following sections, I give you an idea of what you need in terms of strength (high-card points) and distribution (the number of cards you have in each suit) to enter the bidding. I dive into the details of these issues in the rest of Part III.

Adding up your high-card points

Your honor cards (the ace, king, queen, jack, and ten in each suit) contribute to the strength of your hand. When you pick up your hand, assign the following points to each of your honor cards:

- ✔ **Aces:** For every ace, count 4 points (A = 4 points).
- ✔ **Kings:** For every king, count 3 points (K = 3 points).
- ✔ **Queens:** For every queen, count 2 points (Q = 2 points).
- ✔ **Jacks:** For every jack, count 1 point (J = 1 point).

The 10 is also considered an honor card, but, alas, it doesn't count when adding your points initially. Patience.

These points are called *high-card points* (HCP). Most players use this barometer to measure the *initial* strength of their hand.

Each suit contains 10 HCP, totaling 40 HCP in the deck. When you know from the bidding the total number of HCP your partnership has, you'll have an easier time deciding how many tricks to contract for.

Looking for an eight-card trump fit

Why should you care about the *distribution* of the cards (that is, how many cards you or your partner has in any one suit)? For you and your partner to land in a safe trump-suit contract, you want to have at least eight cards in the same suit between the two hands, called an *eight-card trump fit*. Bidding, to a great extent, is geared toward locating such a fit, hopefully in a major suit.

Chapter 10

Making a Successful Opening Bid

tarting off on the right foot is the first step to success at the bridge table, and it all starts with the opening bid. In this chapter, I tell you everything you need to know about the opening bid — the first bid made at the table. If you aren't familiar with the basics of bidding, check out Chapter 9 to pick up some fundamentals.

Working Through the Basics of Opening the Bidding

After the cards are dealt, you pick them up, sort them, and evaluate the strength of your hand. Depending on how strong your hand is, you may get a chance to make the first bid, called the *opening bid*. But how do you decide whether your hand is worth an opening bid? Read on.

Knowing when to get your feet wet

Two factors determine whether you have an opening bid:

  ✔ **Your high-card points (HCP):** Barring exceptions, you should have at least 12 HCP to make an opening bid. (See Chapter 9 for more information on calculating your HCP.)

  ✔ **Your distribution (the way your cards are divided):** Normally, you open the bidding in your longest suit, which typically has four or more cards.

Suppose that you deal yourself either of the hands you see in Figure 10-1. You can open the bidding with either of these hands; both hands contain at least 12 HCP, and each has a suit with four or more cards. So life is easy: You open the bidding in your long suit, 1♠ and 1♣, respectively.

The player who makes the opening bid eventually tries to show both strength and distribution to her partner. For example, if a player makes an opening bid of 1♦, you know that she has at least 12 HCP in her hand and figures to have four or more diamonds.

Figure 10-1:
Add up your HCP to determine whether you can make an opening bid.

♠ A K J 7 4 2 ♥ K J 5 ♦ J 4 2 ♣ 8
(13 HCP)

1

♠ K Q 5 4 ♥ A 3 ♦ 5 4 ♣ K 10 7 6 2
(12 HCP)

2

Understanding when to bend the rules

In the previous section I tell you that you need at least 12 HCP to make an opening bid. I try to give you definitive rules, but not all bridge concepts are cut and dried. As a case in point, the strength requirements for an opening bid can sometimes be shaded a little.

For example, if you have a six-card suit or two five-card suits, you can open the bidding with as few as 11 HCP. If your partner complains about you opening with fewer than 12 HCP, just tell your partner that you don't need as many points because you play so well.

Having the option of passing

The dealer has the first chance to make a bid. If she has sufficient strength, she opens the bidding. She can also choose to pass ("pass" isn't a bid).

When it's your turn to bid (you may be first if you're the dealer, or you may get a chance to make the opening bid if the players before you pass), if your hand doesn't have enough strength to open, just say one word, "Pass," and don't look glum. Even if you aren't strong enough to open the bidding, you can still join in later.

Remembering your goal: The eight-card fit

The first few bids in most bidding sequences are exploratory, like two fighters feeling each other out in the early rounds. Usually on the second bid, called the *rebid,* one of the players comes clean and shows his strength within a few points, which is called *limiting one's hand.* Then his partner can add the total HCP between the two hands to get a feel of how high to bid.

While all this telling and adding is going on, the partnership is trying to locate a suit that both players like (one in which they have at least eight cards between the two hands, also known as an *eight-card fit*); if they find one, they try to make that suit the trump suit. Because hearts and spades (the major suits) are the most rewarding suits to play in (turn to Chapter 20 for more information on scoring), the partnership initially tries to find an eight-card (or longer) major-suit fit. Much of the bidding depends on whether an eight-card or longer major-suit fit exists. If a partnership doesn't have such a fit, the partners may play the hand at notrump, in an eight-card or longer minor-suit fit (diamonds or clubs), or possibly a seven-card major-suit fit.

When you open the bidding in a suit, your partner can't possibly know exactly how many cards you have in the suit. The opening bid is just the beginning of your picture. After you make your rebid (which you can read more about in Chapter 12) and, perhaps, a third bid, the picture of your hand starts to come into focus. Even the greatest of paintings begins with a single stroke of the brush.

The language of bidding: Talking to your partner

Bidding is an exchange of information. During the bidding, you're trying to telegraph details about your cards to your partner. But what about your opponents? What are they doing while you pass this coded information back and forth? They're not reading a book, you know — they listen to the bidding, too! The coded information that you pass to your partner may be in a foreign language (the language of bidding), but your opponents also speak this language. Whatever you tell your partner, your opponents hear and understand.

Your first impulse may be to develop some special bidding conventions that only you and your partner know. However, according to the rules of the game, you can't have any bidding secrets with your partner; the same goes for your opponents. So even though the opponents may be bidding their heads off, you at least will know what their bids mean. You, too, can be a major league "buttinski," as you see in Chapter 14.

Opening the Bidding with 12 to 20 HCP in Your Hand

In theory, opening bids can be made at any level you like (see Chapter 9 for more information on bidding levels). In practice, if you have enough points to open the bidding, you usually start the bidding at the one level, the "seventh floor." Don't forget that the elevator can't stop on the first six floors!

If your hand has 12 to 20 HCP, you usually trot out your longest suit at the one level. If you have 21 HCP or more, turn to "Opening the Bidding with 21 or More HCP" later in this chapter to see how to handle such hands. If you keep picking up hands with 21 or more HCP, give me a call — I need partners like you.

If both your HCP and your distribution help you decide whether to make an opening bid, which factor is more important? One simple fact answers this question: The longer the suit you have, the more tricks you're likely to take. And that's why you bid your longer — not necessarily your stronger — suit first. This approach also helps you reach your partnership's ultimate goal: locating that all-important eight-card major suit fit. Remember: length before strength.

The distribution of your cards (the length of your suits) plus your partner's distribution plays a major part in determining how high you bid. You use an established bidding method, called a *system,* to communicate your strength and distribution. I discuss various common distributions, or *hand patterns,* and how to handle them in the following sections.

If you don't have three people to play with, dig up a deck of cards, shuffle it, and deal out four hands. Count the points and notice the distribution of each hand. See whether a hand is strong enough to open the bidding. Check the distribution and ask yourself which suit you would bid first if the hand were strong enough to open. It's a quick-start way to get a feel for counting points and checking hand patterns.

Eyeballing different distribution types

The distribution of your cards determines which suit you bid first. Every hand you pick up is one of the following types:

✔ **One-suited:** A hand with one five-, six-, or seven-card suit.

✔ **Two-suited:** A hand with two five-card suits (5-5), or a five- and a four-card suit (5-4), or a six- and a four-card suit (6-4), or even some wilder two-suited patterns like 6-5 or 7-4.

> ✔ **Three-suited:** Three suits with at least four cards (such as 4-4-4-1 or 5-4-4-0).
>
> ✔ **Balanced:** A hand with no long suit and no really short suit. Balanced hands come in three types: a hand with only one four-card suit, a hand with two four-card suits, and a hand with a five-card suit. You can refer to balanced hands numerically in terms of the suit length, putting the long suit first: for example, *any* 4-3-3-3 shape, *any* 4-4-3-2 shape, or *any* 5-3-3-2 shape. All these distributions are considered "balanced."

Astute readers may note that hands with a 5-3-3-2 distribution belong to two different families because they can be put in the one-suited hand type as well as the balanced hand category. Who gets custody of the 5-3-3-2 hands? Should they be considered one-suited hands or balanced hands? See "Opening with a balanced hand," later in this chapter, to find out the answer.

Opening with a one-suited hand

With rare exception, to open the bidding in any suit, you need at least four cards in the suit. However, to open the bidding with 1♥ or a 1♠, you need at least five cards in the suit. In the Standard American system (used by most players in the United States), an opening bid of 1♥ or 1♠ promises at least five cards in the suit. This understanding is called *five-card majors*. (When I first started, everyone played four-card majors!) The appendix at the back of this book covers Acol, a four-card major bidding system still used primarily in the United Kingdom.

If your hand has only one suit with five cards or more, you have a one-suited hand. Take a look at the hands in Figure 10-2 to see some great-looking one-suited hands.

Figure 10-2: With a one-suited hand, open the bidding in your longest suit.

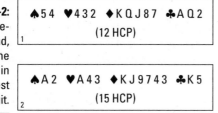

♠54 ♥432 ♦KQJ87 ♣AQ2
(12 HCP)

♠A2 ♥A43 ♦KJ9743 ♣K5
(15 HCP)

When you have a one-suited hand and 12 to 20 HCP, you open with a one-level bid in your longest suit. For example, in Figure 10-2, both hands are strong enough to open 1♦; both have at least 12 HCP and at least four diamonds.

If you have a one-suited hand and between 12 and 20 HCP, you usually open at the one level and bid your longest suit. But if you have a six-card suit, you can open the bidding with 11 HCP — another example of length trumping strength.

Opening with a two-suited hand

Hands with one five-card suit and one four-card suit (or two five-card suits) are the most common two-suited distributions (5-4 or 5-5 shape). However, hands with one six-card suit and one four- or five-card suit (6-4 or 6-5 shape) are also two-suited hands. Figure 10-3 shows you some two-suited hands.

Figure 10-3:
Two suits are definitely better than one when you open the bidding.

♠43 ♥QJ987 ♦K6 ♣AKQ2
(15 HCP)
1

♠KJ543 ♥2 ♦AK1098 ♣82
(11 HCP)
2

When you have a two-suited hand, you want to let your partner in on this little secret. You open with the longer of the two suits, intending to bid (mention) the other suit at your next opportunity. By the way, your second bid is called your *rebid* (you hear more about rebidding in Chapter 12).

If you have two five-card suits, bid the higher-ranking suit first (the rank of the suits is spades, hearts, diamonds, clubs). See Chapter 9 for more information on ranking the suits.

Listen closely to this sage piece of advice from one of the all-time bridge greats, Edgar Kaplan. He has said in print many times, "The answer to most bidding problems is to bid your longest suit." If you remember that you need 12 or more HCP to open the bidding and that you bid your longest suit first, you will be a survivor.

In the first hand in Figure 10-3, you open the bidding with 1♥ because your hearts are longer than your clubs. Yes, I can see that the clubs are stronger (clubs have more honor cards). Never mind — bid the longer suit first. Length comes before strength both in the dictionary and in the bidding.

In the second hand in Figure 10-3, you have two five-card suits. Which one should you bid first? You didn't think you were going to get out of this chapter without any rules, did you? With two five-card suits, bid the higher-ranking suit first. Open 1♠ with the intention of showing your diamonds next.

Opening with a three-suited hand

This category is composed of hands that have three four-card suits and a *singleton* (a suit with one card), or one five-card suit, two four-card suits, and a *void* (no cards in the fourth suit). If your hand contains one of these distributions, you have a *three-suited hand* or a *three-suiter.* Lucky you! These hands come along rarely. But when they do, you'll be prepared.

The cards in Figure 10-4 show you some classic examples of three-suited hands.

♠4 ♥K Q 5 4 ♦A J 5 4 ♣Q 9 7 6
(12 HCP)
1

♠Q J 4 3 ♥4 ♦A K 7 6 ♣A K J 4
(18 HCP)
2

Figure 10-4:
Three-suited
hands are
rare in
bridge.

♠A 9 8 6 ♥Q J 4 3 ♦2 ♣A K 10 9
(14 HCP)
3

♠K J 4 3 ♥A Q J 3 ♦A J 9 8 ♣3
(16 HCP)
4

Three-suiters present a unique challenge. Bridge should offer a special opening bid that tells your partner, "You won't believe this, but I have three four-card suits!" Some bidding systems cater to such an opening bid, but not Standard American. However, you can follow a very simple rule when opening with a three-suited hand.

When you have three four-card suits, open 1♦. However, if your singleton is a diamond, open 1♣. This rule doesn't mean that every time you open 1♦ your partner expects you to have three four-card suits. But he will be at least alive to that possibility.

Opening with a balanced hand

Balanced hands include hands with the following distributions in any suits:

- ✔ **4-3-3-3:** One suit with four cards and three suits with three cards

- ✔ **4-4-3-2:** Two suits with four cards each, one suit with three cards, and one suit with two cards

- ✔ **5-3-3-2:** One suit with five cards, two suits with three cards, and one suit with two cards

In the following sections, I discuss the opening bid with balanced hands that have 15 to 17 HCP. I then focus on opening balanced hands with fewer HCP (12 to 14 HCP) and those with more HCP (18 to 19 HCP).

Opening a balanced hand with 15 to 17 HCP (1NT)

With 15 to 17 HCP, life is so easy you won't believe it. Open 1NT. You've just gotten your hand off your chest with one bid by telling your partner your strength and distribution. You can open 1NT with any hand in Figure 10-5.

Figure 10-5:
Opening
1NT tells
your part-
ner your
strength and
distribution
in one bid!

> ♠ K 4 ♥ A J 6 5 ♦ Q J 4 ♣ A 10 8 7
> (15 HCP)
> 1

> ♠ J 6 5 3 2 ♥ A K J ♦ K 5 4 ♣ A 10
> (16 HCP)
> 2

> ♠ 10 9 4 3 ♥ A Q J ♦ A Q 2 ♣ K J 5
> (17 HCP)
> 3

Each of the hands in Figure 10-5 is balanced, and each falls within the designated range of 15 to 17 HCP. Open any balanced hand pattern that has between 15 and 17 HCP with 1NT.

In the interest of simplicity, open 1NT even with a five-card major suit and 15 to 17 HCP and a balanced hand. When you learn to *hedge* (or use your own judgment), you can pick and choose between opening 1NT and opening with your five-card major suit.

Opening with a 5-3-3-2 hand pattern outside the 1NT range

With a 5-3-3-2 pattern outside the range of a 1NT opening bid (15 to 17 HCP), bid your five-card suit first.

Opening with a 4-4-3-2 hand pattern outside the 1NT range

The 4-4-3-2 hand pattern (any 4-4-3-2 distribution) is the most common of all hand patterns. You pick up this pattern about 20 percent of the time. Your main concern when you open with a 4-4-3-2 hand pattern is to bid the right four-card suit first.

If the hand contains a four-card major and a four-card minor, bid the minor first, because you can't open with 1♠ or 1♥ unless you have five cards in the suit. So with clubs and hearts, or clubs and spades, bid the clubs first. With diamonds and hearts, or diamonds and spades, bid the diamonds first. Figure 10-6 shows you two 4-4-3-2 hand patterns with both a minor and a major suit.

In both of the hands shown in Figure 10-6, bid the minor suit first. In the first example, open 1♦, and in the second, open 1♣.

Figure 10-6:
Bid the four-card minor suit first with a four-card minor, a four-card major, and a 4-4-3-2 hand pattern.

♠ A K J 6   ♥ 6 5 3   ♦ A J 8 7   ♣ 6 5
(13 HCP)

1

♠ A 4   ♥ K Q 8 7   ♦ A Q 4   ♣ K 10 7 6
(18 HCP)

2

When you have two four-card majors in a 4-4-3-2 hand pattern, open the bidding in your three-card minor. Consider the hands in Figure 10-7.

Figure 10-7:
Open with a three-card minor when you have two four-card majors.

♠ K Q 8 7   ♥ A J 6 5   ♦ K J 8   ♣ 10 5
(14 HCP)

1

♠ A 9 8 7   ♥ A K 9 7   ♦ J 9   ♣ A K 4
(19 HCP)

2

In these two 4-4-3-2 hand patterns, you would open with 1♦ and 1♣. Why? You normally open the bidding in your longest suit. Why would you bid a three-card suit when you have two four-card suits? When you open with a major suit, you guarantee at least five cards in the suit. So when you have a hand with two four-card major suits, you don't have enough length to open in either suit. Opening the three-card minor is considered the lesser evil.

Playing a five-card major system means making adjustments when you have an opening bid with one or two four-card majors. The compromise solution with 4-4 in the majors is to open the bidding with your *three*-card minor. You tell a small lie, but you hope that your deception is temporary. On a good day, your partner responds in a major suit, allowing you to come out of the woodwork and support the suit. (See Chapter 11 for more on responding.)

Opening the bidding with a three-card minor is rare and is driven by the requirement that a major-suit opening shows five cards. A three-card minor opening is called a *short club* — or, even rarer, a *short diamond.* If anyone asks whether you play "a short club," your answer should be, "Yes, but only when I have to."

When you have two four-card minors with a 4-4-3-2 hand pattern, open 1♦.

Opening with a 4-3-3-3 hand pattern outside the 1NT range

The 4-3-3-3 hand pattern is so blah: no long suits, no short suits, no nothing. Fittingly, these patterns are called *flat hands* — kind of like a flat tire. Treat these hands as balanced hands and follow the guidelines outlined in this section.

Figure 10-8 shows you a few flat hands. In each case, you have enough HCP (at least 12) to open the bidding. You have no long suit, but you do have too little (or too much) to open 1NT, which shows 15 to 17 HCP (I discuss opening 1NT earlier in this chapter). What to do?

> ♠KJ43 ♥AQ3 ♦654 ♣K65
> (13 HCP)
> 1

> ♠A104 ♥K652 ♦Q65 ♣AKQ
> (18 HCP)
> 2

Figure 10-8: You have two options for getting a handle on flat hands.

> ♠KJ4 ♥QJ3 ♦QJ42 ♣K97
> (13 HCP)
> 3

> ♠KQ3 ♥AQ2 ♦K87 ♣10876
> (14 HCP)
> 4

Being on your best behavior during the bidding

You must follow bridge etiquette during the game — especially during the bidding. Here are a few important points:

✔ Try to use the minimum number of words possible when you bid. If you want to pass, say just one word: "Pass." If you want to bid 3♣, say "Three clubs." No more, no less.

✔ Be careful about how you use your voice. You may be tempted to bid softly if you have a weak hand or loudly if you have a strong one. Remember to keep all your bids at the same decibel level.

✔ If your partner makes a bid that you don't like, don't throw any looks and don't use any negative body language. If your partner makes a bid that you do like, you also must refrain from any telltale signs of glee.

✔ No matter what happens during the bidding, keep an even keel. No emotional breakdowns. Bridge is too great a game to mess it up with illegal signals.

You have two options:

✔ **If the four-card suit is major:** With a 4-3-3-3 distribution and the four-card suit a major, open 1♣. (You can't open 1♥ or 1♠ unless you have five cards in the suit, remember? See "Opening with a one-suited hand," earlier in this chapter.)

✔ **If the four-card suit is minor:** If the four-card suit is a minor, open the bidding in the four-card minor.

With the first and second hands in Figure 10-8, open 1♣; with the third hand, open 1♦; with the fourth hand, open 1♣.

Open 1♣ with any 4-3-3-3 outside the range of 15 to 17 HCP, unless the hand has four diamonds — in that case, open 1♦.

Opening the Bidding with 21 or More HCP

Sometimes you pick up such a wonderful hand that you think you must be dreaming; you can't believe that you have 21 HCP or more in your hand. Your heart starts pounding a little faster, but you can't do or say anything to let on what you have — it isn't ethical.

When you get a great hand like this, you usually open with 2♣, the strongest opening bid in bridge. The 2♣ bid basically tells your partner that you can make game in your own hand. With a little help from your partner, you may even be able to bid a slam! (See Chapter 20 for the details on making game and scoring slams.)

The 2♣ opening is completely artificial, which is to say that the bid has nothing to do with the clubs in your hand; you may or may not have clubs. Your second bid tells your partner the reason for your strong opening bid: It may be because you have a very long suit.

In the following sections, I show you when to open with 2♣ when you have unbalanced and balanced hands. You also find out about the exception to opening with 2♣.

Opening 2♣ with an unbalanced hand

You open many unbalanced hands with 21 or more HCP with 2♣. (Unbalanced hands include all hands that don't fit into the balanced-hand shapes as discussed in "Opening with a balanced hand," earlier in this chapter.) Some hands that have 19 or 20 HCP also should open 2♣, such as hands with a six- or seven-card major suit. These hands can take close to ten (or more) tricks in their own hand facing nada. 2♣ opening bids featuring a long *minor* suit usually start with 22 HCP.

Very strong unbalanced hands may look like the examples shown in Figure 10-9. You would open each of the hands in Figure 10-9 with 2♣.

If you have a six- or seven-card major suit with 20 or more HCP, you probably have a 2♣ opening bid. If you have an unbalanced hand with a five-card suit with 21 or more HCP, you also have a 2♣ opening bid. (If you have a five-card suit and a balanced hand, open 2NT with 20 to 21 HCP. See "Knowing when not to open 2♣ with a balanced hand," later in this chapter, for details.)

Figure 10-9:
If you have 20 or more HCP in an unbalanced hand, you can open with 2♣.

> ♠A 10 9 ♥A K Q 8 7 4 2 ♦2 ♣A K
> (20 HCP)
> 1

> ♠K Q J 10 5 4 ♥A ♦A K Q J ♣9 5
> (20 HCP)
> 2

> ♠4 ♥A K Q 4 ♦A 3 2 ♣A K Q 5 2
> (22 HCP)
> 3

Even a sleepy partner wakes up when the sound of a 2♣ opening bid comes from across the table. A 2♣ opening bid means that big happenings are in the air. All the hands in Figure 10-9 are very powerful. These hands can do great things, no matter what garbage may be in their partner's hand.

- ✔ The first hand in Figure 10-9 shows a 20-point hand that can take ten tricks: seven hearts, two clubs, and one spade.

- ✔ The second hand is another 20-point hand that can take ten tricks: five spades, four diamonds, and one heart.

- ✔ The third hand is a 22-point hand that has a strong potential for ten tricks: four hearts, one diamond, and five clubs. Here you could use a little help from your partner. For example, a good partner will have the jack of hearts, and a really great partner will have the jack of clubs as well.

Notice that the first and second hands are stronger than the third, even though they have fewer HCP. Why? Because the first two have longer suits and can take more tricks.

The first hand would also open 2♣ with the AQ of clubs instead of the AK even though it has 19 HCP. This hand can take close to ten tricks all by itself.

If you open with 2♣, you have aces and kings coming out the kazoo. You want to make a forcing opening bid that tells your partner, "Partner, if you value your life, do not pass until we reach at least a game contract. I have enough tricks in my own hand to make game."

I know that this chapter is about opening bids, but I want to go a little further with the 2♣ opening bid to show you how it really works. The 2♣ opening bid is completely *artificial* — you may or may not have clubs. You just use the 2♣ opening bid to tell your partner that you have a knockout of a hand. You show your partner your "real" suit on your next bid.

Unless your partner has a five- or six-card suit of her own with seven or more HCP, your partner's initial response will be 2♦, an artificial "waiting" response (you find out more about responses in Chapter 11). Your partner responds with this artificial bid because she's waiting to hear your real suit.

Nine times out of ten, your partner's response to your 2♣ opening will be 2♦. After those first two bids of 2♣ and 2♦, everything is on the up-and-up. You and your partner then start bidding suits you really have. When your turn to bid comes around again, bid your longest suit.

For example, consider the following bidding sequence. *Note:* When the opponents' bids are not mentioned, it's because they are passing throughout.

You	Your Partner
2♣	2♦
2♥	

In this sequence, your 2♣ bid says, "Partner, I'm loaded — don't you dare pass!" Your partner's 2♦ bid says, "I wouldn't dream of it — tell me more." Then your 2♥ bid says, "Hearts is my real suit. I was kidding about clubs."

Why not just open 2♥ and be done with it? Bidding takes place through conventions, and the meaning of an opening 2♥ bid is that you have a weak hand (see "Making a Preemptive Opening Bid with 6 to 10 HCP," later in this chapter, for more information on opening the bidding with a weak hand). You open with 2♣ because that's the conventional bid to show that you have some real firepower in your hand. You also open 2♣ so that you can smoothly arrive at a game or a slam contract without worrying that your partner will get cold feet and pass prematurely.

Opening 2♣ with a balanced hand

About half the time that you open 2♣, you have a balanced hand in the range of 22 to 24 HCP. When the 2♣ bidder has a balanced hand in the normal range of 22 to 24 HCP, the opener rebids 2NT to show his strength. When you have such a hand, the bidding sequence looks like this:

You	Your Partner
2♣	2♦
2NT	

Your opening 2♣ bid says, "I have a great hand." Upon hearing your 2♣ bid, your partner responds 2♦, a "waiting" response that doesn't say anything about her hand (she just wants to get the bidding back to you to hear more about your hand). When it's your turn to bid again, you rebid 2NT, which tells your partner "My great hand is balanced and I have 22 to 24 HCP."

When your partner hears your 2NT rebid, your partner becomes the *captain* (the one who makes the final decision of how high to bid) because you have *limited* your hand. *Limiting one's hand* means showing your partner both your point count and your distribution.

If your partner opens 2♣ and rebids 2NT, you can pass. This is the only rebid after a 2♣ opening that can be passed. However, do bear in mind that even a pitiful hand with only three HCP is enough to try for a game contract (see Chapter 20) if your partner opens 2♣ and rebids 2NT.

If you have a hand like the one shown in Figure 10-10 — one with 27 or 28 HCP — open 2♣ and rebid 3NT to show your mammoth strength. If you play day and night and you get lucky, you may get a hand like this once or twice a year.

Figure 10-10:
Rebidding
3NT when
you have a
balanced
hand with 27
to 28 HCP.

♠A K Q J ♥A Q ♦A Q J 3 ♣K J 5
(27 HCP)

In Figure 10-10, the bidding would go like this:

You	Your Partner
2♣	2♦
3NT	

The sequence shows that you have a balanced hand with 27 or 28 HCP. After you bid 3NT, your partner can pass or do whatever he pleases.

Because it takes about 33 HCP to make a slam (slams involve bidding and making at least 12 of the 13 tricks; see Chapter 16 for more about slam bids), your partner looks for a slam holding as little as six HCP, facing your 27 points. What you have together counts most. Togetherness.

Knowing when not to open 2♣ with a balanced hand

Some strong balanced hands don't open 2♣. With a balanced hand and 20 to 21 HCP, open 2NT. With 25 to 26 HCP, open 3NT.

Figure 10-11 shows you three hands primed for 2NT and 3NT opening bids. In the first two hands, open 2NT; in the third, open 3NT.

Figure 10-11:
You have
a bunch
of serious
notrump
opening
bids on your
hands: 2NT
and 3NT.

♠ A K 4 ♥ Q 10 8 7 ♦ A K J 4 ♣ K 3	
(20 HCP)	1

♠ A Q ♥ K 9 6 5 4 ♦ K Q 4 ♣ A Q 3	
(20 HCP)	2

♠ A 6 5 ♥ A K Q ♦ A K Q ♣ Q J 6 5	
(25 HCP)	3

Making a Preemptive Opening Bid with 6 to 10 HCP

The less you have, the more you bid. Sounds crazy, right? Not so crazy. If you don't have enough HCP to open the bidding at the one level (you need at least 12 points to open), you may still have enough in your hand to open the bidding.

With only six to ten HCP in your hand and a strong six-, seven-, or eight-card suit, consider making a *weak opening bid,* also called a *preemptive opening bid.* A preemptive bid bypasses the one level and goes directly to the two, three, or four levels. When you make such a bid, you are *preempting* your opponents by stealing their bidding space. They don't like it. They hate it.

Preemptive opening bids are based primarily on tricks, not on HCP. That is, your bid is based on a long suit (of at least six cards). Such a hand is worth something if that suit is the trump suit, but otherwise it may be worthless. The purpose of preemptive bids is to obstruct the opponents from arriving at their proper contract by forcing them to enter the bidding at an uncomfortably high level.

In the following sections, I talk about the various opening preemptive bids at your disposal as well as the mega-importance of counting your tricks.

Understanding your goals

When you have a very weak hand (ten HCP or less), it figures that your opponents have the majority of the strength in the hand. This strength means that your opponents can usually make some contract, perhaps a game contract, or perhaps even a slam contract (see Chapter 16 for more on slam contracts). Of course, a preempt can make life tough for your partner as well because it involves a risk. Nevertheless, when looking at a long suit without many HCP, you want to make that suit trump, if possible. Bid it!

Think of a preemptive opening bid (an opening bid that starts at the two, three, or four levels) as a sacrifice. When you make a preemptive opening bid, you are prepared to lose several hundred penalty points if you don't make your bid (see Chapter 20 for more on penalty points). But losing those several hundred penalty points is peanuts compared with what you can lose if the opponents bid and make game or a slam.

Face it: When you hold a weak hand, you probably will lose points. The best way to hold down your losses is to strike first with a preemptive opening bid if you have the right type of hand to pull one off.

A preemptive opening bid frequently prevents your opponents from arriving at a reasonable contract, let alone their best contract. To arrive at a reasonable contract (that is, to know how many tricks to bid for), a partnership has to exchange information. Ideally, this exchange takes place at the one and two levels. However, if you start the bidding at the two, three, or four levels, you've stolen these levels from your opponents. Without these levels to exchange information, your preemptive bid often reduces your opponents to guesswork. Even the best players have difficulty arriving at their optimum contract when they have to start the bidding at high levels.

Opponents hate preempts — and if they hate your preempts, you know it must be right to make them. By the way, what's good for the goose is good for the gander; they love to preempt you as well!

Counting your tricks

Tricks form the foundation of preemptive bidding. If you know approximately how many tricks you have and about how many tricks your partner has, you get a good idea of how many tricks your side can take.

Try to make as accurate a preempt as possible to combine maximum safety with the maximum ability to mess up your opponents. You want to show your partner approximately how many tricks you can take; your partner already knows that you have a weak hand, pointswise, when you preempt.

Suppose that you hold the hand shown in Figure 10-12.

Figure 10-12:
This weak-ish hand has only nine HCP.

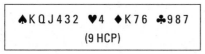

♠K Q J 4 3 2   ♥4   ♦K 7 6   ♣9 8 7
(9 HCP)

The hand in Figure 10-12 is nothing to write home about. True, the hand has a six-card spade suit, but it has only nine HCP. With a six-card suit, you need at least 11 HCP to open the bidding with a one-level bid. If the number of HCP was the only criterion for opening, you would have to pass.

But take a closer look at that spade suit. Pretend that spades are trump and that your partner has a couple of little spades — average expectancy when you have a six-card suit. How many spade tricks do you think you can take with this hand shown in Figure 10-13?

Figure 10-13:
Count the tricks in your long suit to decide whether a preemptive bid is worthwhile.

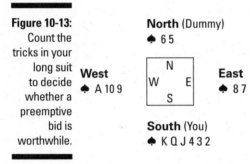

North (Dummy)
♠ 6 5

West
♠ A 10 9

East
♠ 8 7

South (You)
♠ K Q J 4 3 2

When you have eight cards total in a suit between your hand and your partner's hand, your opponents' five cards are usually divided 3-2. In other words, one opponent has three spades and the other two spades. Suppose that you lead the ♠K and West takes the trick with the ♠A. Later you play the ♠Q and ♠J. Now your opponents have no more spades. Your three remaining little spades are all tricks. You have taken five tricks from this spade suit. And what about the ♦K? That king isn't chopped liver, you know. It will take a trick about half the time. You actually have five and a half tricks. Any hand worth five-plus tricks may be grounds for a preemptive bid.

Counting tricks in long suits is relatively easy. Assume that you have a six-card suit and that you want to guesstimate the number of tricks that you can take from the suit (you can never be 100 percent sure, because you can't see your partner's cards). Just follow these steps:

1. **Look at the honor cards at the head of your suit and estimate how many tricks you think you can take with those honors.**

2. **Add an automatic three to that number.**

   The three represents the fourth, fifth, and sixth cards in the suit. After you play a long suit three times, the fourth, fifth, and sixth cards figure to be tricks because normally nobody else at the table has any more cards in that suit.

Suppose that you have a suit like this: AKQ*xxx* (*x* means any small card). The AKQ are three sure tricks — add the three length-tricks to equal six tricks. Or try this suit, for example: QJ10*xxx*. The QJ10 is worth one trick, so 1 + 3 = 4 — you can estimate four tricks. Estimating tricks is easiest when you have three equal honors at the head of your suit, such as AKQ = 3, KQJ = 2, or QJ10 = 1.

Just to give you an idea of approximately how many tricks you can expect to take with some other six-card suits, consider this little guide:

Cards	Tricks
AKJ*xxx* or AQJ*xxx*	Five to six tricks
AK*xxxx*, AQ10*xxx*, AJ10*xxx*, KQ10*xxx*	About five tricks
AQ*xxxx*, AJ9*xxx*, KQ*xxxx*, KJ10*xxx*	Four to five tricks
A109*xxx*, K109*xxx*, Q109*xxx*, KJ*xxxx*, or QJ10*xxx*	Four tricks

Any 109 (the 10 and the 9) combination in the middle of a suit enhances the suit. Suits headed by the A109, K109, Q109, or even J109 can take more tricks than you may expect because of the 10 and the 9.

Determining when to make a weak two bid

In the Standard American system that you're playing, an opening bid of 2♦, 2♥, or 2♠ is called a *weak two bid*. You use a weak two opening bid to tell your partner that your hand has the following characteristics:

✔ A six-card suit, headed by two of the top four honor cards, any three honors, or the A109, K109, or Q109. In other words, if this suit becomes the trump suit, you can expect to take four or five trump tricks.

✔ A hand with six to ten HCP (never more than ten HCP).

✔ A hand with no five-card side suit, no side four-card major suit, and no void suit. A weak two bid is not supposed to show a two-suited hand.

An average opening weak two bid can take five to six tricks. If a hand can take more than six tricks, it's too strong for a weak two bid.

Notice that you don't see an opening bid of 2♣ on the weak-two-bid list. An opening bid of 2♣ is reserved for a truly powerful hand — hands in the range of 21 or more HCP (see "Opening the Bidding with 21 or More HCP," earlier in this chapter, for information on opening with strong hands). Don't open 2♣ with a weak hand unless you're into catastrophes!

Suppose that you pick up the hand shown in Figure 10-14.

Figure 10-14:
This hand
is ripe for a
weak two
bid.

♠4 ♥A K 6 5 4 3 ♦6 5 4 ♣9 4 3
(7 HCP)

You have fewer than ten HCP, a six-card suit, no void suit, no five-card side suit, and no side four-card spade suit (the other major) — looking good. Count your tricks. At the head of the hearts (your longest suit), you have the ♥AK, worth two tricks. The fourth, fifth, and sixth hearts are all considered tricks (because of your length), so you have about five tricks. You have a perfect hand for a preemptive bid. Open 2♥.

You may also pick up a hand like the one shown in Figure 10-15.

Figure 10-15:
Make a
weak two
bid with this
weak hand.

♠6 5 ♥5 4 ♦Q J 10 8 4 3 ♣K Q J
(9 HCP)

In the hand shown in Figure 10-15, you have fewer than ten HCP, a six-card suit, no void, no side five-card suit, and no four-card major. Count your tricks — in diamonds you have four tricks (the QJ10 combination is one, and the three little cards are three more), and in clubs you have two tricks. You have a six-trick hand, the maximum for making a weak two bid. Open 2♦.

Keeping within the parameters of the weak two bid

If you have more than six tricks, your hand is too strong (in tricks) to open a weak two bid. If you have 11 or more HCP, your hand is too strong (in point count) to open a weak two bid. When making a weak two bid, stay within your trick and point count ranges. If you do, your partner can get an accurate picture of what you have; he can add his tricks to your tricks and start working out the best contract. When making any preemptive bid, being too strong is just as dangerous as being too weak.

A weak two bid should tell your partner that your hand is of interest only in the suit you have just bid. If you have a side four-card major, your preemptive bid may preempt your side out of uncovering your best fit!

Take a gander at the cards in Figure 10-16 to see some hands that may fool you into thinking that you could open with a weak two bid.

Figure 10-16:
A side four-card major disqualifies your hand for a weak two bid.

| ♠ A 10 9 7 6 5   ♥ 5 4   ♦ 2   ♣ Q J 10 9 |
| (7 HCP) |

1

| ♠ A 10 9 7 6 5   ♥ Q J 10 9   ♦ 5 4   ♣ 2 |
| (7 HCP) |

2

Both hands in Figure 10-16 may look ripe for a weak two bid, but only the first hand qualifies. It can take about six tricks (four in spades and two in clubs); it has no side four-card major and no void. The second hand contains a side four-card major (hearts), so it's a no-no as far as opening 2♠.

Don't open a weak two bid with a side four-card major. You may miss a four-four fit in that suit if your partner has length in that suit. Open 2♠ with the first hand in Figure 10-16; pass with the second.

Opening with a preemptive bid at the three level

An opening three bid (3♠, 3♥, 3♦, or 3♣) is similar to an opening weak two bid, except for the following two tiny differences:

✔ You have a seven-card suit.

✔ You can have a void (a suit in which you have no cards) in the hand.

If opening at the two level makes your opponents uncomfortable, imagine their aggravation level when you open at the three level. The higher you open, the more space you take away, and thus the more difficult you make it for them to communicate efficiently. They may not be able to bid at all.

You can make opening three bids in all four suits. The club suit finally gets to join the party, unlike with the weak two bid. You can open with a three bid as long as you have a seven-card suit, but again, no side four-card major.

Figure 10-17 shows a hand in which you can open with a preemptive three bid.

Figure 10-17:
Stifle the opponents with your opening three bid.

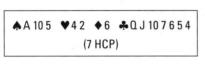

♠ A 10 5   ♥ 4 2   ♦ 6   ♣ Q J 10 7 6 5 4
(7 HCP)

In Figure 10-17, you have seven HCP; your club suit offers the chance to take five tricks (the ♣QJ10 are worth one trick, and count the four little clubs as tricks as well). Throw in the ♠A, and you have a six-trick hand; open 3♣.

When you have a seven-card suit, count four tricks for the fourth, fifth, sixth, and seventh cards in the suit, no matter how small the cards are. The length of the suit turns those cards into tricks.

Opening with a preemptive bid at the four level

An opening four bid is like an opening three bid, except that the four bid features an eight-card suit (or a 7-4 hand pattern). If an opening weak two irritates your opponents, and an opening three bid drives them up the wall, an opening four bid sends a dagger straight into their hearts. Few partnerships can recover from one of these monster preempts.

To open with a four bid (4♠, 4♥, 4♦, or 4♣), your hand must have

✔ Between six and ten HCP (no more than ten)

✔ Seven or eight tricks (count an automatic five tricks for length)

✔ An eight-card suit or a seven-card suit with a four-card side suit

When you get a hand like this, make your opponents pay by opening with a four bid. I show you how in the following sections.

If you make disciplined preempts (that is, your hand fulfills the criteria for making the bids you make), you'll be a feared opponent. If you make undisciplined preempts (yielding to temptation), you'll be a feared partner! Although you can have fun opening with a bombshell such as a 4♥ bid in the hope of messing up the opponents, if you have the wrong sort of hand for the bid (not enough tricks), you run the risk of losing a zillion points, not to mention your partner's trust — the one thing you can't afford to lose. On a bad day, your partner may also have a really weak hand, and you may lose big-time when you preempt.

When you have an eight-card suit

The cards in Figure 10-18 give you a taste of the great feeling you get when you open a four bid.

Figure 10-18:
Your opponents won't like your opening four bid.

♠5 ♥A 8 7 ♦5 ♣Q J 10 7 6 4 3 2
(7 HCP)

The combination of ♣QJ10 is worth one trick. Added to that, you get five length tricks — and don't forget to count the ♥A. You have a seven-trick hand — open 4♣ and watch the suffering begin.

Why will your opponents suffer? Either they have to pass and possibly let you steal them blind, or one of them has to take a huge risk and come in at the four level before knowing what their partner has. If their partner has a terrible hand, how do you spell "a disaster in the making"?

When you have a 7-4 hand pattern

Opening with a four bid gives you a feeling of power. Take a look at the cards in Figure 10-19 as an example of a show of force.

You have a 7-4 hand pattern, acceptable for an opening four bid. You also have ten HCP, also acceptable. Count your tricks. In hearts, you have six tricks, missing only the ♥A. In diamonds, you have a trick, and that fourth diamond has some potential to become a trick. At the very least, you have seven tricks, possibly more. Open 4♥.

Figure 10-19:
Seven and
four, close
the door
— on your
opponents!

♠ 3 ♥ K Q J 10 8 7 3 ♦ A 4 3 2 ♣ 4

(10 HCP)

Chapter 11

Responding to an Opening Bid

. . . .

In This Chapter

▶ Responding to your partner's opening bid

▶ Responding at the two level

▶ Responding in notrump

▶ Hinting at slam with a jump shift

. . . .

*Y*our partner has opened the bidding. Congratulations! Your side has made the first step toward determining the best contract. Now you're at bat. Get ready to tell your partner, the opener, some details about your strength and distribution. In this chapter, I explain what you need to respond at the one and two levels to your partner's opening bid. I also show you a neat trick called a jump shift. For more details about opening bids, head to Chapter 10.

Knowing When You Can Respond to an Opening Bid

When your partner opens the bidding in any suit, the opening bid tells you some important information:

✔ Your partner usually has between 12 and 20 high-card points, or HCP (11 HCP is possible but relatively rare).

✔ With some exceptions, assume your partner is bidding his longest suit.

Unless your partner marches to the beat of a different drum or hasn't read this book, you can bet that the preceding points accurately describe your partner's hand.

After the opening bid, you have some picture of what your partner's hand looks like, but it isn't very sharp. The preceding points cover a wide range of possible hands. Typically, you need to start describing your own hand and wait for your partner to further describe his strength and distribution.

After your partner opens the bidding, the person to your right gets a chance to bid. Then you, the *responder,* begin to describe your hand with your response to the opening bid.

To make any response to an opening bid, you *usually* need at least six HCP in your hand (see Chapter 9 for details on figuring HCP). If you have fewer than six HCP, just pass. If you have six or more HCP, your first obligation is to bid your longest suit. Not necessarily your strongest suit — your longest suit. Sometimes, however, you may want to respond in notrump or support your partner's suit. I discuss all three of these options in this chapter.

If you have six or more HCP, you must make some kind of response. You may have to get creative with your response, but with six HCP, you owe your partner at least one noise.

Responding to a 1♣ Opening Bid

Imagine that your partner opens the bidding with 1♣. Read on to find out what to do when your turn to bid comes around.

With six or more HCP and at least four cards in your suit

To respond to an opening bid of 1♣, you should have

- ✔ Six or more HCP
- ✔ Four or more cards in the suit you want to bid

If you have fewer than six HCP, pass. If you have a strong five-card suit (three honor cards) such as KQ10*xx,* cheat one point and show the suit at the one level with five HCP.

If you have six or more HCP, your plan is to show your partner your longest suit at the one level. The suit you bid must have at least four cards — hopefully five or six.

Suppose that you're gazing at the cards shown in Figure 11-1.

You have six or more HCP, and hearts is your longest suit, so you respond 1♥. (You're allowed to stay at the one level because hearts is ranked higher than clubs.)

Figure 11-1:
Respond to an opening bid of 1♣ in your longest suit at the one level.

♠Q54 ♥AJ654 ♦J432 ♣3
(8 HCP)

When you respond to a one-level bid with another one-level bid, you are said to be bidding *one over one.* This response shows that you have six or more HCP and length in the suit you bid. Because this bid doesn't show any maximum number of HCP, your bid is called an *unlimited response.*

When you respond in any new suit, such as a 1♥ response to a 1♣ opening bid, your partner must bid again. Your partner can't pass; as the opener, he must honor any unlimited response with another bid. You may turn out to hold a mountain (a great hand) and be on your way to the stratosphere. In that case, you won't be too happy if your partner passes and play grinds to a halt at the one level. Sure, at the one level, you would make your contract, but you would also miss out on much tastier rewards, such as a game or slam contract. (See Chapter 20 for more about scoring these contracts.)

With suits of equal length

Responding at the one level in your longest suit first, as I describe in the previous section, may become second nature. However, sometimes you may have two or even three suits of equal length, as the hands in Figure 11-2 show. In the first hand in Figure 11-2, you have two five-card suits; in the second hand, you have two four-card suits; in the third hand, you have three four-card suits.

Figure 11-2:
You may have to choose between suits of equal length when responding to an opening bid.

♠3 ♥A9432 ♦AK765 ♣94
(11 HCP)
1

♠AK54 ♥QJ54 ♦976 ♣32
(10 HCP)
2

♠Q843 ♥10876 ♦AJ108 ♣2
(7 HCP)
3

With two five-card suits, you always bid the higher-ranking suit first. A simple rule — no exceptions.

With two or three four-card suits, you normally, but not always, bid the suit closest in rank to your partner's suit. That call is the most economical one. It's known as bidding your suits *up the line.* In other words, with four spades and four hearts, bid 1♥ in response to a 1♣ opening bid.

In the first hand in Figure 11-2, you respond 1♥; in the second hand, you also respond 1♥; and in the third hand, you respond 1♦. That wasn't so bad, was it?

With 6 to 18 HCP and a balanced hand

A *balanced hand* has no really long suit and no really short suit. When you have a balanced hand with no four- or five-card major suits (spades or hearts), respond with some number of notrump according to the following scale:

- ✔ Respond 1NT if you have 6 to 10 HCP.
- ✔ Respond 2NT if you have 13 to 15 HCP.
- ✔ Respond 3NT if you have 16 to 18 HCP.

If you have four or five cards in a major suit, respond in the major at the one level (if possible) first, reserving the option of bidding notrump later.

You can use this scale to respond to opening bids of 1♦, 1♥, and 1♠, as well as the 1♣ opening.

If you have precisely 11 or 12 HCP with a balanced hand (as you do in Figure 11-3), your hand is too strong to respond 1NT and not strong enough to respond 2NT. What to do? You bid your longest suit and then bid 2NT the next chance you get.

Even if you have the proper number of high-card points, don't jump to 2NT or 3NT directly with a small doubleton in an unbid suit. This move is just too dangerous. Instead, respond in a four-card suit.

In Figure 11-3, respond 1♦ and then bid 2NT the next time you get a chance to bid (see Chapter 13 for more information on bidding again when you are the responder).

If you have 17 HCP or more, you should be thinking that a possible slam is in the offing, which you can read more about in Chapter 16.

Figure 11-3:
Make the best of an awkward situation by bidding in your longest suit at the one level.

> ♠ A 7 5   ♥ K 4 3   ♦ Q J 6 4   ♣ J 10 5
> (11 HCP)

Take a look at the hands in Figure 11-4 to get some practice responding to a 1♣ opening with a balanced hand.

- ✔ In the first hand shown in Figure 11-4, respond 1♠, bidding the major suit first. Priority number one!

- ✔ In the second hand, respond 1NT because you have four cards in your longest suit, a minor suit, and notrump takes precedence when you have the necessary HCP.

- ✔ In the third hand, respond 2NT; once again, your four-card suit is a minor, and you have between 13 and 15 HCP.

- ✔ In the fourth hand, respond 1♦. With 11 HCP, you are too strong to respond 1NT and not strong enough to respond 2NT. You must bide your time by bidding your longest suit.

> ♠ A J 5 4   ♥ 6 5 4   ♦ 6 5 4   ♣ A 10 4
> (9 HCP)
>
> 1

Figure 11-4:
These hands are balanced, but the possession of a four-card major and/or your point count enter into your response.

> ♠ Q 4 3   ♥ Q 7 6   ♦ K J 5 4   ♣ 6 4 3
> (8 HCP)
>
> 2

> ♠ A J 5   ♥ K 10 4   ♦ K 10 6 2   ♣ Q 5 4
> (13 HCP)
>
> 3

> ♠ Q J 2   ♥ Q 7 4   ♦ A 10 7 5   ♣ Q 10 4
> (11 HCP)
>
> 4

Adding support points to your HCP

Every so often, you get four or more clubs, the suit your partner has opened. If your partner opens 1♣ and you don't have four or five cards in a major suit and you don't have a balanced hand with some strength in the unbid suits, you raise clubs, sort of like a last option. The reality is that, when holding four clubs, you have several other more desirable options than supporting clubs. The bottom line is that you usually have five clubs when you do support the suit directly.

When you have support for the suit your partner bids, you can add extra points, called *support points* (SP), to your hand for side-suit shortness (voids, singletons, or doubletons). Short suits offer your partner a chance to trump his losing cards in that suit in your hand. How does this upgrade work? It all depends on how short your short suit is and how many trumps you have (and you can never have too many trumps). In the following sections, I show you an easy scale to use when you factor in support points, and I warn you about the wrong times to use support points.

Using a support-point scale

When supporting your partner's suit with four or more cards, use the one-three-five support point scale and add the following SP to your HCP (the final total is expressed in SP):

✔ Add one SP for each doubleton (a two-card holding in a side suit).

✔ Add three SP for a singleton (a one-card holding in a side suit).

✔ Add five SP for a void (a side suit in which you have zero, nada, zilch, zip cards).

After you add these SP, think in terms of your "new" support point total. But remember, you can add SP to your HCP *only* when you're supporting a suit that your partner has bid. Shortness in side suits becomes valuable only when you have trump support; your shortness allows your partner to trump his losers in that suit with your trumps (see Chapter 8).

After you count up your SP and add them to your HCP, respond to a 1♣ opening bid according to the following scale:

✔ **6 to 9 SP:** Raise your partner from 1♣ to 2♣.

✔ **10 to 12 SP:** Raise your partner from 1♣ to 3♣.

✔ **13 or more SP:** Bid your longest side suit, planning to strongly support clubs next. However, if the hand is balanced with stoppers in the other three suits and has 13 to 15 HCP, start with 2NT.

Take a peek at the cards in Figure 11-5 to see how adding SP figures into responding to a 1♣ opening bid.

 ✔ In the first hand in Figure 11-5, you pick up one point for having a doubleton, and your proper response is 2♣.

 ✔ In the second hand, you can add three support points for the singleton, which means that you should respond 3♣.

 ✔ In the third hand, you pick up five support points for the void you have in hearts; your response is 1♦ (diamonds are your longest side suit), and you intend to jump in clubs at your next opportunity. You're too strong to bid 3♣ directly.

 ✔ In the fourth hand, you have four spades, so show the major first (major suits always get the red carpet treatment); respond 1♠ and then bid clubs next.

♠54 ♥654 ♦1076 ♣AK543
(7 HCP + 1 = 8 SP)

1

♠A ♥Q65 ♦10952 ♣Q10754
(8 HCP + 3 = 11 SP)

2

Figure 11-5:
Factor in points when you have support for the suit that your partner bids.

♠K53 ♦A975 ♣J108643
(8 HCP + 5 = 13 SP)

3

♠KQ87 ♥43 ♦52 ♣KJ976
(9 HCP + 2 = 11 SP)

4

Avoiding the premature addition of support points

Some bridge players fall in love with singletons and voids. They love them so much that they count extra points for them right off the bat. Do everything you can to avoid becoming one of these players. They are a tragedy waiting to happen because they fail to appreciate that short suits are good *only when you have support for your partner's suit.* You need a good fit before you can count extra for short suits.

Figure 11-6 illustrates the dangers of adding SP to your HCP prematurely. You have eight HCP plus four cards in each of three suits — potentially excellent support for your partner if he bids any of those suits. Feel free to add three SP (for your singleton club) if your partner opens 1♦, 1♥, or 1♠.

Figure 11-6:
Don't get
smitten
with your
singletons,
double-
tons, and
voids until
you know
whether
they support
your part-
ner's bid.

♠ A 6 5 4 ♥ J 1 0 8 7 ♦ K 8 7 4 ♣ 2
(8 HCP)

But some partners (mine included) have the irritating habit of bidding your short suit. When this happens, keep your cool and don't add any SP to your hand. Only if your partner later mentions one of your four-card suits do you count extra points for shortness.

Unless you have X-ray vision and can see through the backs of the cards, you can't tell whether your short suits are worth anything until you hear the bidding. The bidding tells you whether your short suits are valuable or worthless. Remember, support in your partner's suit makes your short suits more valuable; don't count for shortness until you find a fit.

Making the call: Problem hands

You can't always find one "right" bid for a hand. If only it were so. Many hands present close-call decisions. For many hands, you become like the baseball umpire who decides whether each pitch is a ball or a strike. Some calls are obvious; others raise the dander of the pitcher or the batter.

One of the most popular bridge magazines, *Bridge World,* features a great monthly column called "Master Solver's Club." In this column, 25 or so top bridge experts are shown a hand and told how the bidding goes up to a certain point, where it is now the experts' turn to bid. Each expert makes what he thinks is the right bid and usually makes a comment to justify the bid. You'd think that most of

the experts would come up with the same bid for the same hand, but it never happens. Each sample hand attracts at least three, four, and sometimes as many as eight different bids, plus lively (and funny) comments about the hand.

Sometimes the magazine tries to trick the experts by feeding them the same hands they gave them 20 or more years ago, to see if they come up with the same bids. Most of the experts don't recognize the hands and come up with different bids and different comments, sometimes even ridiculing bids they themselves suggested in the past for the same hand! (See Chapter 24 for more on bridge magazines from all around the world.)

Responding to a 1♦ Opening Bid

When your partner opens 1♦, you respond almost the same way you would respond if your partner opens 1♣ (as described in the previous section). In fact, your response differs in only one case — when your long suit is clubs.

When clubs is your longest suit

Clubs is a lower-ranking suit than diamonds, so you can't respond 1♣ to show clubs. Remember, during the bidding, each successive bid must be higher than the last bid. After your partner opens 1♦, you can't backtrack and respond 1♣.

If you want to respond with clubs, you have to bid 2♣. However, to make this response, which pushes up the level of the auction by a step, from one to two, you need 11 or more HCP (or 10 HCP if you have a strong six-card suit headed by the two of the top three or three of the five honor cards). A bid of 2♣ is an unlimited response (this bid has no upper limit as far as HCP). In short, it shows a respectable hand.

Naturally, problems arise when your long suit is clubs and you aren't strong enough to respond with 2♣. If you have fewer than six HCP, you can always pass, but if you have more than six HCP, you have to come up with some response.

If you have at least four cards in a major suit (spades or hearts), you can respond with a one-level bid in that suit. But if your only long suit is clubs, you don't have enough strength to respond 2♣, and you don't have four cards in either major suit, respond 1NT.

The 1NT response to a 1♦ opening bid doesn't necessarily guarantee a balanced hand; only the 1NT response to a 1♣ opening bid promises a balanced hand (see "With 6 to 18 HCP and a balanced hand," earlier in this chapter).

For example, the hand shown in Figure 11-7 is strong enough to respond (you have six HCP) but not nearly strong enough to respond 2♣. Solution: Respond 1NT and hope that you can show your clubs later. When you bid clubs later, your partner will know you have a weak hand because you bid 1NT first.

Figure 11-7:
You can
respond
1NT to a 1♦
opening bid
when you
have a long
club suit.

♠A 5 4   ♥5 4 3   ♣Q 10 8 7 4 3 2
(6 HCP)

The cards in Figure 11-8 show several hands in which clubs is your longest
suit. Your partner has opened the bidding 1♦. What do you do?

✔ In the first two hands in Figure 11-8, you meet the requirements to
respond 2♣, although the first hand just barely makes the cut because
of the six-card suit.

✔ On the third and fourth hands, you don't have enough HCP to respond
2♣ (you need at least 11 HCP). However, you need to make a bid
because in both cases you have more than six HCP.

- On the third hand, respond 1♠; although spades isn't your longest
suit, at least it's a suit that can be shown at the one level.

- Respond 1NT on the fourth hand because you don't have a four-card
major suit to bid and you aren't strong enough to respond 2♣.

♠A 5 4 3   ♥6   ♦K 4   ♣Q J 10 9 5 4
(10 HCP)
1

Figure 11-8:
These
hands
require
different
responses
to a 1♦
opening bid
when clubs
is your lon-
gest suit.

♠A 5 4 3   ♥5 4   ♦6 5   ♣A K J 5 4
(12 HCP)
2

♠K J 9 7   ♥5 4 3   ♦2   ♣Q J 8 7 3
(7 HCP)
3

♠Q 10 8   ♥4 3 2   ♦J 5   ♣A Q 8 4 3
(9 HCP)
4

How to get to game after a two-level response

Because you usually need at least 11 HCP to make a 2♣ response to a 1♦ opening bid, more often than not, you will have opening bid strength when you respond at the two level (a *two-over-one* response).

Partners love to hear two-over-one responses, especially when you have what you're supposed to have for the bid. When you respond two over one, your partner knows that you almost always have enough strength for an opening bid. Your partner's opening bid strength combined with your opening bid strength is usually enough to arrive at a game contract. See Chapter 20 for more about game contracts.

Responding to a 1♥ Opening Bid

When your partner opens the bidding with 1♣ or 1♦, he may have five, six, or even seven cards in the suit. He may also have a balanced hand with four (or, in emergencies, even three) cards in the suit. When your partner opens a major suit (1♥ or 1♠), your partner must have five or more cards in the suit.

Many times, you make the same response to a 1♥ opening bid as you do to a 1♠ opening bid. Turn to "Responding to a 1♠ Opening Bid" later in this chapter to see how responding to a 1♠ opening bid differs slightly from responding to a 1♥ opening bid.

During the bidding, you and your partner want to locate a suit in which you have eight or more cards between the two hands (an eight-card fit). You may not always have an eight-card fit, but if you do, happiness is just around the corner when you make that suit the trump suit.

If your partner opens 1♥ and you have three or more hearts, you have found your eight-card fit. It's blasphemous not to show your partner this fit at some point during the bidding!

Because locating an eight-card fit in a major suit is so important (you can score tons of points with such a fit), place your hand in one of the three following categories (covered in the following sections) when you're formulating your response to a 1♥ opening bid:

- ✔ Hands with fewer than three hearts
- ✔ Hands with exactly three hearts
- ✔ Hands with four or more hearts

Playing bridge would be so much easier if you could just lean over and whisper the number of hearts and HCP that you have, but the rules of the game forbid such direct communication. You have to use the special language of bidding — a bidding system — to tell your partner what you have.

With fewer than three hearts

Oh, great. Your partner has just opened with 1♥, and you have fewer than three hearts in your hand. What should you do?

When you have fewer than three hearts and at least six HCP, you have to come up with some response. Your first instinct should be to look for your longest suit. If you have to go to the two level to bid your longest suit, you need 11 or more HCP. If you don't have that strong of a hand but you do have four spades, respond 1♠ because spades is a higher-ranking suit than hearts.

If your longest suit is clubs or diamonds, you need 11 or more HCP to respond 2♣ or 2♦. If you don't have the necessary HCP (you have six to ten HCP), cough up a 1NT response, the catch-all response for all weak hands that don't have support for your partner's suit and don't have a four-card or longer suit to bid at the one level.

Each of the hands shown in Figure 11-9 shows a hand with fewer than three hearts.

- ✔ In the first hand in Figure 11-9, respond 1♠, your longest suit, showing six or more HCP.

- ✔ In the second hand, also respond 1♠; with two four-card suits (spades and diamonds, in this case), go up the bidding ladder starting with the suit your partner has opened, 1♥, and bid the first suit you come to. The first suit after hearts is spades and you have four spades. Perfect. Respond 1♠.

- ✔ In the third hand, respond 1♠; with two five-card suits, bid the higher-ranking suit first.

The cards in Figure 11-10 also feature some possible responding hands with fewer than three hearts.

- ✔ In the first hand in Figure 11-10, respond 1NT, showing six to ten HCP. You aren't strong enough to bid 2♦, which shows 11 or more HCP.

- ✔ In the second hand, respond 1♠. You aren't strong enough to respond 2♦, but you are strong enough to respond 1♠, which shows six or more HCP.

✔ In the third hand, respond 2♦ — although you have only ten HCP, you have a strong six-card suit.

✔ In the fourth hand, respond 1NT. You don't have the ten HCP you need to introduce a six-card suit at the two level.

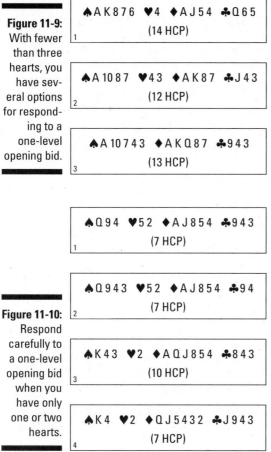

Figure 11-9: With fewer than three hearts, you have several options for responding to a one-level opening bid.

♠ A K 8 7 6   ♥ 4   ♦ A J 5 4   ♣ Q 6 5
(14 HCP)
1

♠ A 10 8 7   ♥ 4 3   ♦ A K 8 7   ♣ J 4 3
(12 HCP)
2

♠ A 10 7 4 3   ♦ A K Q 8 7   ♣ 9 4 3
(13 HCP)
3

♠ Q 9 4   ♥ 5 2   ♦ A J 8 5 4   ♣ 9 4 3
(7 HCP)
1

Figure 11-10: Respond carefully to a one-level opening bid when you have only one or two hearts.

♠ Q 9 4 3   ♥ 5 2   ♦ A J 8 5 4   ♣ 9 4
(7 HCP)
2

♠ K 4 3   ♥ 2   ♦ A Q J 8 5 4   ♣ 8 4 3
(10 HCP)
3

♠ K 4   ♥ 2   ♦ Q J 5 4 3 2   ♣ J 9 4 3
(7 HCP)
4

If you have fewer than three hearts plus a balanced hand, you can use the 2NT and 3NT responses with the following HCP ranges, providing you have honor cards in the other three suits:

✔ Respond 2NT if you have 13 to 15 HCP.

✔ Respond 3NT if you have 16 to 18 HCP.

With exactly three hearts

If your partner opens the bidding with 1♥ and you have three hearts in your hand, you have just located that all-important eight-card fit. An eight-card fit often produces an extra trick or two in the play of the hand. When you find an eight-card fit, never let it go.

When you realize that you have an eight-card fit, this is what you do:

✔ **Revalue your hand upward.** Even with three-card support, you get to add points (support points, or SP) for short suits, but not as many. Instead of the one-three-five support-point scale you use when you have four or more cards in your partner's suit (see "Using a support-point scale," earlier in this chapter), you use a more modest one-two-three support-point scale when you have three-card support.

✔ **As ever, add your HCP to your SP to get the true value of your hand expressed in SP:**

• Add one point for each doubleton.

• Add two points for a singleton.

• Add three points for a void.

✔ **Show your partner your support and your strength.**

You can make one of three responses, depending on how many SP you have after you revalue your hand:

✔ **6 to 10 SP:** Respond 2♥.

✔ **11 to 12 SP:** Respond in your longest suit. If your longest suit is spades, bid 1♠ and then 3♥ at your next opportunity. If your longest suit is clubs or diamonds, respond 2♣ or 2♦ and then bid the cheapest number of hearts possible at your next turn.

✔ **13 to 16 SP:** Respond in your longest suit and then bid 4♥ at your next opportunity.

The cards in Figure 11-11 show a few examples of responding hands with three hearts.

✔ In the first hand, add one point for the doubleton diamond, bringing you to nine SP and a response of 2♥.

✔ In the second hand, add two points for the singleton club. Your hand now weighs in at 11 SP, enough to bid 2♦. Then bid 3♥ next time around.

✔ You don't have any short suits in the third hand, but you have enough HCP to respond 2♥.

Signals create scandals

Most bridge players bend over backward to be ethical, but every once in a while, you run across partners who can't resist the temptation to cheat by using illegal signals.

Many years ago, a famous cheating scandal arose at a World Championship. One partnership was accused of using illegal signals to tell each other how many hearts they had. It was alleged that they signaled each other by holding their cards so that a certain number of fingers showed when they had a certain number of hearts. The accused partnership denied the charges, even though the captain of the accused team forfeited all matches. The case eventually went to a court of law, and the accused were found not guilty.

I was once witness to a famous cheating scandal during the 1975 World Championship in Bermuda. We were playing against two Italians

who were accused of passing information by kicking each other under the table. To prevent this illegal spread of information, a huge board was secretly placed under the table. Not knowing about the board, I inadvertently crashed my leg into it the next day. Ouch.

Despite the use of the board to prevent cheating, the United States team considered withdrawing from the tournament. The offending pair was barred from play, so we stayed. The Italians did, however, go on to win the championship in a very exciting finish. My friend Walter Bingham, who covered the event for *Sports Illustrated,* wrote a great article about the scandal called "The Foot Soldiers."

Because of scandals such as these, some people watch every move they make at the bridge table to avoid any suspicion of signaling.

♠ A 4 3   ♥ Q 5 4   ◆ 4 3   ♣ Q 8 7 6 5

(8 HCP + 1 = 9 SP)

1

Figure 11-11:
Three
hearts make
an eight-
card fit.

♠ A 4 3   ♥ K Q 4   ◆ 10 8 7 6 5 4   ♣ 2

(9 HCP + 2 = 11 SP)

2

♠ A 6 5   ♥ K 5 4   ◆ J 5 4 3   ♣ 9 8 4

(8 HCP)

3

With four or more hearts

Having four or more hearts when your partner has opened with 1♥ should be near the top of your wish list. When you have such great support for your partner's major suit, you know you have a great fit: at least nine hearts between you. You get to add even more SP to your hand because your short-side suits pay even higher dividends for your partner, who should be able to trump at least one or two of his losing cards in your hand (see Chapter 6 for the details on trumping losers).

If you have four or more hearts, return to the one-three-five scale of SP (as I discuss in "Using a support-point scale," earlier in this chapter):

✔ Add one point for each doubleton.

✔ Add three points for a singleton.

✔ Add five points for a void.

After you revalue your hand, your response depends on your new total. Your original HCP count is out-of-date; you add the old HCP to your SP and get a new, improved SP product.

When you have four or more hearts, make one of the following responses based on your new point total:

✔ **With 6 to 9 SP:** Respond 2♥.

✔ **With 10 to 12 SP:** Respond 3♥.

✔ **With 13 to 16 SP:** Respond in another suit and then leap to 4♥ at your next opportunity.

The cards in Figure 11-12 show you several hands with four or more hearts.

♠A876 ♥J876 ♦43 ♣872
    (5 HCP + 1 = 6 SP)
1

♠K876 ♥KJ54 ♦J954 ♣2
    (8 HCP + 3 = 11 SP)
2

Figure 11-12:
You can
respond in
several dif-
ferent ways   ♠4 ♥A8743 ♦J98432 ♣3
when you   3   (5 HCP + 6 = 11 SP)
have four or
more hearts.

♠92 ♥KQ43 ♦AQ976 ♣86
    (11 HCP + 2 = 13 SP)
4

In the first hand, after revaluing your hand, you clock in with enough points (six) to squeak out a 2♥ response. In the second hand, your hand grows from 8 to 11 HCP. You can jump to 3♥. This jump support for a partner is called a *limit raise;* this bid shows a fair hand, but it doesn't force your partner to bid again. Your partner can pass if you make a limit raise, but only if he has a very minimum hand for his opening bid.

The opener passes a limit raise with only a minimum opening bid. Because the responder shows a pretty fair hand, the opener normally bids game with any hand that has a singleton or two doubletons. The opener passes with 12 to 13 HCP and a 5-3-3-2 distribution (no singleton and no two doubletons).

The cards in the third hand in Figure 11-12 show a case in which you can respond 4♥ with a *weak freak,* a response that catapults you directly to game! You have a hand with plenty of trump support, not much in the way of high cards, and a side suit of five or six cards. To make a weak-freak jump response to game in your partner's suit, your hand must have

- Five or more hearts
- Two to seven HCP
- A total of 10 or 11 cards between your hearts and your long side suit

In the case of the third hand in Figure 11-12, your hand meets all three of these criteria — thus, the weak-freak response of 4♥.

Weak freaks take a huge number of tricks. You don't have to worry about points when you have a freak hand. Just get thee to a game contract of four of partner's major.

In the fourth hand in Figure 11-12, your hand blossoms from 11 HCP to 13 SP. In this case, you're too strong to make a limit raise of 3♥. To get this message across to your partner, respond 2♦ (diamonds is your side suit), and then leap to 4♥ on your next bid. The rest is up to your partner; you have shown your strength and your support. At least your partner can't sue you for nonsupport.

Responding to a 1♠ Opening Bid

Spades is the boss suit. Whichever partnership has the majority of the spades rules the world. If your partnership has the spades and your opponents want to compete against your spade bids, they have to increase the level of the bidding. If you want to compete against any suit they bid, you don't have to worry about increasing the level because you have spades, the highest-ranking suit in the deck. Having spades can make your day.

Basically, you respond to a 1♠ opening bid exactly the same way you respond to a 1♥ opening bid. Do I hear a big cheer in the background?— see "Responding to a 1♥ Opening Bid," earlier in this chapter, for the details. In the following sections, I show you several responses to a 1♠ opening bid.

With at least six HCP but no spade support

When your partner opens the bidding with 1♠, you can't mention your longest suit at the one level — period. Lacking spade support but having six or more HCP, you have to bid something. If you aren't strong enough to respond in your longest suit with a two-level response (you don't have 11 or more HCP), you must respond 1NT. This means that responding 1NT to a 1♠ opening bid can show some really strange distributions, such as the one in Figure 11-13.

Figure 11-13:
Responding
1NT with
a crazy
distribution.

♥42 ◆K65432 ♣K9743
(6 HCP)

Suppose that your partner opens 1♠ and you have the hand shown in Figure 11-13. You aren't strong enough to respond 2◆, by a long shot, but you have to bid something (you do have six or more HCP). Welcome to the 1NT garbage-can response. You can make a 1NT response to a 1♠ opening bid with some really bizarre hands. When you respond with 1NT to a 1♠ opening bid, your partner can expect anything!

With two five-card suits

If you have enough strength to bid at the two level (11 or more HCP), your responses are identical to those to a 1♥ opening bid.

For example, with two five-card suits, respond in the higher-ranking of the two suits. The cards in Figure 11-14 provide a few examples of hands with two five-card suits.

In the first hand, respond 1NT because you don't have the 11 HCP necessary to respond with 2♥. In the second hand, respond 2♥ because you have the necessary HCP to make a two-level response, and hearts outrank clubs.

Figure 11-14:
Bid the higher-ranking suit if you have two five-card suits.

♥ A J 5 4 3 ♦ 6 5 4 ♣ Q 9 7 4 3
(7 HCP)

1

♥ A J 10 5 4 ♦ A 9 4 ♣ Q 9 7 4 3
(11 HCP)

2

With two or more four-card suits

If you have two or more four-card suits, bid the lower-ranking suit at the two level first. Check out Figure 11-15 for examples of hands with two or more four-card suits.

✔ In the first hand, respond 2♣ — the first four-card suit you come to when starting from spades and working your way up the ladder from the bottom rung.

✔ In the second hand, respond 2♦, the first four-card suit you come to.

✔ Respond 1NT with the third hand because you aren't strong enough to bid any of your four-card suits; you have only nine HCP.

Figure 11-15:
With two or three four-card suits, respond in the cheapest four-card suit, going up the ladder from the suit partner opened.

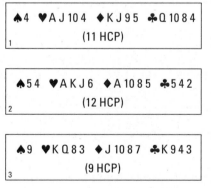

♠ 4 ♥ A J 10 4 ♦ K J 9 5 ♣ Q 10 8 4
(11 HCP)

1

♠ 5 4 ♥ A K J 6 ♦ A 10 8 5 ♣ 5 4 2
(12 HCP)

2

♠ 9 ♥ K Q 8 3 ♦ J 10 8 7 ♣ K 9 4 3
(9 HCP)

3

Supporting your partner's spades or responding 1NT, 2NT, or 3NT is identical in meaning to those responses for a 1♥ opening. See "Responding to a 1♥ Opening Bid," earlier in this chapter, for more information on making those responses.

Responding to a 1NT Opening Bid

When your partner opens 1NT, you have a pretty clear picture of what he has: a balanced hand and 15 to 17 HCP — no more, no less.

When your partner opens 1NT, assume he has 16 HCP — that way, you can never be off by more than a point.

When your partner opens 1NT, your own long suits take on extra luster because you know that your partner has at least two cards in your suit (your partner must have a balanced hand to open 1NT; see Chapter 10 for more details). If your partner has two cards in your suit, at least one is probably an honor card.

After you estimate the strength of your partner's hand, you can start looking at your own hand. The fact that your partner has a strong hand and at least something in every suit means that your long suits are worth more than usual. In fact, you can upgrade or *revalue* your hand by using the following scale:

- A five-card suit headed by two honors is worth one extra point. For example, KJ976 = five points, not four.

- A five-card suit headed by three honors is worth two extra points. For example, KQJ42 = eight points, not six.

- A six-card suit headed by the ace or king is worth two extra points. For example, A97632 = six points, not four.

- A six-card suit headed by two of the top three honors or any three honors is worth three extra points. AQ8432 = nine points, not six. AK10875 = ten points, not seven.

In this book, I use the abbreviation *RP* (revalued points) instead of *HCP* to show the new value of a hand. For more on how to count points, see Chapter 9.

Revaluing *long, strong* suits upwards facing a known balanced hand is a no-brainer. It's also a no-brainer to count extra points for short suits (SP) when you are *supporting* your partner's suit. Check "With exactly three hearts" earlier in this chapter.

Responding to 1NT is much easier than responding to any other bid because your partner's high-card range is so narrowly defined. With other opening bids of one of a suit, the range of the opening is really wide, but 1NT has a range of only three points. Because this bid tells you so much about your partner's hand, you can formulate a pretty specific plan of attack when responding:

✔ If you have ten points or more (using the preceding revaluation scale), you want to play in a game contract.

✔ If you have nine points, you want to invite game by asking your partner to bid game if he has 16 or 17 HCP, or stay out of the game with only 15 HCP.

✔ If you have zero to eight points, you want out either in 1NT or at the cheapest possible level in another suit.

Your distributional strategy, which I cover in the following sections, works like this:

✔ If you have a balanced hand lacking a four- or five-card major, keep the bidding in notrump.

✔ If you have six cards in a major suit (spades or hearts), make that suit trump.

✔ If you have four or five cards in a major suit, you have ways of finding out if you have an eight-card fit before returning to notrump.

With a balanced hand or a six-card minor suit

In this section, I discuss how to respond to the 1NT opening if you have a balanced hand or a hand that includes a six-card minor suit (clubs or diamonds). The cards in Figure 11-16 show some sample balanced hands.

Figure 11-16:
Use your revised point count when holding a five- or six-card minor suit in response to partner's 1NT opening bid.

1 ♠K J 5 ♥A 7 5 ◆9 8 7 ♣10 5 4 3
(8 HCP)

2 ♠K 4 ♥3 2 ◆A 10 8 4 2 ♣J 9 8 4
(8 HCP + 1 = 9 RP)

3 ♠Q 6 5 ♥5 4 ◆A Q 7 6 4 2 ♣8 7
(8 HCP + 3 = 11 RP)

When you have a balanced hand, you can add extra points to your HCP tally according to the scale mentioned at the start of this section. After you revaluate your points, you can respond to a 1NT opening bid according to the following scale:

- ✔ **With 0 to 8 RP:** Pass
- ✔ **With 9 RP:** Bid 2NT
- ✔ **With 10 to 15 RP:** Raise to 3NT

These counts assume that you have made the upward adjustments necessary for your long, strong suits. With a better hand, you can start thinking about slams, which you hear more about in Chapter 16.

In the first hand in Figure 11-16, pass because you need nine points to respond 2NT and look for a game; you have no reason to assume that game will be sensible here, so stay low. On the second hand, you have nine points (you've given yourself an extra point for the five-card diamond suit headed by two honors), which is enough to raise to 2NT.

A 2NT response is called an *invitational bid.* When you respond 2NT, you show your partner nine points and "invite" your partner to bid for game if he has enough points (he needs 16 to 17 points). If your partner has only 15 points, he should decline your invitation and pass.

With the third hand in Figure 11-16, respond 3NT to show 10 to 15 points; you have eight HCP and three extra points for the six-card diamond suit, headed by two of the top three honors.

With a five- or six-card major suit

With a five-card major suit, you consider making your suit the trump suit. When you have a six-card major suit, your strategy is to definitely make the six-card suit the trump suit — no matter how weak your hand is. If you have a six-card major suit, you can respond with zero points! After all, the 1NT bid shows a balanced hand, so you know that you have an eight-card fit.

The cards in Figure 11-17 show you a prime example of a six-card major suit.

You may look at the cards in Figure 11-17 and think, "Why do I need to end up with spades as the trump suit? Can't I just pass and end up taking just as many tricks at notrump?" Besides, I don't want to play this hand with only one jack! To answer this question, count the number of tricks your partner would take at notrump with this hand (see Chapter 2 for more about counting tricks in notrump). Here's a list by suit:

> ✔ **Spades:** Zero tricks (no ♠A, no ♠K)
>
> ✔ **Hearts:** Two tricks (you have the ♥AK)
>
> ✔ **Diamonds:** One trick (the ♦A)
>
> ✔ **Clubs:** One trick (the ♣A)

Responder (You)

♠J 10 9 8 3 2

♥8 7

♦3 2   (1 HCP)

♣10 7 6

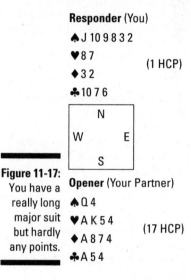

Figure 11-17:
You have a
really long
major suit
but hardly
any points.

Opener (Your Partner)

♠Q 4

♥A K 5 4

♦A 8 7 4   (17 HCP)

♣A 5 4

Even though your spades are long and reasonably strong, you can't take a single spade trick. After you drive out the opponents' ♠A and ♠K, even a blowtorch can't get the lead into the dummy, and the established spade tricks wither on the vine. However, if you played this hand with spades as the trump suit, you can count the following number of tricks for each suit:

> ✔ **Spades:** Four tricks (the ♠10983 after the ♠AK are driven out)
>
> ✔ **Hearts:** Two tricks (the same ♥AK)
>
> ✔ **Diamonds:** One trick (the same ♦A)
>
> ✔ **Clubs:** One trick (the same ♣A)

You end up taking four more tricks if spades is the trump suit. Clearly, you need the bidding to end with spades as the trump suit, without getting your partner too excited about your bid so that he heads for the stratosphere while you're trying to get out with your life at as low a level as possible.

Six-card suits don't have to be headed by high honors to take tricks when they're trumps. By attrition, three or four of the little ones will be good. Why? After the suit has been played two or three times, nobody else at the table will have any!

When your responding hand has a six-card major suit facing an opening 1NT bid, that suit must be made the trump suit. The 1NT bidder will always have at least two cards for you — sometimes even three or four cards to help you. So play the final contract in your suit at all costs. But how do you do that? Ah, there's the rub.

Responding in the suit beneath your real suit

I'm about to tell you something rather shocking. For a moment, put yourself in my hands and trust me as you have never trusted me before.

When you have a six-card major suit, however many HCP you have, you use a very strange convention to show your major suit to your partner: You respond in the suit *beneath* your real suit! This means that you respond 2♥ if you have six spades and 2♦ when you have six hearts.

Responding in the suit beneath your real six-card suit (you do the same with five-card majors) may seem outlandishly strange to you. However, this response is an established convention with a compelling reason behind it. After your partner bids your real suit, your partner, the stronger of the two hands, will be the declarer, which is a huge advantage.

You find out pretty quickly that the stronger of the two hands in a partnership should be the declarer (by bidding the trump suit first) whenever possible. When the declarer is the stronger hand, high cards are concealed from the opponents and the opening lead comes up to rather than through declarer's honor strength, a big advantage.

For the cards shown in Figure 11-17, the bidding goes like this: (Assume the opponents are silent, as they usually are after a strong 1NT opening bid.)

Opener (Your Partner)	Responder (You)
1NT	2♥
2♠	Pass

During this bidding sequence, you and your partner communicate important information. When your partner opens with 1NT, he says, "I have 15 to 17 HCP and a balanced hand." Your 2♥ response says, "I can't believe that I'm doing this, but I have spades, not hearts! Can you hear me over there? Eddie Kantar told me to make this bid, and I hope that you understand it!" Your partner stays cool and bids 2♠, which says, "Will you please stop panicking? I know you have spades. That's the convention. I hear you loud and clear and

I'm bidding 2♠ as requested." You then pass, winding up in the best contract played by the stronger of the two hands. Mission accomplished.

When you respond to a 1NT opener by bidding the suit beneath your major suit, you end up *transferring* the play to the strong hand. Instead of you playing the hand in your long suit, your partner does; you show the suit, and your partner bids it. Your partner becomes the declarer, and you get the coffee.

Using the Jacoby transfer

Due to the convention of transfers, your partner is programmed to bid 2♠ when you respond 2♥ and is similarly programmed to bid 2♥ when you bid 2♦. Your partner's programmed responses are called *completing the transfer*. By transferring, you achieve a number of aims, but the simplest of them is to make the strong hand the declarer.

Transfers are the brainchild of Oswald Jacoby and are often called *Jacoby transfers*. Jacoby was one of the top players in the world in his day. To see a Jacoby transfer in action, take a peek at the cards in Figure 11-18.

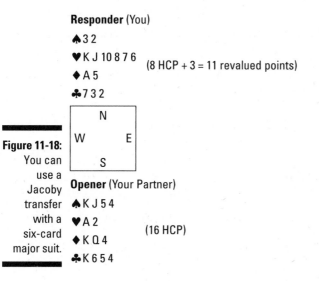

Responder (You)

♠ 3 2
♥ K J 10 8 7 6   (8 HCP + 3 = 11 revalued points)
♦ A 5
♣ 7 3 2

Opener (Your Partner)

♠ K J 5 4
♥ A 2   (16 HCP)
♦ K Q 4
♣ K 6 5 4

Figure 11-18: You can use a Jacoby transfer with a six-card major suit.

For the cards in Figure 11-18, the bidding looks something like this:

Opener (Your Partner)	Responder (You)
1NT	2♦
2♥	4♥
Pass	

When the bidding opens with 1NT, you respond with 2♦, which tells your partner, "I want to play the hand in hearts. Eddie told me to bid 2♦, and he promised me that you would come through for me by bidding 2♥." Your partner responds, "Yes, sir," and bids 2♥. You have enough points and length in hearts to contract for game, so you rebid 4♥. Your partner then passes.

Notice how much easier it is to play 4♥ from the strong hand (the hand with the majority of the high-card points). Whatever suit the opponents lead comes right up to your partner's strength. It's an advantage for the stronger hand to be the last person to play to a trick.

You can also use the Jacoby transfer with a five-card major suit. If you have a five-card major and a balanced hand, the bidding may go something like this:

Opener (Your Partner)	Responder (You)
1NT	2♦ (transfer to 2♥)
2♥	Pass (0 to 8 points)
	2NT (9 points)
	3NT (10 to 15 points)

Check out the cards in Figure 11-19 to see a hand in which you can use the Jacoby transfer with a five-card major suit.

Responder (You)

♠ K Q 8 7 3

♥ 9 4 3

♦ A J 2   (10 HCP + 1 = 11 revalued points)

♣ 4 2

```
        N
   W         E
        S
```

Figure 11-19:
Transferring
with a five-
card major
suit is a
smart move.

Opener (Your Partner)

♠ A J 3

♥ 6 5

♦ K Q 8 7   (16 HCP)

♣ A Q 8 7

For the cards shown in Figure 11-19, the bidding goes like this:

Opener (Your Partner)	Responder (You)
1NT	2♥
2♠	3NT
4♠	Pass

Your 2♥ response tells your partner, "I have at least five spades. I hope you remember that this response means that I have spades." Your partner's 2♠ response confirms that he has, in fact, remembered. Your next bid of 3NT tells your partner, "I'm giving you a choice of contracts. I have a balanced hand with five spades. You decide whether to play in 4♠ or 3NT."

Your partner has three spades, making his bid of 4♠ a very easy choice to make. If he had only two spades, he would pass 3NT, knowing of only a seven-card fit.

If you've never played with someone, it doesn't hurt to ask whether that person uses Jacoby transfers before you start playing. Bidding conventions work only when both players in a partnership know and use the same conventions!

You can also use Jacoby transfers after your partner opens 2NT. Again, a bid of 3♦ shows at least five hearts, and a bid of 3♥ shows at least five spades. Again, the target is to get the strong hand to be the declarer as often as possible. When your partner completes the transfer, he isn't showing support for your suit; he often has a doubleton. So if you've transferred with a five-card suit, go back to notrump. Your partner will know what to do.

With one or two four-card majors (the Stayman convention)

Your partner has just bid 1NT. If you have one four-card major with nine or more HCP, or two four-card majors with eight or more HCP, you're strong enough to respond. The question is, with what bid?

Your goal is to find out whether your partner also has four cards in the same major suit you do (you're looking for that magical eight-card major-suit fit). Thank goodness you can use a convention (oh no, not another one!) to find out just what you need to know.

A Jacoby story

Oswald Jacoby was one of the world's most famous players, and he always retained his sense of humor. Near the end, he began bidding more and more with less and less strength.

When he was asked about this tendency, he answered, "Yes, I bid every time it is my turn. At my age, the bidding may not get back around to me again."

Pull up your chair a little closer; you're about to join a group of millions of bridge players who use the *Stayman convention,* an artificial response of 2♣ that has nothing to do with clubs but that asks your partner if he has a four-card major. The object of the bid is to find out at the lowest level possible whether your partnership has a fit in either spades or hearts.

Artificial responses are bids that don't mean what they say. Instead, an artificial response conveys a preprogrammed message to your partner.

When you respond with 2♣ to a 1NT opening bid, you're asking your partner if he has a four-card major suit. If he does, he responds at the two level in the major suit in which he has four cards by bidding 2♥ or 2♠. With both majors, he bids 2♥. If he doesn't have a four-card major, he bids 2♦, which tells you, "Sorry. I don't have a four-card major."

When the Stayman convention works

The cards in Figure 11-20 show you a hand in which you can use the Stayman convention quite effectively.

Responder (You)

♠ K Q 8 6
♥ 9 4   (11 HCP)
♦ Q 9 8 7
♣ A 5 4

```
      N
  W       E
      S
```

Figure 11-20: Tell your partner about your four-card major(s) with the Stayman convention.

Opener (Your Partner)

♠ A J 4 3
♥ 6 5 2   (17 HCP)
♦ A K 6 5
♣ K Q

The bidding for the cards shown in Figure 11-20 goes like this:

Opener (Your Partner)	Responder (You)
1NT	2♣
2♠	4♠
Pass	

In this hand, your 2♣ response is made with this in mind: "I have enough power in my hand to bid 3NT because I have 11 HCP, but first I want to check to see if you have four spades. I hope you know I'm not trying to show you clubs." Your partner's response of 2♠ says, "Of course I know you're not showing clubs. Everybody in the world plays the Stayman convention. I know you're asking whether I have a four-card major. I sure do, and it's spades. Is that the major suit you're looking for?" Your 4♠ bid joyfully proclaims, "That's the major suit I'm looking for!" And you're right to be happy; 4♠ is the best game contract for these two hands.

When the Stayman convention doesn't work

You can't expect to find the four-card suit you need each time you use the Stayman convention. Sometimes your partner has the other four-card major; sometimes your partner doesn't have a four-card major at all. The cards in Figure 11-21 show you a case in which using Stayman doesn't make the desired connection.

Responder (You)

♠ K Q 7 6

♥ 6 4

♦ Q 9 8 7   (11 HCP)

♣ A 5 4

```
      N
  W       E
      S
```

Figure 11-21: Your Stayman response doesn't make a connection in this hand.

Opener (Your Partner)

♠ A 4 3

♥ Q J 10 9

♦ A 6 5   (15 HCP)

♣ K J 9

For these two hands, the bidding goes like this:

Opener (Your Partner)	Responder (You)
1NT	2♣
2♥	3NT
Pass	

Your 2♣ says, "I hope you remember that we use the Stayman convention, and I'm asking you if you have a four-card major." Your partner's 2♥ bid says loud and clear, "I have four hearts. How does that grab you?" That's not the response you were looking for, so you bid 3NT, which says, "Sorry, man, that's not the major I was looking for. I'm heading back to notrump because we don't have an eight-card major suit fit." Your partner then passes, telling you, "You're the boss." If your partner has four hearts and four spades, it is safe to bid 4♠ over 3NT because you must have four spades (you don't have four hearts) to have used Stayman.

When your partner doesn't have the four-card major suit you're looking for, bid 2NT with 9 HCP, or bid 3NT if you have 10 to 15 HCP.

If you open the bidding 1NT, your partner's response of 2♣ asks if you have a four-card major. For example, if you bid 2♥ and your partner goes back to notrump, you know that his four-card major is spades. If you bid 2♠ and he goes back to notrump, you know that he has four hearts. Good thinking. The only problem is that now the opponents also know that, and it may help them make a strong opening lead.

A Sam Stayman story

Many years ago, I was on a six-man team (only four play at a time) and we were playing a big match against the Stayman team, also playing six-handed. Sam Stayman was playing with Vic Mitchell, a fabulous player. Their team was so far ahead of us at halftime that Sam and Vic decided to retire early so they could rest up for the next day's match. We were so far behind we were thinking of conceding the match and having a nice dinner.

But we didn't. As it happened, everything went our way: We played well, they didn't, and we had all the luck in the world. We actually pulled out the match by a trifling amount — delirium in our camp, silence in theirs.

Somebody had to call Sam and tell him what happened. Nobody dared. Finally, Vic's wife, Jacqui, said she would. When Sam answered, she said, "Sam, I have some terrible news for you." "What, something awful has happened to Vic?" "No," said Jacqui, "worse."

Responding with a Jump Shift

When your partner opens the bidding and catches you with 17 or more HCP, not only is game a certainty, but slam is also a strong probability. To tell your partner the good news, you usually *jump shift*, responding one level higher than necessary in another suit. Your jump shift is a game force (neither player can pass until a game contract is reached). Indeed, you frequently wind up in a slam contract after a jump shift. (See Chapter 16 for more about slam bidding.)

The two most frequent reasons for jump shifting are

- ✔ To show a hand with a strong five- or six-card suit with 17 or more HCP. (You can jump shift with 16 HCP if you have a seven-card suit.)

- ✔ To show a hand with four- or five-card support for your partner's suit, plus 17 or more SP.

Figure 11-22 shows you an example of a jump shift with a six-card suit.

Figure 11-22:
You can jump shift when you have a six-card suit and at least 17 HCP.

♠ A K J 9 5 2   ♥ A 8 2   ♦ K Q 4   ♣ 7
Responder (You)
(17 HCP)

As you are busily adding up your points, you hear your partner open 1♣. Respond 2♠ (not 1♠), a jump shift that alerts your partner that game is a certainty and slam is on the horizon. At your next opportunity, repeat your spades (telling your partner that your jump shift was based on a long, strong suit).

A jump shift can also be based on support (usually four or more cards) for your partner's suit, plus 17 or more SP. Jump shift in your longest *side* suit, and then return to your partner's suit. Figure 11-23 gives you another chance to make your partner happy.

♠ A 2   ♥ K 10 8 5   ♦ A J 8 5 4   ♣ K 4
Responder (You)
(15 HCP + 2 = 17 SP)

Your hand has just blossomed to 17 SP (add 1 for each doubleton), enough to jump shift. After your partner bids 1♥, respond 3♦ and then return to hearts.

Chapter 12

Rebidding by the Opener

In This Chapter

▶ Deciding whether or not to make a rebid

▶ Figuring out what to rebid after different responses

After you open the bidding and your partner makes a response, do you have to bid again, or can you just pass? In this chapter, I tell you everything you need to know about your second bid, called your *rebid,* including when you can just pass and forget the whole thing.

Note: What happened to your opponents? Have they taken a vow of silence not to come in and confuse your bidding? Of course not! However, I give your opponents the day off in this chapter. You may find working through the principles of rebidding easier without any interference from your opponents. You can read about the nasty things your opponents can do to you (and what you can do to your opponents) during the bidding in Chapter 14.

Knowing When to Rebid and When to Pass

You made the opening bid (see Chapter 10) and listened to your partner's response (see Chapter 11). After that, do you absolutely have to bid again? Your decision depends on the response your partner makes.

Your partner's response can be *unlimited,* meaning that it shows a minimum number of points with no upper limit of high-card points. You can't pass an unlimited response. Or your partner's response can be *limited,* a bid that shows a narrow range of points. You're allowed to pass a limited response if you believe that you're in a sensible contract.

Consider this sequence featuring an unlimited response:

Opener (You)	Responder (Your Partner)
1♣ (12 to 20 HCP)	1♥ (6 or more HCP)

Your partner has made an unlimited response by changing suits, so you can't pass. Your partner may have a very strong hand, and a game or a slam may be in your future (see Chapter 16 for more about slams). When your partner makes an unlimited response, your rebid further describes your hand. Many times your rebid limits your hand, describing your strength and distribution and allowing your partner to figure out the combined assets of the partnership.

Listen to your partner's response to your opening bid very carefully, because you employ two completely different rebid strategies depending on your partner's response.

As soon as your partner makes a limited bid (raises your suit, bids 1NT), you can pass if you have nothing more to say.

Rebidding After a One-Over-One Response

When your partner responds to an opening bid at the one level, she makes what is called a *one-over-one* response.

Before you rebid, classify your hand by strength by totaling your high-card points (HCP; see Chapter 9 for details):

- ✔ **11 to 14 HCP:** Minimum zone (11 is an exception)
- ✔ **15 to 18 HCP:** Intermediate zone
- ✔ **19 to 20 HCP:** Rock crushers, or hands with mondo points (a few awesome 18-point hands sneak into this category)

Distributions, or *hand patterns* (the way your cards are divided), also influence your rebid. You may have

- ✔ **A one-suiter:** A hand with a six- or seven-card suit
- ✔ **A two-suiter:** A hand with nine or more cards in two suits (the shorter suit must have at least four cards)
- ✔ **A three-suiter:** A hand with three four-card suits, or one five-card suit and two four-card suits

> ✔ **A hand with support for your partner's suit:** Typically three- or four-card support for your partner's major suit
>
> ✔ **A balanced hand:** Hands that are divided with any 4-3-3-3, any 4-4-3-2, or any 5-3-3-2 hand pattern

When you open the bidding, you often have two or three chances to describe your hand. You have 1 of 635,013,559,600 possible hands, so describing your hand to your partner can be perplexing. But when you get the hang of that daunting task, you can give your partner a pretty clear picture of your hand. Read on to figure out how to plan your next move after a one-over-one response.

With a one-suited hand

You've got one long suit (with six, maybe seven cards), and one long suit only. You open the bidding with a one-level bid in your long suit, and your partner makes a one-over-one response. Now you want to show your partner that you have a one-suited hand.

However, you also must show your strength. If you have a minimum hand (11 to 14 HCP), you rebid your suit at the two level. If you have intermediate strength (15 to 18 HCP), you rebid your suit at the three level with a jump bid.

Figure 12-1 shows you a couple of hands that allow you to test these strategies.

Figure 12-1: Only one of your suits is long enough to rebid.

♠K 4 3 ♥3 2 ♦Q 4 ♣A K 9 7 3 2
(12 HCP)
1

♠K 4 3 ♥3 ♦A 5 4 ♣A K J 9 8 7
(15 HCP)
2

For each of the hands shown in Figure 12-1, suppose that the bidding begins as follows:

Opener (You)	Responder (Your Partner)
1♣	1♥
?	

In the first hand in Figure 12-1, you have a minimum-range opening bid, 12 to 14 HCP, so make a minimum rebid. Rebid 2♣, the cheapest club bid you can make, to show that you have long clubs — usually a six-card suit.

In the second hand, you have an intermediate-range hand, 15 to 18 HCP. When you have an intermediate one-suiter, jump to the three level in your suit. In this case, rebid 3♣ to tell your partner that your hand is in the 15 to 18 HCP range.

After you rebid your suit, you have made a limited rebid. At that point, your partner knows quite a bit about your strength and distribution. Your partner becomes the *captain.* After either player makes a limited bid, the partner is considered the captain of the hand . . . at least temporarily. The captain knows his partner's strength and distribution and is frequently in a position to pass, bid game, or even try for a slam! However, if the captain still doesn't know how high to bid, he can make an *invitational bid,* reversing the captaincy and asking his partner to make the final mistake — I mean, decision.

Notice that in the cards in Figure 12-1, you rebid a six-card club suit. You can also rebid a five-card suit, but you rarely do because you almost always have something better to tell your partner. As a general rule, the responder assumes that the opener has a six-card suit when the opener rebids his original suit.

You can voluntarily rebid a five-card suit that's dripping with royalty — a suit with four honor cards and one small card: AKJ107, for example. When your five-card suit reeks of honor cards, treat it as a six-card suit and rebid it.

With a two-suited hand

When you have two five-card suits or one five-card and one four-card suit, you have a two-suited hand. When rebidding a two-suited hand, you tend to show your second suit (you have already shown your first suit with your opening bid). In the following sections, I describe rebidding your second suit at the one and two levels. (See "With a rock crusher," later in this chapter, for details about bidding a two-suited hand with 19 or 20 HCP.)

Bidding your second suit at the one level

Count your blessings if you have a two-suited opening bid. Bidding two suits is great because it gives your partner a choice of trump suits. Bidding two suits can also be a challenge to your partner because it doesn't define your hand's strength all that narrowly — you're showing 12 to 18 HCP, a very wide range. Heaven is being able to bid both of your suits at the one level. However, you often find yourself in Hades because the rank of your partner's response makes it impossible to show the second suit at the two level, let alone the one level!

The cards in Figure 12-2 allow you to spend some time in seventh heaven because you can show your second suit at the one level.

Figure 12-2:
Whenever possible, rebid your second suit at the one level.

> ♠A J 6 5   ♥3 2   ♦9 2   ♣A K 5 4 3
> (12 HCP)
> 1

> ♠A J 6 5   ♥3 2   ♦K 8   ♣A K Q 5 4
> (17 HCP)
> 2

> ♠A J 6 5   ♥3 2   ♦4   ♣A Q 9 7 6 5
> (11 HCP)
> 3

For each of the hands shown in Figure 12-2, suppose that the bidding begins as follows:

Opener (You)	Responder (Your Partner)
1♣	1♥
?	

In Figure 12-2, you should rebid 1♠ with all three hands; the rank of your second suit allows you to bid your second suit at the one level. In other words, you can bid spades (your second suit) at the one level because spades rank higher than hearts (the order of the suits, from highest to lowest, is spades, hearts, diamonds, and clubs). You have just bid both of your suits at the one level, very economical. Nice going. You've told some of your story and not climbed too high in the bidding; your partner now has a better idea of what to do and where to go starting from the first floor of the bidding elevator.

When the opener bids two suits, the second suit is almost always a four-card suit. As responder, if you have four cards in partner's second suit, you have found a 4-4 fit.

After opening 1♣ or 1♦ and then rebidding ♥ or 1♠, the opener could have two four-card suits. However, if opener's first is bid is 1♥ or 1♠ and then she rebids a second suit, she must have at least 5-4 distribution.

Bidding your second suit at the two level

The rank of your two suits may not allow you to bid your second suit at the one level, and you may have to bid the second suit at the two level. Guess what? Bridge has a little rule for whether you are strong enough to rebid your second suit at the two level.

Assuming that your partner has made a response at the one level, if your second suit is lower ranking than your first suit, you have no problem. Just bid your second suit at the two level. But if your second suit is *higher* ranking than your first suit, you must have 17 HCP or more to show the second suit at the two level, called a *reverse*. I tell you more about reverses later in this chapter. If you don't have 17 HCP, you need to come up with some other rebid: perhaps 1NT, perhaps supporting your partner's suit, perhaps rebidding your own suit. What you can't do is show your second suit or, worse, pass out of frustration.

The cards in Figure 12-3 ask you to decide whether you're strong enough to show your second suit at the two level.

> ♠54 ♥65 ♦A K 5 4 3 ♣A Q 4 3
> (13 HCP)
> 1

Figure 12-3:
Whether
you can
bid your
second suit
depends on
the ranks
of your first
and second
suits.

> ♠54 ♥A Q 4 3 ♦A K 5 4 3 ♣4 3
> (13 HCP)
> 2

> ♠54 ♥A K J 8 ♦A Q J 8 6 ♣K 3
> (18 HCP)
> 3

> ♠4 ♥K Q 9 4 ♦A K J 9 7 6 ♣A 2
> (17 HCP)
> 4

Assume that the bidding begins like this:

Opener (You)	Responder (Your Partner)
1♦	1♠
?	

In the first hand in Figure 12-3, your second suit, clubs, is lower ranking than your first suit, diamonds. When your second suit is lower ranking than your first suit, you have no headache: Just bid the suit at the two level — 2♣.

In the second, third, and fourth hands in Figure 12-3, your second suit, hearts, is higher ranking than your first suit, diamonds. When your second suit is higher ranking than your first suit, you need 17 or more HCP to bid the second suit. If you don't have those 17 HCP, you can't show your second suit. You have to find some other rebid.

- ✔ In the second hand, you don't have nearly enough strength to show your second suit, hearts, because you have only 13 HCP. Instead, rebid 2♦ as a last resort.

- ✔ In the third and fourth hands, you're strong enough to show your second suit, so rebid 2♥.

Bidding a higher-ranking second suit at the two level is called *reversing*. After a one-level response, reverses show a minimum of 17 HCP with 5-4 distribution. Your partner can't pass a reverse. In other words, a reverse is a *forcing* bid, and your partner must bid again. As a responder, hearing your partner reverse is always music to your ears.

When you have a 6-4 hand pattern, such as the one shown in the fourth hand in Figure 12-3, you can reverse with as few as 16 HCP. (With 6-4, bid some more!) You can also reverse with 16 HCP if all your points are in your two long suits. When all your strength lies in your two long suits, award yourself an extra "purity" point, which brings you up to the 17 points you need to rebid a second, higher-ranking suit.

With a three-suited hand

You have a three-suited hand when you have three suits with four cards in them and a singleton in the fourth suit (a suit with one card). Lucky you.

Are you the gambling type? If you are, you can bet that when you have a three-suited hand, your partner's response will be in your short suit. It never fails. However, if your partner responds in one of your four-card suits, your birthday has come early.

Figure 12-4 shows two example hands in which you have a three-suited hand.

Figure 12-4:
With three
four-card
suits and
one short
suit, you
may have to
bid up the
line.

♠ A J 6 5 ♥ K Q 6 5 ♦ 2 ♣ A 9 8 4
(14 HCP)

1

♠ K Q 9 8 ♥ 4 ♦ A K 9 8 ♣ 10 8 7 6
(12 HCP)

2

In the first hand in Figure 12-4, the bidding has gone as follows:

Opener (You)	Responder (Your Partner)
1♣	1♦
?	

When your partner responds in your short suit (what else is new?), bid the next highest-ranking four-card suit (called *bidding up the line*). In the case of the first hand in Figure 12-4, you would rebid 1♥.

In the second hand in Figure 12-4, the bidding has gone as follows:

Opener (You)	Responder (Your Partner)
1♦	1♥
?	

In this case, you would rebid 1♠, your next-highest-ranking four-card suit.

The bad news scenario is a 1-4-4-4 pattern, 12 to 14 HCP, with a singleton spade. The proper opening bid is 1♦, and when partner responds the inevitable 1♠, you have a choice of evils. You can either (1) rebid 1NT with a singleton (you promise a balanced hand), or (2) rebid 2♣ with eight cards in your two suits (you promise nine). The short answer is to rebid 1NT with a singleton queen and king or ace of spades, and rebid 2♣ with any lower spade.

With support for your partner's one-level major-suit response

Whenever your partner makes a major-suit response of 1♥ or 1♠, go out of your way to support your partner's suit. In the following sections, I discuss raising your partner's major suit to the two and three levels.

Raising to the two level

REMEMBER

You can support a one-level major-suit response with either three or four cards in your partner's suit. However, if you have three-card support, you must have a side-suit singleton or a small doubleton (two small cards). If you don't have a side-suit singleton or a small doubleton, don't support your partner's suit just yet.

TIP

If you make a simple raise from the one level to the two level, you show a minimum hand with 13 to 15 support points (SP). You get to add SP to your hand for short suits whenever you support your partner's suit. (See Chapter 11 for more information on support points.)

Take a look at the hands in Figure 12-5 to decide whether you can support your partner's one-level major-suit response.

Figure 12-5: Look for the proper rebid after a one-level major-suit response.

1. ♠ A 4 3   ♥ K 10 5   ♦ 4 3   ♣ A Q 8 7 6 (13 HCP + 1 = 14 SP)
2. ♠ A 4   ♥ K 10 4 3   ♦ 4 3   ♣ A J 8 7 6 (12 HCP + 2 = 14 SP)
3. ♠ A 4 3   ♥ K 10 5   ♦ J 9 8   ♣ A J 5 4 (13 HCP)

For each of the hands in Figure 12-5, the bidding has gone as follows:

Opener (You)	Responder (Your Partner)
1♣	1♥
?	

In the first two hands, you can comfortably raise your partner's response of 1♥ to 2♥. The raise from one to two shows a minimum hand (13 to 15 SP) with three- or four-card support.

Be sure to revalue your hand when raising your partner. With the first hand in Figure 12-5, add one extra point for your doubleton diamond; with the second hand, add two extra points, one for each doubleton. In the third hand, you have no side-suit singleton or weak doubleton, so don't raise.

With a "flat" hand in the third hand in Figure 12-5 (a 4-3-3-3 distribution), a 1NT rebid showing 12 to 14 HCP more accurately describes your hand. Don't even think about raising your partner with a flat hand! (See "With a 4-3-3-3 pattern," later in this chapter, for more about rebidding with this type of balanced hand.)

Raising to the three level

In Figure 12-6, you can *jump raise* your partner's suit from the one level to the three level to show your extra strength. However, for a jump raise you need four-card support, called primary support. Happiness is having primary support for one of partner's suits.

Figure 12-6:
Jump
over the
two level
straight
to the
three level
when you
have extra
strength.

♠A 7 2 ♥A K 6 5 ◆3 ♣K 8 7 4 3
(14 HCP + 3 = 17 SP)

The bidding for this hand has gone about its merry way like this:

Opener (You)	Responder (Your Partner)
1♣	1♥
?	

The hand in Figure 12-6 starts out as a minimum hand (you have 14 HCP). If your partner had responded 1◆, your short suit, the hand would stay a minimum and you would rebid 1♥.

Never add extra points to your hand when your partner bids your short suit.

However, if your partner responds 1♥, a suit for which you have four-card support, your stock goes way up. You can add three extra points for your singleton diamond, so your minimum hand has now blossomed into an intermediate hand. The hand now evaluates to 17 SP. With 16 to 18 SP, jump raise to the three level; in this case, jump to 3♥.

Partners love to hear you raise their major-suit responses, particularly with a jump. It means that your side has found a great fit and your partner gets to play the hand if the final contract ends in the "agreed" major suit.

With a balanced hand

Three classic shapes form a balanced hand: the 4-3-3-3 shape, the 4-4-3-2 shape, and the 5-3-3-2 shape. Balanced hands don't offer many options when it comes to rebidding. You can support your partner's suit, rebid notrump, or introduce a second four-card suit at the one level. I explain how to respond with each balanced pattern in the following sections.

With a 4-3-3-3 pattern

If your partner responds in your four-card major, raise it. If your partner responds in any other suit, rebid some number of notrump depending on your point count.

The cards in Figure 12-7 let you rebid with a flat 4-3-3-3 hand pattern.

Figure 12-7:
You have very few options for making a rebid with a flat hand.

♠ K J 4   ♥ Q 10 7   ♦ K 5 4   ♣ A 8 7 2
(13 HCP)

1

♠ K J 4   ♥ Q 10 7 2   ♦ K 5 4   ♣ A 8 7
(13 HCP)

2

You open 1♣ with both hands in Figure 12-7. How do you rebid?

- ✔ On the first hand, rebid 1NT over any one-level response because you don't have four-card support for whichever suit your partner responds with.

- ✔ On the second hand in Figure 12-7, rebid 1NT if your partner responds 1♦ or 1♠; raise a 1♥ response to 2♥.

If you have 18 or 19 HCP with this distribution, jump to 2NT on your second bid. This bid will be music to your partner's ears!

Even with a flat hand, you can raise your partner's major-suit response when you have four-card support, but not with three-card support. Make your partner happy and tell him about the fit. Did you know that bridge is a game of fits and misfits? (You can take that any way you like!)

With a 4-4-3-2 pattern

Far and away the most common balanced hand distribution is some 4-4-3-2 pattern. With 15 to 17 HCP and this hand pattern, you limit your hand immediately and open 1NT. If you open one of any suit with a balanced hand, your hand should be in the 12 to 14 or 18 to 19 HCP range (see Chapter 10 for details).

The hands in Figure 12-8 show you a couple of 4-4-3-2 hand patterns.

Figure 12-8: You usually rebid at the one level with a 4-4-3-2 hand pattern.

♠ A J 4 2   ♥ 3 2   ◆ K J 6 2   ♣ A 10 7
(13 HCP)

1

♠ K Q 5   ♥ 3 2   ◆ A 10 3 2   ♣ A 9 7 6
(13 HCP)

2

In both of the hands in Figure 12-8, the bidding sequence is this:

Opener (You)	Responder (Your Partner)
1◆	1♥
?	

Anytime you can rebid your second suit at the one level with minimum or intermediate zone hands (with 12 to 18 HCP), do it. On the first hand in Figure 12-8, rebid 1♠. If your partner responds in your doubleton suit and you would have to introduce your other suit at the two level, rebid 1NT instead, as in the second hand in Figure 12-8.

To rebid a second suit at the two level, you need at least nine cards between your two suits. If you have only eight cards, rebid 1NT instead.

With a 5-3-3-2 pattern

In this section, I discuss only 5-3-3-2 patterns with 12 to 14 HCP. With 15 to 17 HCP, you would have opened 1NT in the first place.

When you make a rebid with a 5-3-3-2 pattern, either rebid some number of notrump or raise your partner's suit. To raise your partner's suit directly with three-card support, your trump suit should be headed by at least the ace, the king, the queen, or the J10.

The cards in Figure 12-9 allow you to rebid with a 5-3-3-2 hand pattern.

Figure 12-9:
You can rebid notrump or raise your partner's suit with a 5-3-3-2 hand pattern.

♠ A J 4   ♥ K 10 4   ♦ 5 4   ♣ A J 6 5 4
(13 HCP)

Open the bidding with 1♣. If your partner bids your doubleton suit, diamonds, rebid 1NT. If your partner responds with 1♥ or 1♠, raise to 2♥ or 2♠. In each case, you've limited your hand and your partner usually has enough information about your hand to decide what contract is best. Notice that you don't rebid your five-card club suit. Raising your partner or rebidding notrump is the higher priority.

Finally, if your partner responds 1NT or raises to 2♣, both limited responses, you become the captain (the partner of the player who first limits her hand). As captain, your duty is to decide whether to go on or pass. Because you have a minimum hand and your partner has advertised a weak hand, just pass.

With a rock crusher

Suppose you have a two-suited hand with at least nine cards in the two suits (5-4, 5-5, 6-4), along with 19 to 20 HCP. Open the bidding in your longest suit. Say you have five clubs and four spades with 19+ HCP. You open 1♣, and your partner bids 1♥. If you bid 1♠, showing 12 to 18 HCP, partner could pass, which is something you don't relish. To make sure partner doesn't pass, jump to 2♠. You have just made a *jump shift,* bidding one level higher than you normally would in order to make sure partner doesn't pass. A jump shift is forcing to at least some game contract (3NT, 4♠, 4♥, 5♦, or 5♣).

Now suppose that your second suit is diamonds. Say you have five clubs and four diamonds with 19+ HCP. You open 1♣, and partner bids 1♥. The temptation is to jump to 3♦ to show the strength. However, a rebid of 2♦, a *reverse* (see "Bidding your second suit at the two level"), shows 17+ HCP and is forcing. Jump shifting is counterproductive if your rebid is already forcing. It wastes valuable bidding space.

Do you want to see a typical jump shift? I thought you'd never ask:

Opener (You)	Responder (Your Partner)
1♣	1♦
2♥	

In this sequence, you jumped (skipped one level) in a new suit at your second turn. You could have bid 1♥, but you chose to jump. Why? Because you wanted to show a rock crusher, and a rebid of 1♥ would not be forcing.

When your partner responds at the one level and you want to make sure that she bids again, you want to reverse, if possible. If that's not possible, jump shift instead. A jump shift is a game force that shows a mountain of a hand.

On a good day, you'll pick up a rock crusher that has four-card support for your partner's suit. With that hand, you don't have to jump in a new suit because your partner has just bid your second suit. Make her happy and jump all the way to game. Jumping to game shows a great hand because your partner may have as few as six HCP. In fact, you need at least 19 SP to pull off this leap all the way to game. The cards in Figure 12-10 show a hand with which you can make this fantastic leap of faith.

Figure 12-10:
Jump to game when you have 19 or 20 points.

♠ A K 7 4   ♥ A 7   ♦ K 4   ♣ Q J 8 6 2
(17 HCP + 2 = 19 SP)

For this hand, the bidding has gone as follows:

Opener (You)	Responder (Your Partner)
1♣	1♠
?	

Your partner's response allows you to revalue your hand upward. You can count one additional point for each doubleton, so your point total zooms to 19 SP. Rebid 4♠, a game bid, to reflect that strength.

When you have four-card support for your partner's one-level major-suit response, jump to game in your partner's suit with 19 to 21 SP.

Rebidding After a Two-Over-One Response

Nothing too bad can happen to you if your partner is strong enough to respond in a new suit at the two level after you open at the one level. A *two-over-one response* has no upper limit of HCP; it's an *unlimited* response. A two-over-one response can be a springboard to a game or a slam. Think of hitting the jackpot.

When your partner makes a two-over-one response, you know the following:

- ✔ Your partner has a minimum of 11 HCP (or maybe 10 HCP with a strong six-card suit — an exception).
- ✔ Your partner promises to bid again, unless you jump to game. That promise, written in blood, allows you to relax, knowing that your next bid can't be passed.

After a two-over-one response, you have options, all good ones, which I discuss in the following sections. Possibilities include limiting your hand by rebidding some number of notrump, supporting your partner's suit, or rebidding your original suit. You also can rebid a second suit. *Bidding a second suit does not limit your hand.*

Rebidding 2NT with a balanced hand

REMEMBER

With 12 to 14 HCP and a balanced hand, you plan to rebid 1NT over most one-over-one responses. (See "With a balanced hand," earlier in this chapter, for more about this rebid.) But your partner may double-cross you and respond at the two level. No sweat — rebid 2NT, which still shows 12 to 14 HCP.

Suppose that you deal yourself either of the hands shown in Figure 12-11.

Figure 12-11:
With a balanced hand and 12 to 14 HCP, rebid 2NT after a two-over-one response.

1　♠ A J 4　♥ K 10 8　♦ K Q 6 5　♣ J 6 5
　　　(14 HCP)

2　♠ A J 4 2　♥ K 10　♦ A J 9 6　♣ 8 7 6
　　　(13 HCP)

On the first hand, open 1♦, intending to rebid 1NT over a 1♥ or 1♠ response. However, if your partner crosses you up and responds 2♣, rebid 2NT.

On the second hand in Figure 12-11, you also open 1♦. If your partner responds 1♥, 1♠ is the proper rebid; if your partner responds 1♠, a raise to 2♠ is correct. However, if your partner responds 2♣, 2NT is the proper rebid. The hand isn't strong enough to rebid 2♠; rebidding a higher-ranking suit at the two level after a two-over-one response (reversing at the two level) shows 15 or more HCP. In addition, when you reverse, your first suit is supposed to be longer than your second suit. (See "Bidding your second suit at the two level" earlier in this chapter for more on reversing after a *one* level response.)

Jumping all the way to 3NT

With 18 to 19 HCP, balanced, you're too strong to open 1NT (15 to 17 HCP), and too weak to open 2NT (20 to 21 HCP). The solution: Open your longest suit and then jump in notrump. After a two-level response, jump directly to 3NT.

The cards in Figure 12-12 show you an example of jumping in notrump.

Figure 12-12:
Jump to
3NT with 18
or 19 HCP.

♠ A J 5   ♥ K J 5   ♦ Q 10 8 7   ♣ A K 4
Opener (You)
(18 HCP)

In Figure 12-12, the bidding has gone as follows:

Opener (You)	Responder (Your Partner)
1♦	2♣
?	

If your partner had responded 1♥ or 1♠, you would have jumped to 2NT. However, your partner has responded 2♣, so jump to 3NT.

Raising your partner's suit

If you have three- or four-card support for your partner's two-level response, don't hold back; show this support by raising your partner's suit, particularly when it's a major suit. Bear in mind that the responder can make a two-level response in clubs or diamonds with a four-card suit (fairly rare) but must have five cards to make a two-level response in a major suit. The bottom line is that you normally need four-card support (or three neat ones, such as AKx, AQx, or KQx, where x stands for any small card, like a two or a three) when raising a two-level minor suit response. However, a two-level response of 2♥, for example, guarantees at least five hearts, so you can raise your partner with any three hearts.

The cards in Figure 12-13 show you a neat example of when you have the support you need to raise your partner's two-level response to the three level.

Supporting your partner's major suit is the way to go with the following bidding sequence:

Opener (You)	Responder (Your Partner)
1♠	2♥
3♥	4♥
Pass	

Responder (Your Partner)

♠ 8

♥ K J 9 4 3 2   (11 HCP)

♦ A K 3

♣ 10 9 3

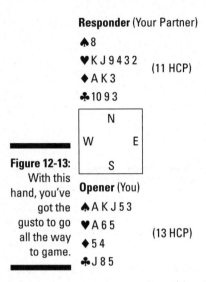

Figure 12-13:
With this
hand, you've
got the
gusto to go
all the way
to game.

Opener (You)

♠ A K J 5 3

♥ A 6 5   (13 HCP)

♦ 5 4

♣ J 8 5

Your partner's 2♥ response promises a minimum of a five-card heart suit
with at least 11 HCP. Your 3♥ rebid tells your partner, "I'm impressed. And
I'm not about to rebid a five-card spade suit with Kantar watching my every
move when I have three-card heart support for your five- or six-card heart
suit." Your partner's 4♥ bid joyfully says, "Thanks for the support, partner."
When you pass, you're telling your partner, "What an easy game. You bid a
suit, I support the suit, and we get to game. What could be better?"

If you want to win at bridge, raise partner's major-suit responses when you
have a three- or four-card fit.

Rebidding a six-card suit

Whenever you have a hand with just one long suit, you normally rebid the suit.
You want to show your partner a six-card suit and, at the same time, show your
strength. If you have a minimum-zone hand of 12 to 14 HCP, make a minimum
rebid; if you have an intermediate-zone hand of 15 to 17 HCP, make a jump
rebid.

For example, rebid your imaginary six-card heart suit as follows:

Opener (You)	Responder (Your Partner)
1♥	2♣
2♥ (12 to 14 HCP)	

Keep in mind that you can open the bidding with 11 HCP and a six-card suit.

Opener (You)	Responder (Your Partner)
1♥	2♣
3♥ (15 to 17 HCP)	

Rebidding a second, higher-ranking suit (reversing)

If you have a two-suited hand, you generally rebid the second suit and tell your partner the glad tidings as soon as you can.

However, after a two-level response, if your second suit is higher ranking than your first, you need 15 or more HCP to show the second suit. If you don't have 15 or more HCP, find another rebid. Your options include rebidding your original suit, raising your partner's suit, or rebidding a minimum number of notrump. Passing isn't an option.

Suppose that you pick up either of the two hands shown in Figure 12-14.

Figure 12-14:
Try reversing with more than 15 HCP.

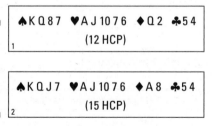

♠ K Q 8 7 ♥ A J 10 7 6 ♦ Q 2 ♣ 5 4
(12 HCP)
1

♠ K Q J 7 ♥ A J 10 7 6 ♦ A 8 ♣ 5 4
(15 HCP)
2

For both of these hands, the bidding has gone as follows:

Opener (You)	Responder (Your Partner)
1♥	2♣
?	

On the first hand, you aren't strong enough to rebid 2♠, a reverse, so you content yourself with a 2♥ rebid. Your hearts are quite chunky, so you're telling a little white lie to suggest that you may have six hearts. If your partner has four spades, he'll rebid 2♠ over 2♥ and the spade fit will be uncovered anyway. On the second hand, you're strong enough to reverse; rebid 2♠.

Rebidding a second suit at the three level (a high reverse)

Sometimes a partner's two-level response forces you all the way to the three level to show your second suit. Bidding a new suit at the three level is called a *high reverse* by some. To make a high reverse, you need 15 or more HCP. If you don't have 15 or more HCP, find another rebid. Three possibilities are rebidding your original suit, rebidding 2NT, or raising partner's suit.

The hands in Figure 12-15 show you when you can reverse at the three level and when you can take an alternative route.

Figure 12-15:
You need at least 15 HCP to bid your second suit at the three level.

♠ A K 10 4 2   ♥ 7 3   ♦ A J 4 2   ♣ 6 5
(12 HCP)
1

♠ A K 10 4 2   ♥ 7 3   ♦ A K J 2   ♣ 6 5
(15 HCP)
2

In both sample hands, the bidding has gone as follows:

Opener (You)	Responder (Your Partner)
1♠	2♣
?	

Perfect. In both cases in Figure 12-15, your second suit is lower ranking than your first, so you don't have to worry. Just rebid your second suit — rebid 2♦ with both hands.

Now assume that you have the same two hands shown in Figure 12-15, but this time, the bidding goes like this:

Opener (You)	Responder (Your Partner)
1♠	2♥
?	

Your partner's 2♥ response forces you to the three level to show your second suit, diamonds. You need 15 or more HCP to show that second suit at the three level. On the first hand, you don't have the HCP you need, so rebid 2♠. On the second hand, you do, so be my guest and show your second suit. Rebid 3♦.

You can't always show your second suit. If showing your second suit after a two-over-one response means going beyond the two level of your first suit, you need 15 or more HCP. With fewer than 15 HCP, find another rebid.

Rebidding After a Limited Response

When your partner makes a limited response, showing her strength within a few points, the fog clears (at least, it's supposed to!). You can add the strength of the two hands together and have a good idea of how high to bid. You then become the captain. The captain makes the decisions of whether to close up shop and pass, to bid game, or to issue an invitational bid to game or even to slam. In the following sections, I discuss what, if anything, to rebid after the two most common limited responses: when your partner supports your suit and when your partner responds 1NT.

When your partner supports your suit

When your partner supports your suit at the two level, assume she has seven to ten SP. (The average strength for a single raise is eight to nine SP.)

Whenever your partner raises your suit, your hand improves because an eight-card (or longer) fit has been found. How do you know you have a fit? If your partner raises you voluntarily, that eight-card fit is like an elephant in your sock drawer — you just can't miss it.

Your partner has already added extra points for short suits to revalue her hand properly. Now you, too, can add extra points when you uncover an eight-card or nine-card fit. How many points should you add?

When you first pick up your hand, you just count your HCP. You don't add for shortness or length because you haven't found a fit yet. However, after you uncover an eight-card fit, you can add extra points to your hand by using the following scale:

- Add one point for each doubleton.
- Add two points for each singleton.
- Add three points for a void.

If you know you have a nine-card fit, make the same calculations but give yourself two additional happiness points. Eight-card fits are nice, but nine-card fits are sublime.

When you've been supported, you get to count extra points for side-suit shortness. The total of your HCP plus your short-suit points is expressed in *revalued points* (RP). Had any alphabet soup lately?

Figure 12-16 shows three hands in which your partner has raised your 1♥ opening bid to 2♥, more often than not showing three-card support. You have to revalue your hand and decide what to do.

♠75 ♥A Q 8 7 6 ♦A Q 4 ♣8 7 6
(12 HCP + 1 = 13 revalued points)
1

Figure 12-16:
Revalue
your hand
upward
after you
find a fit.

♠A Q 2 ♥A K J 8 5 ♦9 8 6 2 ♣2
(14 HCP + 2 = 16 revalued points)
2

♠5 ♥A Q 9 5 3 ♦A K Q 4 2 ♣8 7
(15 HCP + 4 = 19 revalued points)
3

After you find an eight-card fit and revalue your hand, you decide how high to bid by using the following scale:

✔ If you have 15 RP or less, pass. Game is too remote.

✔ If you have 16 to 17 RP, you have a reasonable chance for game. Therefore, with this strength hand, you invite game, perhaps by bidding 3♥. Your partner passes with six to seven SP, bids 4♥ with nine to ten SP, and flips a coin with exactly eight SP. It's that close.

✔ If you have 18 or more RP, take a chance and bid game.

On the first hand, with 13 RP, pass because you have no chance for game, even facing a maximum in your partner's hand. On the second hand, with 16 RP, invite game by bidding 3♥. On the third hand, you can leap all the way to 4♥ because your hand is now worth 19 RP, giving yourself one extra point, a *purity* point, when all of your strength is in your two long suits, enough to bid game. The one who knows goes.

If your partner makes a *limit raise* by jumping directly to 3♥ in her first response, showing 10 to 12 SP with four-card support, pass with 5-3-3-2 distribution and 12 or 13 HCP. Bid game with all other hand patterns, regardless of strength. You would pass a limit raise with the first example hand in Figure 12-16 and bid 4♥ with the other two hands.

When your partner responds 1NT

The 1NT response is a limited response, and, as with all limited responses, the partner of the limited hand has a much better picture of the overall strength of the two hands and becomes the captain. When your partner responds 1NT, this is what you know:

- ✔ Your partner has six to ten HCP.
- ✔ In response to a 1♣ opening bid, the 1NT response promises a balanced hand; in response to any other suit, the bid does not guarantee a balanced hand.
- ✔ When the responder bids 1NT, she may have a long suit but not strong enough to bid it at the two level.
- ✔ Assume your partner's 1NT response to your major suit opening bid denies three-card support.

The opener, the captain, must remember all these things when making a rebid after a 1NT response. In the following sections, I show you how to rebid after your partner's 1NT response, whether you have a balanced or unbalanced hand.

When you have a balanced hand

The cards in Figure 12-17 give you a chance to rebid after your partner has responded 1NT. When you have a balanced hand, use this suggested scale to determine your next bid, keeping in mind that most 15- to 17-point balanced hands open 1NT.

- ✔ With 15 or fewer HCP, pass; game is too remote.
- ✔ With 16 to 18 HCP, raise to 2NT, an invitation to the waltz. If your partner has eight to ten HCP, she accepts and bids 3NT. With six to seven HCP, she passes.
- ✔ If you have 19 HCP, bid 3NT.

So far, the bidding for this hand has gone as follows:

Opener (You)	Responder (Your Partner)
1♠	1NT
?	

Figure 12-17:
You have several options for rebidding with a balanced hand after a 1NT response.

♠ A Q 8 4 2   ♥ A 6 5   ♦ K 6 2   ♣ J 7
(14 HCP)

Because you have a balanced hand and your partner has bid notrump, you should be content with a notrump contract. In Figure 12-17, you have fewer than 16 HCP, the minimum needed for an invitational raise to 2NT, so pass . . . quickly.

The cards in Figure 12-18 give you another chance to rebid after a 1NT response.

Figure 12-18:
After your partner responds 1NT, check your HCP count before rebidding.

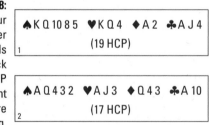

♠ K Q 10 8 5   ♥ K Q 4   ♦ A 2   ♣ A J 4
(19 HCP)
1

♠ A Q 4 3 2   ♥ A J 3   ♦ Q 4 3   ♣ A 10
(17 HCP)
2

In both hands, the bidding has gone as follows:

Opener (You)	*Responder (Your Partner)*
1♠	1NT
?	

On the first hand in Figure 12-18, you have a balanced hand with 19 HCP, enough to go directly to game. Bid 3NT. Even if your partner has a pitiful six count, you will have 25 HCP between the two hands and your partner may have a chance to make the contract. Besides, you don't have to play the hand — your partner does.

On the second hand in Figure 12-18, you have a choice between opening 1♠ and opening 1NT. I advise you (for the time being) to open all 5-3-3-2 hands that have 15 to 17 HCP with 1NT. Later you find out how to pick and choose between opening 1NT with exactly 17 HCP and a five-card suit or opening the five-card suit. With 17 HCP, you have a game facing good news (eight to ten HCP in your partner's hand), but you want to stay low if you're facing bad news (six to seven HCP in your partner's hand). To find out, make the good news/bad news ask of 2NT. If your partner has eight to ten HCP, she raises to 3NT. If she has six or seven HCP, pass is best. Not every story has a happy ending.

When you don't have a balanced hand

What if your partner responds 1NT and you don't have a balanced hand? No sweat. If you have a six-card suit, rebid it; if you have a second, lower-ranking suit, bid it. You know your partner doesn't have support for your first suit; maybe you'll get lucky with your second suit.

The cards in Figure 12-19 show an unbalanced hand.

Responder (Your Partner)

♠ 4
♥ A 8 7 6   (6 HCP)
♦ J 10 7 6
♣ J 9 7 6

```
      N
  W       E
      S
```

Figure 12-19:
Make a
rebid of your
six-card suit
or a second,
lower-
ranking
suit with an
unbalanced
hand.

Opener (You)

♠ A K 8 7 6
♥ 4 3 2   (12 HCP)
♦ K Q 8 7
♣ 4

Look how the bidding has gone so far with this hand:

Opener (You)	Responder (Your Partner)
1♠	1NT
?	

You have an unbalanced hand, and you know that your partner doesn't have spade support (if she had support, she would have raised to 2♠). Look for a home in another suit. Show your second suit and bid 2♦. Bidding a new lower-ranking suit doesn't necessarily show extra strength. The range of that 2♦ bid is 12 to 18 HCP.

Guess what? You have found a home. Your partner is allowed to pass your second suit with a weak hand that likes your second suit more than your first, and you end up in a very cozy contract, thank you very much.

Good bidders rebid only a six-card major suit after a 1NT response. After all, a 1NT response denies three-card major suit support. Rebidding a five-card major suit after a 1NT response has all the earmarks of a death wish.

Chapter 13

Rebidding by the Responder

. . . .

In This Chapter

▶ Determining which player is the captain

▶ Making the most descriptive rebid

. . . .

*Y*our partner has opened the bidding, and you have responded. Your partner has bid again, and now it's your turn to bid again. You can either pass or make another bid, called a *rebid*. In this chapter, I give you all kinds of tips and hints on what to bid at this stage of the game. (See Chapter 10 for more about opening bids, Chapter 11 for more about responding, and Chapter 12 for more about rebidding by the opener.)

Becoming the Captain

During the bidding, each player tries to determine his partner's strength and distribution. After opening the bidding and making a rebid, your partner's hand can fall into any of the following ranges:

> ✓ **12 to 14 high-card points (HCP):** Minimum range (11 HCP is an exception)
>
> ✓ **15 to 18 HCP:** Intermediate range
>
> ✓ **19 to 20 HCP:** Rock-crusher range

Your hand, as the responder, can fall into any of the following four ranges:

> ✓ **6 to 10 HCP:** Minimum range
>
> ✓ **11 to 12 HCP:** Invitational range
>
> ✓ **13 to 17 HCP:** Game, or possible slam range
>
> ✓ **18 or more HCP:** Likely slam range

After either player reveals her range, which is called *limiting one's hand,* that player's partner becomes the *captain.* The captain knows how many total points are held by the partnership and uses that number to help determine how high to bid. The captain can sometimes determine which trump suit is best for the hand after his partner has limited her hand. During the bidding, your first objective is to try to locate an eight-card (or longer) major-suit trump fit. If you find one, your quest is over; make that suit your trump suit.

As the responder, you frequently have a pretty clear picture of your partner's hand after you hear partner bid twice. Any rebid of the original suit, any raise of your suit, or any notrump rebid are all considered *limited* bids. Any change of suit is considered an *unlimited* bid. Before you rebid, the topic of this chapter, ask yourself the following two questions:

- ✔ What has my partner already told me with her first two bids?
- ✔ What have I already told my partner about my hand with my original response?

Your rebid depends on your answers to these two questions. In the following sections, I explain what happens to the captaincy when you limit your own hand and when your partner limits her hand.

Limiting your hand

You may have already limited your hand with your first response. For example, you may have raised your partner's suit, or you may have responded some number of notrump, both limit bids. After you limit your hand, your partner becomes the captain. You're off the hook; no more decision making for you to add to the gray hairs — unless your partner turns the tables on you by making an *invitational bid.* An invitational bid basically asks whether you want to go game or get out in a lower level contract called a *partscore contract* (see Chapter 20 for more about partscores). Such an invitation transfers the responsibility (and also the blame) back to you; you are now about to become the hero . . . or the goat.

Pretend that you and your partner have exchanged the following info:

Opener (Your Partner)	Responder (You)
1 ♥	2 ♥

Your response shows seven to ten support points (SP), and it's a limited response because you have limited your hand by showing your strength and distribution. Your partner has just become the captain. In this case, your partner usually makes one of the following three rebids:

- ✔ **Pass:** Telling you that the partnership doesn't have enough for game
- ✔ **3♥:** An invitational bid, telling you that your partner isn't sure whether enough points exist to bid game
- ✔ **4♥:** Telling you that the partnership has 25 or more revalued points between the two hands (remember that both hands can add extra points when a fit has been uncovered)

The 3♥ asks for more information. It invites you to bid game (4♥) if you have a maximum raise (nine to ten SP) and suggests you pass if you have a minimum raise (seven to eight SP).

An invitational bid in this sequence reverses the captaincy. After an invitational bid, you, not your partner, must decide whether your partnership has enough total game.

When your partner limits her hand

Your partner, the opener, can also limit her hand by supporting your suit, rebidding her original suit, or bidding some number of notrump. If your partner limits her hand, you become the captain. I give you a few sample hands to bid in the following sections.

With an eight-card fit

In each of the hands in Figure 13-1, it's up to you to decide whether you have enough points to bid game. Remember the following scale if you have a five-card suit that has been supported, indicating a likely eight-card fit:

- ✔ Add one point for each doubleton.
- ✔ Add two points for a singleton.
- ✔ Add three points for a void.

However, if there is a known nine-card fit, add two more points. A nine-card fit often plays one trick better than an eight-card fit.

♠ A J 6 5   ♥ 6 5   ♦ K J 6   ♣ A 10 9 7
Opener (Your Partner)
(13 HCP)

♠ K Q 9 3 2   ♥ Q 8 3   ♦ 9 4 3 2   ♣ 3
Responder (You)
(7 HCP + 2 = 9 points)
1

♠ K Q 9 7 3   ♥ A J 4 3 2   ♦ 10 8   ♣ 8
Responder (You)
(10 HCP + 3 = 13 points)
2

Figure 13-1:
Listen to
your part-
ner's rebid
before
revaluing
your hand.

♠ K Q 9 3 2   ♥ A 10 4   ♦ 10 9 3   ♣ J 5
Responder (You)
(10 HCP + 1 = 11 points)
3

For each of the hands in Figure 13-1, the bidding has gone as follows:

Opener (Your Partner)	Responder (You)
1♣ (12 or more HCP)	1♠ (6 or more HCP)
2♠ (13 to 15 SP)	?

In each case in Figure 13-1, you've made an unlimited response that shows six or more HCP. Your partner still doesn't know which range your hand is in. However, when your partner raises your suit to 2♠, she makes a limit bid that shows a minimum-range hand, and you become the captain.

If you feel that you have found a home for your partnership (an eight-card fit), add the two hands together and see whether you have a total of 25 or more revalued points between the hands. If you do, bid game. If you can't have 25 or more revalued points, pass. If you can't be sure, ask your partner for more information, perhaps by bidding 3♠, promising at least five spades. When you ask your partner for more information, she then becomes the captain.

In each of the hands in Figure 13-1, you have found a home. Even though your partner can have three spades to raise your one-level major-suit response, you know that you have at least eight spades between the two hands. Time to add the two hands together — almost.

Before you can add the two hands together, you must revaluate your hand after your suit has been supported and you know that you have an eight-card fit (or longer).

After revaluating your hand, you can decide what to do with each of the hands in Figure 13-1.

- ✔ For the first hand, which revalues to nine points, you don't have enough for game, so you pass.
- ✔ For the second hand, which revalues to 13 points, you have enough for game, so you bid 4♠.
- ✔ For the third hand, which revalues to 11 points, you have invitational strength, so you bid 3♠.

After your suit has been raised from the one level to the two level, a three-level bid in that suit by you invites your partner, the opener, to bid game. Your partner passes with a minimum hand (13 SP) and bids game with a maximum (14 or 15 SP). With the hand in Figure 13-1, which revalues to 14 SP, your partner bids 4♠.

With at least a seven-card fit

When your partner raises your suit, she shows a minimum opening bid with at least three-card support. This makes you the captain; you know her range — but she doesn't know yours. You can settle down at the two level if that seems high enough, or you can look for more if you aren't satisfied with a low-level contract. In Figure 13-2, you see two hands in which your partner raises your four-card major suit.

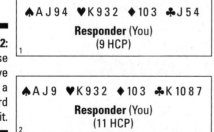

Figure 13-2:
These hands have at least a seven-card heart fit.

♠ A J 9 4   ♥ K 9 3 2   ♦ 10 3   ♣ J 5 4
Responder (You)
(9 HCP)
1

♠ A J 9   ♥ K 9 3 2   ♦ 10 3   ♣ K 10 8 7
Responder (You)
(11 HCP)
2

The bidding has gone as follows:

Opener (Your Partner)	Responder (You)
1♦ (12 or more HCP)	1♥ (6 or more HCP)
2♥ (13 to 15 SP)	?

After your partner raises your suit, you have found a seven-card heart fit (at least). At this point, you can either put up or shut up. In the first example in Figure 13-2, you have only nine HCP. Facing a maximum of 15 SP, you have no ambition for game because you can't have more than 24 revalued points between the two hands, and you need at least 25 revalued points to bid game. When your four-card suit is raised to the two level, you can't be sure of an eight-card fit, so just count your HCP. You're in a comfortable spot, so why look for trouble? Pass. If it turns out that you wind up in a four-three trump fit, so be it. It builds character to play an occasional seven-card trump fit.

When the opener's second bid shows a minimum-range hand (12 to 14 HCP), the responder needs 11 or more HCP to consider making a forward-going second bid.

With the second hand in Figure 13-2, you have enough to bid on, but not enough to drive to game. You can describe your hand accurately by bidding 2NT. What does this sound like to you? You have just found a fit in hearts, and here you are veering off into notrump. Did you mis-sort your hand and suddenly find that two of your red cards were diamonds, not hearts? No. Your 2NT rebid says, "Do you really want to play hearts? I have only four hearts, and if you raised me with three hearts, maybe we belong in notrump. I also have enough to try for game. Make the decision: game or partscore, hearts or notrump?" All those questions and inferences from just one bid!

After the opener raises your major suit, a 2NT rebid by you, the responder, shows 11 or 12 HCP and four cards in your major suit.

Rebidding After Your Limited Response of 1NT

When you respond 1NT to your partner's opening bid, you limit your hand, showing six to ten HCP, and your partner is captain. Nevertheless, developments may force you to make yet another decision. I show you a few of those developments in the following sections.

Sticking with notrump

Take a look at the cards in Figure 13-3 to see some hands in which your partner's rebid may force you to bid again.

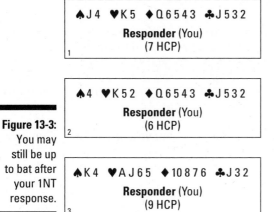

Figure 13-3:
You may still be up to bat after your 1NT response.

For each of the hands in Figure 13-3, the bidding has gone as follows:

Opener (Your Partner)	Responder (You)
1♠	1NT
?	

If your partner has a balanced hand and wants to keep the bidding in notrump, she'll make one of the following bids:

- ✔ **Pass:** Your partner has no hope for game (has 15 or fewer HCP).

- ✔ **2NT:** This invitational bid shows 17 to 18 HCP. If you like notrump, bid 3NT with eight to ten HCP and pass with six or seven HCP.

- ✔ **3NT:** Your partner counts 25 points between the two hands (she must be looking at 19 or more HCP). The one who knows goes!

Note: With 16 HCP and some hands with 17 HCP, your partner opens 1NT to begin with.

If your partner invites you to game by bidding 2NT, refuse the invitation by passing with the first two hands. With the third hand, accept and bid 3NT.

Choosing between two of your partner's suits

After your 1NT response, your partner may choose to bid a second suit. Unless you have a six-card suit of your own (see the following section), your partner wants to know which of those two suits you prefer.

If you have an equal number of cards in both suits, you absolutely must return to your partner's first suit, which is the longer one.

The cards in Figure 13-4 show you a hand in which you must choose between two suits that your partner bids.

Responder (You)

♠ 9 3
♥ A K
♦ 9 7 4 3
♣ J 9 5 3 2

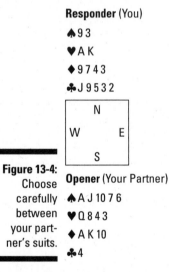

Opener (Your Partner)

♠ A J 10 7 6
♥ Q 8 4 3
♦ A K 10
♣ 4

Figure 13-4:
Choose carefully between your partner's suits.

For this hand, the bidding has gone as follows:

Opener (Your Partner)	Responder (You)
1♠	1NT
2♥	2♠
Pass	

In this bidding sequence, your partner's opening bid of 1♠ says, "I like this chapter. I get an opening bid on every hand." Your 1NT response says, "Stop your crowing; I have nothing again." When your partner rebids 2♥, she asks you, "Which of my suits do you like better?" Your 2♠ response says, "I don't like either one, but I prefer spades to hearts because I have an equal number of cards in both suits. Besides, Kantar is watching my every move."

When your partner passes, the unspoken message is, "Thanks for giving me a break and allowing me to play this hand in spades, where we have seven trumps between our two hands, not in hearts, where we have only six." Obviously, you need to outgun the opponents in the trump suit — not necessarily in terms of the high cards, but more in the numerical department. You must have more trumps than they do, or else bad things can happen, very bad things. Don't ask.

Ideally, you want to have eight or more trump cards between the two hands every time you play a trump contract. However, in the real world, you don't always have an eight-card fit. You may have to make do with a seven-card trump fit. If you wind up playing a contract with fewer than seven trump cards between the two hands, the wheels have come off. So when giving preferences to your partner, make sure that you concentrate on playing in the trump suit in which you expect to have the *most* cards, not the one in which you have the highest cards.

Going with your own long suit

In Figure 13-5, you get a second chance to bid your own long suit.

Responder (You)

♠ 7
♥ 4 2   (6 HCP)
♦ K 9 4 3
♣ Q J 10 8 7 4

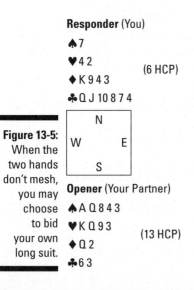

Figure 13-5: When the two hands don't mesh, you may choose to bid your own long suit.

Opener (Your Partner)

♠ A Q 8 4 3
♥ K Q 9 3   (13 HCP)
♦ Q 2
♣ 6 3

The expert and his watch

I've heard the story of a young up-and-coming player playing for the first time with a wily old veteran, an expert who was taking the young man under his wing. The first time they played together, the veteran opened 1♠, the next hand passed, and the young man looked at this hand: ♠104, ♥AQJ, ♦Q954, ♣J1087. He correctly responded 1NT, showing six to ten HCP. The expert rebid 2♥, and the young man, with such strong hearts, raised to 3♥. The veteran bid 4♥. When the opening lead was made, the young man proudly put down his strong trump support on the table. The veteran immediately looked at his watch. The young man asked him why he was looking at his watch, and the wily old veteran replied, "I will give you exactly 10 seconds to produce a fourth heart!" So much for raising a second suit directly without four-card support.

In this hand, the bidding has gone as follows:

Opener (Your Partner)	Responder (You)
1♠	1NT
2♥	3♣
Pass	

If your bids could talk, they'd be shouting the following messages to each other:

1♠: "I have five or more spades with 12 or more HCP."

1NT: "Good for you. I have a weak hand with only six HCP, but I have to respond, or you'll disown me. I'm not nearly strong enough to bid 2♣ with my six-card suit, which would show ten or more HCP, so I am hedging with 1NT."

2♥: "Hey, there. Hearts is my second suit. Which of my two suits do you like better?"

3♣: "I hate both of your suits, but I have a strong six-card suit of my own, which is clubs."

Pass: "This is the end of the trail, amigo. You have shown six or more clubs, and we have an eight-card fit, but because you guarantee a weak hand and I have a minimum hand, I know enough to get out of this mess right now."

When your partner bids two suits, just remember the following points:

🖉 With an equal number of cards in each suit, take your partner back to her first suit. However, if you have a strong six-card suit of your own without support for either of your partner's suits, bid it!

🖉 To raise your partner's second suit directly, you need four-card support because you always assume that your partner has four cards in her second bid suit, and you're looking for an eight-card trump fit.

Rebidding After Your Partner Rebids 1NT

A 1NT rebid comes up frequently because balanced minimum hands are very common. Thus, the following chart shows a typical sequence:

Opener (Your Partner)	Responder (You)
1♣	1♥
1NT	?

Take a good look at this sequence. You hear this type of sequence so often that you may start to hum it in your sleep.

When your partner rebids 1NT, here's what you know about your partner's hand:

🖉 It's a minimum-range hand (12 to 14 HCP).

🖉 It's a balanced hand with a likely four clubs and three cards in the other three suits, or perhaps five clubs with some 3-3-2 distribution.

If you, too, have a balanced hand, add your points to your partner's (the 1NT rebid shows 12 to 14 HCP, so assume 13 points as a ballpark figure). Your next move is to decide whether the two hands have a combined total of 25 HCP, enough to try for game, 3NT (see Chapter 20 on scoring). Don't forget to tack on an extra point if you have a five-card suit headed by two honor cards or two extra points if you have a five-card suit headed by three honors.

The three examples in Figure 13-6 give you a chance to decide what to do after your partner's 1NT rebid.

♠ A J 6 ♥ 65 ◆ K J 6 ♣ A 10 9 7 2
Opener (Your Partner)
(13 HCP)

♠ 10 4 3 ♥ A Q 8 3 2 ◆ Q 7 4 ♣ 64
Responder (You)
(8 HCP + 1 = 9 RP)

1

♠ K 3 2 ♥ A K 8 3 2 ◆ 10 7 5 ♣ K 4
Responder (You)
(13 HCP + 1 = 14 RP)

2

♠ K 3 2 ♥ A Q 8 3 2 ◆ 10 7 5 ♣ J 4
Responder (You)
(10 HCP + 1 = 11 RP)

3

Figure 13-6: You can respond to your partner's 1NT rebid in one of several ways.

You have a balanced hand in all the examples in Figure 13-6, so notrump is your home (you want the bidding to end in a notrump contract). Now you just need to decide how high to bid.

✔ In the first hand in Figure 13-6, you have nine revalued points and should pass because you have no chance for the 25 HCP you need for game.

✔ In the second hand, you have 14 revalued points and should raise to 3NT because you know of at least 25 HCP between the two hands.

✔ In the third hand, you have 11 revalued points and should invite game by bidding 2NT; you may or may not have 25 HCP between the two hands — you have to let your partner tell you whether you do. If your partner has 13 HCP and a good five-card suit or 14 HCP, your invitation will be accepted; with less, it should be passed.

Rebidding Notrump After Your Partner Shows Two Suits

If your partner bids two suits and you're not thrilled with either, you may want to veer off into notrump. A notrump rebid gets you out of the awkwardness of playing in a trump suit with only seven cards between the two hands. Just be sure to tell your partner your strength.

If you want to make a notrump rebid, show your HCP according to the following scale:

> ✔ **7 to 10 HCP:** Rebid 1NT, a minimum-range hand.

> ✔ **11 to 12 HCP:** Rebid 2NT, an invitational-range hand.

> ✔ **13 to 17 HCP:** Rebid 3NT — go straight to game with this count.

The cards in Figure 13-7 show some hands in which rebidding notrump is on target.

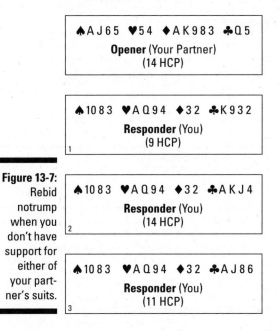

♠ A J 6 5　♥ 5 4　♦ A K 9 8 3　♣ Q 5
Opener (Your Partner)
(14 HCP)

♠ 1 0 8 3　♥ A Q 9 4　♦ 3 2　♣ K 9 3 2
Responder (You)
(9 HCP)
1

Figure 13-7:
Rebid notrump when you don't have support for either of your partner's suits.

♠ 1 0 8 3　♥ A Q 9 4　♦ 3 2　♣ A K J 4
Responder (You)
(14 HCP)
2

♠ 1 0 8 3　♥ A Q 9 4　♦ 3 2　♣ A J 8 6
Responder (You)
(11 HCP)
3

For each of the following hands, the bidding has gone as follows:

Opener (Your Partner)	Responder (You)
1 ♦	1 ♥
1 ♠	?

You have no support for either of your partner's suits, but you do have a balanced hand with strength in the unbid suit, clubs. A notrump rebid is called for in each of the responder hands shown in Figure 13-7.

✔ In the first hand, rebid 1NT, showing 7 to 10 HCP.

✔ In the second hand, rebid 3NT, showing 13 to 17 HCP.

✔ In the third hand, rebid 2NT, showing 11 to 12 HCP.

The 2NT rebid showing 11 to 12 HCP is one of your best friends. You use it in many sequences to invite game.

Raising Your Partner's Second Suit with Four-Card Support

When the opener bids two suits, the second suit is presumed to be a four-carder. To support a second suit directly, the responder (you) needs four-card support. In fact, you promise it in blood!

Consider this oh-so-typical bidding sequence:

Opener (Your Partner)	Responder (You)
1♣	1♥
1♠	?

If you're sitting over there with four spades, by all means let your partner in on the secret.

✔ With 7 to 10 SP, raise to 2♠.

✔ With 11 to 12 SP, raise to 3♠.

✔ With 13 to 16 SP, raise to 4♠.

Figure 13-8 gives you a chance to look over some second-suit raises. The first responding hand in Figure 13-8 has nine SP, counting one support point for each doubleton, so a raise to 2♠ fills the bill. The second hand revalues to 12 SP, again adding one point for each doubleton, enough to invite game with a jump to 3♠. The third hand revalues to 14 SP, enough to bid game directly by leaping to 4♠.

♠ A J 4 3   ♥ 7 4   ♦ K 5   ♣ A Q 9 7 4
Opener (Your Partner)
(16 HCP)

♠ K 7 4 2   ♥ A 6 5 3 2   ♦ 9 8   ♣ 3 2
Responder (You)
(7 HCP + 2 = 9 SP)

1

♠ K 9 8 4   ♥ A 6 5 3 2   ♦ 9 8   ♣ K 2
Responder (You)
(10 HCP + 2 = 12 SP)

2

Figure 13-8:
Raising a
second suit
promises
four-card
support.

♠ K Q 8 4   ♥ A K 5 3 2   ♦ 9 8   ♣ 3 2
Responder (You)
(12 HCP + 2 = 14 SP)

3

Rebidding After Your Partner Repeats Her Suit

If your partner has a six- or seven-card suit, you can expect her to bid that suit at least twice, maybe three times. When your partner rebids a suit, she has limited her hand, meaning that you're the captain. If you have support for the suit, you have found a home, but how high should you bid? It depends on your partner's strength added to your strength.

Consider the following two bidding sequences:

Opener (Your Partner)	Responder (You)
1♥	1♠
2♥ (11 to 14 HCP)	?

Opener (Your Partner)	Responder (You)
1♥	1♠
3♥ (15 to 17 HCP)	?

In these two sequences, you know that your partner has at least six hearts, possibly seven. In the first sequence, your partner makes a simple rebid at the two level, showing a minimum hand; in the second sequence, she jumps to the three level, showing an intermediate hand.

Point-count ranges aren't written in stone when it comes to long suits. Experienced players upgrade their hands when they hold a long, strong suit because such suits take many tricks in the play of the hand.

The cards in Figure 13-9 illustrate your partner making a jump rebid.

Responder (You)

♠ K 4

♥ A J 5 2   (8 HCP)

♦ 8 7 4 3

♣ 10 8 2

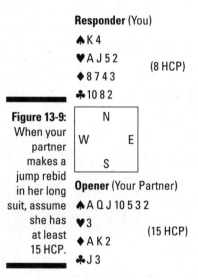

Figure 13-9:
When your partner makes a jump rebid in her long suit, assume she has at least 15 HCP.

Opener (Your Partner)

♠ A Q J 10 5 3 2

♥ 3   (15 HCP)

♦ A K 2

♣ J 3

In Figure 13-9, the bidding has gone as follows:

Opener (Your Partner)	Responder (You)
1♠	1NT
3♠	4♠
Pass	

Your partner's opening bid of 1♠ shows five or more spades with 12 or more HCP. You respond 1NT because you aren't strong enough to bid at the two level. Besides, you don't have three-card support for your partner's suit.

When your partner bids a suit and then jumps the bidding in that suit, assume she has an intermediate-strength hand (15 to 17 HCP) but, more important, one that can take about eight tricks. Because you have two taking tricks in your hand, go for it: Bid 4♠.

Rebidding Your Long Suit

Sometimes you (the responder) have a long, strong suit of your own. Strong six-card suits, especially major suits, were put on this earth to be bid and rebid. But don't forget that you also have to tell your partner your strength as well. Any hand that has a six-card suit has extra trick-taking potential; even more so if a fit is uncovered.

So what's the best rebid when you have a long suit typically headed by three of the top five honors, or two of the top four honors? Long suits in the responding hand are grouped according to this scale:

- ✔ If you have a minimum-range hand (six to nine HCP), rebid your six-card suit at the cheapest level possible.

- ✔ With an intermediate-range hand of 10 to 11 HCP, jump to the three level in your suit, an invitational rebid.

- ✔ With a game-going range hand of 12 to 16 HCP, get thee to game by jumping to game in your long suit.

- ✔ With 17 or more HCP, responder frequently jump shifts immediately. (See Chapter 11 for info on jump shifts.)

The cards in Figure 13-10 give you a chance to decide whether your long suit is long enough to rebid, and how high to rebid if it is strong enough.

For each of the hands in Figure 13-10, you and your partner have the following dialogue:

Opener (Your Partner)	Responder (You)
1♥	1♠
2♦	?

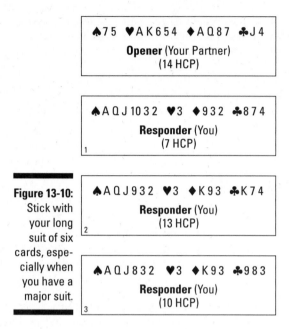

Figure 13-10:
Stick with your long suit of six cards, especially when you have a major suit.

On the first hand in Figure 13-10, rebid 2♠ to show your minimum-range hand. Your partner passes. No game in sight. On the second hand, jump to 4♠ to show a game-going range hand. And on the third hand, jump to 3♠ to invite your partner to bid game. Your partner, with 14 HCP, accepts and bids 4♠, thank you very much.

Rebidding After a Two-Over-One Response

Most of the responder's rebidding headaches arise after a one-over-one response, followed by the opener mentioning a second suit. At that point, three bids have been made, and neither player has made a limit bid. Both hands have problems determining each other's strength.

However, if the initial response is two over one, the opener already knows of 11 or more HCP, eliminating the possibility that you (the responder) have a weak hand. The responder figures to have a hand that fits into one of the following ranges:

✔ **11 to 12 HCP:** Invitational strength

✔ **13 to 17 HCP:** Game-going strength, at least

The examples in Figure 13-11 show you how the responder defines her hand after a two-over-one response. Remember, the responder already has shown at least 11 HCP.

Figure 13-11:
The responder completes the picture after the two-over-one response.

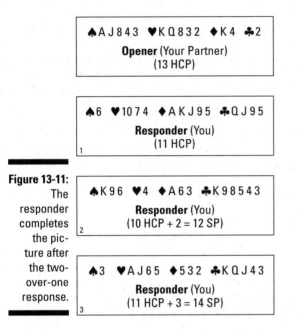

♠A J 8 4 3 ♥K Q 8 3 2 ♦K 4 ♣2
Opener (Your Partner)
(13 HCP)

♠6 ♥10 7 4 ♦A K J 9 5 ♣Q J 9 5
Responder (You)
(11 HCP)

1

♠K 9 6 ♥4 ♦A 6 3 ♣K 9 8 5 4 3
Responder (You)
(10 HCP + 2 = 12 SP)

2

♠3 ♥A J 6 5 ♦5 3 2 ♣K Q J 4 3
Responder (You)
(11 HCP + 3 = 14 SP)

3

The bidding for this hand has gone as follows:

Opener (Your Partner)	Responder (You)
1♠	2♣
2♥	?

You must make a rebid because a two-over-one response promises a second bid. In addition, both hands are unlimited. No one has rebid a suit, raised a suit, or bid notrump, so the traffic light is set firmly on green.

Ask yourself what you know about your partner's hand. So far, your partner has shown you the following information:

✔ A range of 12 or more HCP (an unlimited range)

✔ The likely possibility of five spades and four hearts

What does your partner know about your hand? So far, you have revealed the following details:

- ✔ 11 or more HCP, possibly 10 HCP with three spades and side suit shortness — a hand too strong to raise to 2♠
- ✔ Four or more clubs

In the first responding hand in Figure 13-11, rebid 2NT, showing 11 to 12 HCP. Notice that you can rebid 2NT with a singleton in your partner's first-bid suit. When you don't like either of your partner's suits and you need to bid again, bidding notrump is an option.

On the second hand, bid 2♠. You have 12 SP for spades (two extra for the singleton with three-card support), and now is the time to let your partner in on that little secret. In the third hand, you have four-card support for your partner's second suit. You can revalue your hand, bringing it to 14 SP (three extra for the singleton) — go ahead and jump to 4♥.

After you make a two-over-one response, your partner already knows that you have at least 11 HCP. With 11 or 12 HCP, don't do any jumping — just make a minimum rebid.

Playing the Waiting Game

After the opener bids twice, the responder may still not have enough information to place the final contract. In such cases, the responder usually bids a new suit, a waiting response, which forces the opener to bid again. The waiting response gives the opener another chance to further describe her hand.

The opener can't pass when the responder bids a new suit, which is an unlimited bid. The opener cannot pass an unlimited bid. However, most notrump bids are limited bids, so they can be passed.

The cards in Figure 13-12 show an example of this waiting response in action.

Assume that the bidding has gone as follows:

Opener (Your Partner)	Responder (You)
1♠	2♥
2♠	3♣
3NT	Pass

Responder (You)

♠ 5
♥ A K 9 5 4   (15 HCP)
♦ 3 2
♣ A K J 3 2

```
      N
  W       E
      S
```

Figure 13-12: Wait for more information from your partner when you can't place the final contract.

Opener (Your Partner)

♠ A K 9 4 3 2
♥ 2   (12 HCP)
♦ K Q 6
♣ 9 8 5

Here's how this bidding sequence unfolds:

1♠: "I have at least five spades."

2♥: "Of course, I don't know you actually have six spades. In the meantime, I want to tell you that I have a minimum of 11 HCP with at least five hearts, so I'm expecting some action here."

2♠: "I'm suggesting a six-card spade suit or five strong spades. I have a minimum-range hand, so don't get too carried away. I have just limited my hand, making you the captain. Good luck!"

3♣: "I have some more to tell you about my hand. I'm bidding a new suit, which does not limit my hand, so you have to bid again."

3NT: "I have strength in the unbid suit, diamonds, and I'm not in love with either of your suits. After all, you have two suits under control, I have the other two suits, and 3NT is game."

Pass: "So be it!"

Bob Hamman, a many-time world champion, says, "3NT ends all auctions." With all due respect (I better say that — he's a former partner!), it doesn't end all auctions, just most of them.

Part IV

Forging Ahead with Advanced Bidding Techniques

The 5th Wave   By Rich Tennant

"Donald, you can double your opponent, but you can't fire him."

In this part . . .

You can't let the opponents push you around in the bidding. You've got to get in their hair and make their lives miserable. In this part, I introduce you to defensive bidding techniques, including overcalling, jump overcalling, and the takeout double. No more Mr. Nice Guy.

In addition, I introduce you to slam bidding, a really exciting part of the game. You and your partner bid all the way to the six or seven level, contracting for 12 or 13 tricks! Of course, you have to take that number of tricks to get the huge bonuses that await you. I show you how to do it in this part. Buckle up.

Chapter 14

Creating Interference: Defensive Bidding

*J*ust because an opponent opens the bidding doesn't mean that you and your partner lose the use of your vocal cords. You may be able to interfere with a bid (or bids) to make it harder for your opponents to reach a good contract.

Indeed, your side may have more strength than your opponents, and you or your partner may wind up playing the hand. However, even if your opponents do play the hand, your interference bid(s) may cause them to reach a lousy contract. They may not be able to locate their best fit, and do they ever hate that! Equally important, your opponents may reach their best contract, but you may have tipped off your partner to the winning opening lead.

In this chapter, you discover how to use defensive bidding to your advantage. In short, you see how to become a difficult opponent. And you see what your opponents' bids mean if they do the same to you; after all, turnabout is fair play.

Getting Nasty with the Bad Guys: Overcalling

No matter how much you like your opponents, don't resist the temptation to mess up their bidding. It's a jungle out there. Here's a short list of ways to really annoy your opponents after they open the bidding:

✔ Bid a different suit, called an *overcall*. If you bid a suit at the one level, you make a *one-level overcall*.

✔ Bid a suit at the two-level, called — surprise — a *two-level overcall*.

✔ Jump the bidding (skipping a level) in another suit, a *weak jump overcall*.

✔ Bid 1NT, a *one notrump overcall*.

You can start harassing the opposition as soon as they open the bidding. At least consider overcalling every time the opponents open the bidding. To overcall, you need a strong five- or six-card suit. If you have that strong suit, high-card points (HCP) become less important.

In this book, you sit in the South position (see Chapter 1 for more about positions in bridge). Overcalls apply whether the player who opened the bidding is on your right (you're second to bid) or on your left (you're fourth to bid).

The following sections show you how to get the most mileage out of your overcalls. When bidding defensively after your opponents have opened, you want to achieve maximum irritation at minimum risk while still hoping to bid constructively when you have a good hand. It's an ambitious target, but you can manage it.

Making a one-level overcall

When your opponents open the bidding, a one-level overcall has an annoyance factor. To bid a suit at the one level after an opponent has opened the bidding, you need

✔ 10 to 16 HCP

✔ A five- or six-card suit headed by two of the top four honors, any three of the five honors (the 10 counts as an honor card too), or the A109, the K109, the Q109, or even the J109 with opening bid values

In other words, you need a decent-looking five-card suit, not one that looks like something the cat dragged home.

Pretend that East, to your right, opens the bidding with 1 ♦:

East	South (You)	West	North (Your Partner)
1 ♦	?		

You know that you want to interfere with East's bid, if at all possible; after all, you want to help your partner find a good lead, bug your opponents, and maybe play the hand, don't you? In Figure 14-1, you see four different hands that you may hold when trying to decide whether to overcall East's opening bid of 1♦.

♠A 4 ♥K Q 10 8 7 ◆8 7 ♣J 8 7 6
(10 HCP)
1

♠A Q 9 4 3 ♥3 ◆9 8 ♣K J 10 8 7
(10 HCP)
2

Figure 14-1:
You need
at least 10
HCP and
a decent
five-card
suit to make
a one-level
overcall.

♠A K J 9 7 ♥9 4 2 ◆K J 3 ♣K 4
(15 HCP)
3

♠A K 8 7 ♥5 4 ◆K 9 8 4 ♣10 8 7
(10 HCP)
4

The first three hands in Figure 14-1 all fit the mold for an overcall: 1♥ in the first instance; 1♠ in the second and third examples.

The second hand in Figure 14-1 has two five-card suits. Whether you're the opener, responder, or overcaller, you always bid the higher ranking of two five-card suits first.

Notice that the third hand in Figure 14-1 has opening-bid strength, which is very common (see Chapter 10 for more about opening bids). With a range of 10 to 16 HCP, many overcalls show opening-bid strength. Just because you have an opening bid doesn't mean that another player won't open before you get the chance to open. After all, a deck has 40 HCP!

Alas, the fourth hand in Figure 14-1 is the black sheep of the family. This hand doesn't have a five-card suit. Don't make one-level overcalls with four-card suits unless they look like AKQ10 or AKJ10. You have to pass with this hand.

You make your one-level overcalls in Figure 14-1 in the second seat. The opponent on your right opened the bidding, and you were second to bid. You can also make overcalls in the fourth seat, when you're the last person at the table to bid.

For example, if you had either the second or third example hands shown in Figure 14-1 and the bidding had gone as shown in the following chart, you would still overcall 1♠ in the fourth seat.

West	North (Your Partner)	East	South (You)
1♦	Pass	1♥	?

Making a two-level overcall

Your opponents' bidding or the rank of your long suit may make it impossible for you to name your long suit at the one level. For example, the opponent on your right may open 1♥ and you have diamonds, a lower-ranking suit, as your long suit. To mention your diamonds, you have to bid 2♦. In other words, you have to make a *two-level overcall.*

A two-level overcall takes away some space from the opponents, but it ups your side's risk — you are at the two level, not the one level, after all. You need a pretty good hand to up the ante with a two-level overcall. Specifically, you need the following:

✔ A hand that would have opened the bidding if you had had the chance

✔ More often than not, a six-card suit headed by at least two of the top-four honor cards or the A109, K109, Q109, or J109, along with 11 HCP

✔ If your overcall is based on a five-card suit, a suit topped by three or more honor cards, along with 12 HCP

Having strong intermediate cards in your suit (8s, 9s, and 10s) is very helpful when you make a two-level overcall. You're sticking your neck out a bit when you make the bid — that's the time to have some stuffing in your suit that the intermediate cards provide.

A world of difference exists between a suit with AQ743 and a suit with AQ1096. With the latter, along with sufficient outside high-card strength, you should make a two-level overcall; the weak intermediates in the first suit make a two-level overcall quite risky. You may get doubled (see Chapter 15 for more on doubling).

To get a better look at some two-level overcalls, take a peek at the hands in Figure 14-2. For each of these hands, East, to your right, opens 1♥. It's your turn.

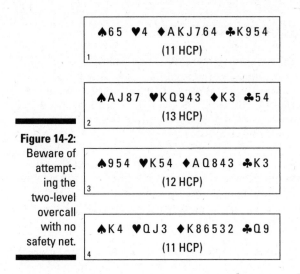

♠ 6 5   ♥ 4   ♦ A K J 7 6 4   ♣ K 9 5 4
(11 HCP)

1

♠ A J 8 7   ♥ K Q 9 4 3   ♦ K 3   ♣ 5 4
(13 HCP)

2

Figure 14-2:
Beware of attempting the two-level overcall with no safety net.

♠ 9 5 4   ♥ K 5 4   ♦ A Q 8 4 3   ♣ K 3
(12 HCP)

3

♠ K 4   ♥ Q J 3   ♦ K 8 6 5 3 2   ♣ Q 9
(11 HCP)

4

In the first hand in Figure 14-2, you can overcall 2♦; you have opening-bid strength plus a strong six-card suit — just what the doctor ordered.

In the second hand in Figure 14-2, you shouldn't overcall, for the following reasons:

- No overcalls with four-card suits (you were looking at that spade suit, weren't you, and not the long hearts?). You can't — and don't want to — bid the opponent's suit. Why bid hearts knowing that the opponent to your right has five or more of them?
- The opponents open in your longest suit.

When the opponents bid your longest suit, the *trap pass* offers your best strategy. The trap pass allows you to hide in the bushes, waiting to pounce later if your opponents have an accident and finish up in hearts. At that point, you can lower the boom on them with a penalty double (which I cover in Chapter 15); but wait until they have climbed a bit higher before you bring down the ax!

With the third hand in Figure 14-2, you should also pass. Your hand is strong enough and your suit is long enough, but, alas, your five-card suit isn't strong enough because you don't have three honors. Where's the meat?

Sadly, on the fourth hand in Figure 14-2, you must also pass. Your hand is strong enough and your suit is long enough, but, again, your suit isn't strong enough. Throw in the 10 of diamonds instead of a little one, and you would have a two-level overcall.

Making a weak jump overcall

A *weak jump overcall,* or preemptive jump overcall, is not a simple overcall, such as a bid of 1♥ over your opponent's opening bid of 1♦. A weak jump overcall skips one entire level of bidding and goes straight to 2♥, 2♠, or 3♣ over an opponent's 1♦ opening bid. (Bidding 2♣ over the opponent's 1♦ is a simple overcall, not a jump overcall because you bid clubs at the lowest legal level. A jump overcall would be to bid 3♣.)

Despite its name, this bid actually has a lot of offensive power. A weak jump overcall forces your opponents to enter the bidding at a higher level than they may want to. A weak jump's main aim is to screw up the opponents' bidding, and you can make one at your first opportunity, regardless of whether the opening bid comes on your right or on your left.

A jump overcall implies that you have a limited number of HCP. Jump overcalls make it that much harder for the opponents to find a fit because you steal bidding space and foul up their constructive bidding. Weak jump overcalls are extremely effective defensive weapons; as usual, the combination of maximum irritation with minimum risk is your goal. Another way to think of a weak jump overcall is to think of an opening weak two bid. They are almost identical. See Chapter 10 for details on weak two bids.

If your hands meet the following conditions, the time is ripe for making a weak jump overcall:

- ✔ Six to nine HCP
- ✔ A six-card suit headed by two of the top four honors, three of the top five honors, or the A109, K109, or Q109

If you have more than nine HCP, make a simple overcall by bidding your suit at the lowest possible level, without jumping.

In the following sections, I show examples of weak jump overcalls at the two, three, and four levels.

Making a two-level weak jump overcall

To see a weak jump overcall in the making, take a peek at Figure 14-3.

With this hand, you would have opened 2♠, a weak two bid if you had been allowed to get your blow in first.

Figure 14-3:
A weak jump over-call is about to be in full effect.

♠K Q J 8 7 6   ♥6   ♦Q 5 4   ♣9 8 7
(8 HCP)

However, an opponent may open the bidding with some suit at the one level before you can bid 2♠. No matter. Jump to 2♠, bidding one level higher than necessary. With ten or more HCP, simply overcall 1♠.

A weak jump overcall takes away bidding space from your opponents. When you have a strong six-card suit with a weak hand in HCP, think "weak jump overcall" and then do it!

Check out the hands in Figure 14-4 to get a better handle on making weak jump overcalls.

♠K Q 9 8 4 3   ♥A J 4   ♦Q 5 4   ♣3
(12 HCP)

1

♠4   ♥A K J 9 7 6   ♦8 7   ♣9 4 3 2
(8 HCP)

2

Figure 14-4:
Count your HCP care-fully before making a weak jump overcall.

♠A 9 7 6 5 3   ♥K 2   ♦K 9   ♣6 5 4
(10 HCP)

3

♠A K Q 10 8 7   ♥6 5 4   ♦4   ♣K Q 4
(14 HCP)

4

Assume that the opponent on your right (East) opens the bidding with 1♦; you are South and, thus, are next to speak.

✔ In the first hand in Figure 14-4, overcall 1♠; you're too strong to make a weak jump overcall.

✔ In the second hand, everything is perfect for a weak jump overcall, so go for it and bid 2♥.

✔ In the third hand, you have too many points and your suit is too weak for a weak jump overcall; overcall 1♠.

✔ In the fourth hand, overcall 1♠; again, you're too strong to make a weak jump overcall.

Making a three-level weak jump overcall

A weak jump overcall at the three level is the equivalent of an opening three bid. Again, your defensive bid robs your opponents of a huge amount of bidding space — generally a good tactic.

To make a three-level weak jump overcall, you need the following bullets in your gun:

✔ Six to nine HCP

✔ A seven-card suit headed by the ace or any two of the top four honor cards

Show your opponents no mercy when you have a seven-card suit. Make them suffer. When you make a three-level weak jump overcall, their wheels are likely to come off.

The cards in Figure 14-5 show you some hands in which you need to decide whether you can make a weak jump overcall at the three level.

Figure 14-5:
Make a three-level weak jump overcall whenever you can.

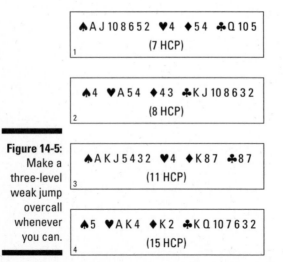

```
♠ A J 10 8 6 5 2   ♥ 4   ♦ 5 4   ♣ Q 10 5
                  (7 HCP)
1
```

```
♠ 4   ♥ A 5 4   ♦ 4 3   ♣ K J 10 8 6 3 2
               (8 HCP)
2
```

```
♠ A K J 5 4 3 2   ♥ 4   ♦ K 8 7   ♣ 8 7
                 (11 HCP)
3
```

```
♠ 5   ♥ A K 4   ♦ K 2   ♣ K Q 10 7 6 3 2
              (15 HCP)
4
```

For the hands in Figure 14-5, assume that the bidding has proceeded as follows:

West	North (Your Partner)	East	South (You)
1♦	Pass	1♥	?

In the first hand in Figure 14-5, all the conditions are right to make a three-level overcall — bid 3♠. In the second hand, you can make a three-level overcall with 3♣ — stick it to them! In the third hand, you can overcall, but only with 1♠; you can't make a weak jump overcall with every seven-card suit. You may be too strong! You intend to bid again the next time your turn comes around. In the fourth hand, overcall 2♣. You're too strong to make a weak jump overcall. You plan to bid again with this hand.

Making a four-level jump overcall

If you hold an eight-card suit (or a seven-card suit with a four-card side suit) in the range of 6 to 12 HCP, make a jump overcall straight to the four level. For example, if you're fortunate enough to have the hand shown in Figure 14-6, bid 4♥ the first time you get a chance to bid.

Figure 14-6:
Thank your lucky stars and go for an overcall at the four level with this hand.

♠3 ♥A Q J 9 7 6 3 2 ♦3 ♣Q 10 4
(9 HCP)

What happens next? You have just jumped to game in the teeth of an opponent's opening bid, and you may find nothing from your partner. Will someone fall off a chair? Will you be doubled and find a heap of garbage coming down in the dummy? Or will the contract roll home with an overtrick or two? Who can say? That's the beauty of a preempt. No one knows how it will work out, but if you make the bid on the right sort of hand, you will usually come out on top. Four-level jump overcalls are devastating!

Making a 1NT overcall

When the opponents open the bidding, you may choose to bid a suit, of course. But you can also overcall 1NT. The overcall of 1NT is almost identical to the opening bid of 1NT (see Chapter 10 for more details). The 1NT overcall shows 15 to 18 HCP, a balanced hand, plus strength in the suit that has been opened. So you need a pretty good hand to make the bid.

The hand in Figure 14-7 shows a typical example of a 1NT overcall.

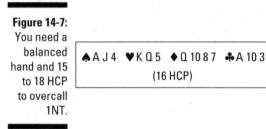

Figure 14-7: You need a balanced hand and 15 to 18 HCP to overcall 1NT.

♠ A J 4   ♥ K Q 5   ♦ Q 10 8 7   ♣ A 10 3
(16 HCP)

In Figure 14-7, you have 16 HCP and a balanced hand pattern of 4-3-3-3. No matter which suit the opponent on your right opens, overcall 1NT.

Respecting a two-over-one response from your opponents

When your opponents respond two over one (a two-level response in a new suit) showing 11 or more HCP, be very careful about making a two-level overcall.

When the responder bids two over one, the opponents usually have 24 or more HCP between them. That leaves the good guys with 16 HCP, max. Face it — you're outgunned. To enter the bidding after a two-over-one response, you need a powerful six-card suit with most of your high cards in that suit. Your overall strength is less important. Basically, you make the bid to indicate a good opening lead because your side is unlikely to play the hand.

Say you're faced with the following bidding sequence:

West	North (Your Partner)	East	South (You)
1♠	Pass	2♦	?

What would you do if you had the cards shown in Figure 14-8?

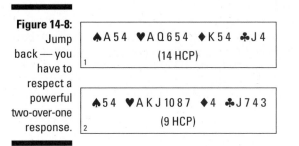

Figure 14-8:
Jump
back — you
have to
respect a
powerful
two-over-one
response.

♠A 5 4   ♥A Q 6 5 4   ♦K 5 4   ♣J 4
(14 HCP)
1

♠5 4   ♥A K J 10 8 7   ♦4   ♣J 7 4 3
(9 HCP)
2

With the first hand in Figure 14-8, pass with the speed of summer lightning. Yes, I see your 14 HCP, but I also see a mangy five-card suit instead of a powerful six-card suit. Also, with this hand, you would be lucky to find your partner with a stray jack or queen because the opponents apparently have at least 24 points between them. You can't take many tricks facing a whole heap of nothing.

Often your opponents' bidding tells you how strong your partner's hand is! When both opponents bid, add their supposed high-card strength to yours and subtract the total from 40, which tells you how strong your partner is. Be prepared to be depressed.

In the second hand in Figure 14-8, bid 2♥. Look at that suit. Strong suits like hearts here are what two-level overcalls are all about. Not a strong hand, only nine HCP, but a great suit; all those high hearts really warm the heart.

If your two-level overcalls aren't all that strong in high cards, nobody will call the cops. However, if the suit that you bid isn't a six-card suit dripping with honor cards, even 911 won't be able to save you.

Listen Carefully: Responding to Your Partner's Overcall

After an opponent opens the bidding and your partner overcalls, you know that your partner has a five- or six-card suit — more often than not, a five-card suit at the one level and a six-card suit at the two level. The strength of your hand plus the number of cards you hold in your partner's suit dictates your response. In the following sections, I explain how to respond to a variety of overcalls from your partner.

Responding to a one-level major suit overcall

If your partner overcalls 1♥ or 1♠, you know that she has at least a respectable five-card suit. If you have three or more cards in your partner's suit, you have found the Holy Grail, an eight-card fit. In the following sections, I show you how to respond when you find yourself in this situation; I also explain how to proceed when you have fewer than three cards in your partner's suit and when you have a balanced hand.

Having three or more cards in your partner's suit

If you have three cards in your partner's overcalled major suit, you have located an eight-card fit. This is no time for secrets; raise your partner's suit! This advice applies whatever the level of overcall you're responding to — in fact, the higher the level of the overcall, the faster you should raise!

You can respond to your partner's one-level overcall according to the following scale:

- **7 to 10 support points (SP):** Raise to the two level.
- **11 to 14 SP:** Raise to the three level.
- **15 or more SP:** Jump to game.

After you locate an eight-card fit, you get to add SP for shortness in the side suits (the nontrump suit). Add one point for every doubleton (two-card suit), two points for a singleton (one-card suit), and three points for a void (no cards in the suit). If you have four-card support, add one point for each doubleton, three points for a singleton, and five points for a void; the identical scale you use when supporting an opening bid. See Chapter 11 for more about SP.

Say that the bidding goes like this:

West	North (Your Partner)	East	South (You)
1♦	1♥	Pass	?

The cards in Figure 14-9 give you a chance to respond to this one-level overcall with a variety of hands.

In the first hand, raise to 2♥. You have eight support points, giving yourself one extra for the doubleton club. Do not bid 1♠. You already have an eight-card major suit fit; be content.

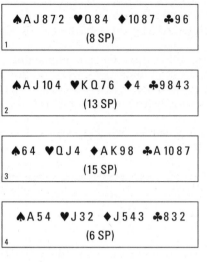

♠ A J 8 7 2   ♥ Q 8 4   ♦ 10 8 7   ♣ 9 6
(8 SP)

1

♠ A J 10 4   ♥ K Q 7 6   ♦ 4   ♣ 9 8 4 3
(13 SP)

2

♠ 6 4   ♥ Q J 4   ♦ A K 9 8   ♣ A 10 8 7
(15 SP)

3

♠ A 5 4   ♥ J 3 2   ♦ J 5 4 3   ♣ 8 3 2
(6 SP)

4

Figure 14-9:
Consider your SP as you decide what to say after your partner makes an overcall.

When your partner overcalls in a major suit and you bid another suit, you usually deny three cards in your partner's major suit.

In the second hand in Figure 14-9, jump to 3♥. Your hand has sprouted to 13 SP, adding three points for that singleton diamond because you have four-card support. The rest is up to your partner — he can pass or bid game, depending on what he has.

In the third hand, jump all the way to 4♥. You have 15 SP, facing at least ten HCP in your partner's hand, putting you in the game zone (your partner has a minimum of ten HCP for the overcall). The player who knows what to do should take the pressure off his partner.

On the fourth hand, you have to pass. You have only six SP, not to mention that your hand is of the hated "flat as a pancake" variety, with the dreaded 4-3-3-3 shape. The disadvantage of this shape is that your partner can't trump anything in your hand because you have no short side suit. Don't punish your partner by raising to the two level with this piece of unmitigated junk.

Having fewer than three cards in your partner's suit

When your partner overcalls and you have fewer than three cards in his suit, you can't support your partner. However, if you have enough points to bid, you may feel like introducing a decent five- or preferably six-card suit of your own. A five-card suit should be topped by at least two of the top four honors plus intermediates. Experienced players know how important intermediate cards are in long suits. All you need is a hand with the following traits:

✔ Eight or more HCP

✔ A respectable five-card suit headed by three of the top five honor cards

If you have 8 to 12 HCP, bid your suit at the lowest level possible; with 13 to 16 HCP, jump the bidding in your suit. A jump response (bidding your suit at one level higher than you need to) to a one-level overcall is a highly invitational bid; your partner can pass only with a minimum hand.

Take a look at the following bidding sequence, where you find yourself responding to your partner's 1♥ overcall:

West	North (Your Partner)	East	South (You)
1♦	1♥	Pass	?

Following is a rundown of what you would respond with each of the hands shown in Figure 14-10:

✔ In the first hand, bid a peaceful 1♠. Your partner will know that you have five decent spades, fewer than three hearts, and 8 to 12 HCP. Your partner can pass your 1♠ bid if he wants.

✔ On the second hand, jump to 2♠. A jump response to your partner's one-level overcall typically shows a strong six-card suit with 13 to 16 HCP. Just what you have! Your bid is highly invitational, meaning that your partner can pass only with a really minimum hand and no spade support.

✔ On the third hand, bid 2♣. Bidding a new suit at the two level strongly hints at a six-card suit, again showing a moderate hand of 8 to 12 HCP. This bid is nonforcing (your partner can pass); your partner can bid with extra values for his overcall or for any other good reason.

✔ On the fourth hand, jump to 3♣, an invitational bid. You want to show your partner that you have the values for an opening bid, plus a strong six-card suit. You just did.

Branching off into notrump

When your partner overcalls at the one level, your hand may lack three-card support or a long suit, which suggests a balanced hand. If you have honor strength in the opponent's suit, you can branch off into notrump by using the following scale (another scale!):

✔ **9 to 12 HCP:** Bid 1NT.

✔ **13 to 15 HCP:** Bid 2NT.

✔ **16 or more HCP:** Bid 3NT.

♠ A K Q 6 5 ♥ 4 ♦ 6 5 4 ♣ 10 8 7 5
(9 HCP)

1

♠ A K J 6 5 4 ♥ 4 ♦ 5 4 3 ♣ A Q 5
(14 HCP)

2

Figure 14-10:
You have
fewer than
three cards
in your
partner's
overcalled
suit.

♠ 6 4 3 ♥ 5 4 ♦ A 4 ♣ K Q 10 8 7 4
(9 HCP)

3

♠ A 5 4 ♥ 4 3 ♦ 6 2 ♣ A K Q J 7 6
(14 HCP)

4

When evaluating your hand, subtract one point if you have a small singleton in your partner's suit. On the other hand, add a point to your hand if you have the ace, king, or queen in partner's suit.

Check your notrump responses to the one-level overcall, shown in Figure 14-11. Assume that the bidding progresses as follows:

West	North (Your Partner)	East	South (You)
1♥	1♠	Pass	?

Here's how you'd respond:

✔ In the first hand in Figure 14-11, bid a quiet 1NT. You have the points and strength in the opponent's suit, hearts.

Any notrump bid after the opponents have bid promises strength in their suit(s). You don't promise strength in the unbid suits (notice your clubs).

✔ On the second hand, you can cough up a 2NT response, showing 13 to 15 HCP. The bid is invitational. Your partner can pass if the hands don't add up to 25 HCP.

✔ On the third hand, don't fool around; bid a direct 3NT. Your partner should have at least ten HCP, bringing the total to 26 points (the magic number for bidding game). Did you remember to give yourself an extra point for the ♠K?

✔ With the fourth hand in Figure 14-11, get out while the getting is good: Pass. You don't have enough to bid. Did you remember to subtract one point for the small singleton in your partner's suit? Just nod.

The best rule in all of bridge is this: When you don't have enough to bid, pass.

♠54 ♥AQ87 ♦KJ54 ♣1093	
(10 HCP)	

Figure 14-11:
Decide
carefully
whether to
respond to
an overcall
in notrump
and how
high.

♠J4 ♥KQ5 ♦AK87 ♣10943	
(13 HCP)	

♠K ♥AJ62 ♦KQ87 ♣Q1087	
(15 HCP + 1 = 16 revalued points)	

♠4 ♥A932 ♦Q543 ♣J632	
(7 HCP – 1 = 6 revalued points)	

Responding to a two-level overcall

Two-level overcalls show the strength of an opening bid, typically with six-card suits. If your partner makes an overcall of 2♣ or 2♦ and you have strength in the opponent's suit, think about the possibility of playing in notrump. If you have a decent holding in the opponent's suit and a balanced hand, respond in notrump according to the following scale:

✔ **10 to 12 HCP:** Bid 2NT.

✔ **13 to 16 HCP:** Bid 3NT.

Of course, you have other options; you may have a strong five- or six-card heart or spade (major) suit that you want to show, or you may raise your partner's suit to the three level if you have seven to ten SP plus three-card support.

The cards in Figure 14-12 give you a chance to test your sea legs when responding to a two-level overcall. For each of the hands in the figure, assume that the bidding has gone like this:

West	North (Your Partner)	East	South (You)
1♠	2♦	Pass	?

In the first hand, trot out 2NT; you have high cards in spades to control the opponent's suit, your ♦K is worth an extra point bringing you up to 12 points, a maximum for your 2NT bid (10 HCP but 12 revalued points). In the second hand, try 2♥, a strong five-card suit. Maybe your partner has heart support. In the third hand, leap to 3NT. Clubs are for peasants. When you have a choice of bidding notrump or bidding a minor suit (clubs or diamonds), notrump prevails. In the fourth hand, raise to 3♦, a typical raise with nine SP (one extra for the doubleton spade).

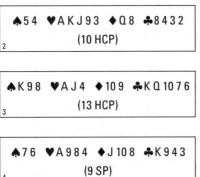

Figure 14-12: Responding in notrump is an option to a two-level overcall from your partner.

```
♠ A J 4   ♥ 8 4 3   ♦ K J 7   ♣ Q 10 7
            (11 HCP)
1
```

```
♠ 5 4   ♥ A K J 9 3   ♦ Q 8   ♣ 8 4 3 2
            (10 HCP)
2
```

```
♠ K 9 8   ♥ A J 4   ♦ 10 9   ♣ K Q 10 7 6
            (13 HCP)
3
```

```
♠ 7 6   ♥ A 9 8 4   ♦ J 10 8   ♣ K 9 4 3
            (9 SP)
4
```

Responding to a weak jump overcall

When responding to any preemptive opening bid or overcall, you're better off adding your tricks to your partner's tricks rather than your HCP to your partner's HCP. When your partner makes a jump overcall at the two level, he promises to take five or six tricks; at the three level, he promises six or seven tricks. So if you have a modicum of support plus a hand that looks like the two hands may add up to ten tricks (assuming your partner has bid a major suit), go for it. Invite your partner by raising to the three level, or bid game (4♥ or 4♠) if you can see a likely ten tricks.

How do you count tricks? Well, an ace is one trick, an ace and a king in the same suit is two tricks, a singleton with trump support is two tricks, and — hang on to your seat belt — a king is worth a half a trick! Why? If you want to take a trick with a king, you lead from weakness to strength and play the king. Half the time it takes a trick, half the time it doesn't! An ace-queen combination is worth a trick and a half. You lead low to the queen, and if the queen wins, you take two tricks; if it loses, you take one trick. (Check out Chapter 4 to see examples of the finesse in action).

Anyway, adding tricks to tricks is the idea. If this is all too much for you, raise your partner to game with 16 or more support points.

Responding to a 1NT overcall

"System is on" — that is, you respond to a 1NT overcall exactly as you do to a 1NT opening bid, which I discuss in Chapter 11. In other words, you can still use the Stayman and Jacoby transfer responses.

Chapter 15

Double Trouble: Doubling and Redoubling

. . . .

In This Chapter

▶ Chalking up extra points by making a penalty double

▶ Showing the two faces of a redouble

▶ Making a takeout double showing support for the unbid suits

▶ Using a negative double to show the unbid major suit(s)

. . . .

The title of this chapter, "Double Trouble," may give you a little hint of what to expect. *Double* can have several possible meanings, and when you say, "Double," your partner is going have to sort out exactly what you mean.

Not to worry; in this chapter I explain all things doubled. For openers, penalty doubles tell your partner to please shut up and pass — the opponents have bid too much. And if you sock it to them with a penalty double, they may stick it right back to you by redoubling, which says, "Brother, you've just made a huge mistake doubling me, and I'm upping the ante to four times what the normal score would have been — one way or the other." Excitement!

On the other hand, takeout and negative doubles ask your partner to please open his mouth and bid! Keep the faith; I know by the end of the chapter you'll have a handle on the doubling possibilities.

Putting Your Money Where Your Mouth Is: The Penalty Double

Knowing when to make a *penalty double,* a bid that tells your partner and the world that the opponents have overreached themselves, is truly the hallmark of a winning player. You're most apt to lash the opponents with a penalty double after they've bid to a game contract or higher. In the following sections, I explain the basics of penalty doubles and show you when to make one.

Understanding the basics of penalty doubles

Nobody bids perfectly. Accidents happen, and signals get crossed. Here's a short list of some of the ways that their (and your) bidding can go awry:

- **Misguided hope:** Some players see every hand through rose-colored glasses. Consequently, they overbid frequently. They wind up in stratospheric contracts that they can't possibly make.

- **Misunderstandings:** Each partner interprets a bid differently — sometimes very differently. Don't be surprised if at some point in an auction your partner thinks that you have a great hand when you've been trying to get the message across that your hand couldn't take a trick even if your opponents got up and left the table. Trouble looms.

- **Sacrifice bidding:** The opponents may decide that their hands just stink. They may prefer to lose points taking the contract away from you (even though they know that they can't make what they bid) instead of letting you bid and make your contract. Because this strategy can be a good defensive move (or a disastrous one), you have to know how to take advantage when it comes up. See Chapter 14 for more on defensive bidding.

When one of the above scenarios takes place, either you or your partner must be on the ready to wield your most potent and dreaded weapon: the penalty double.

A *penalty double* tells your partner (and your opponents) that you think that your opponents have made a big mistake and can't make their contract. Penalty doubles usually take place toward the end or at the end of a bidding sequence (after you've given them enough rope to hang themselves).

After you say "double" (just that one word), your partner usually passes. Of course, you can double them again if they extract themselves (running) from the frying pan by escaping to another contract.

If you double the opponents and they don't make their contract, you get at least twice as many points as you would have received if you had not doubled. Of course, if they make a doubled contract, they rack up twice the points they would normally get for making the contract. (See Chapter 20 for more information about the points you score for making a doubled or redoubled contract.)

Knowing when to double

The penalty double offers a formidable weapon that keeps your opponents from stepping all over you. If they know that you won't ever double them, they will take all kinds of liberties in the bidding.

However, you must use the penalty double wisely. You seldom double "on spec." You need to know the proper times to unleash this lethal weapon, as I show you in the following sections.

Doubling when your opponents overbid to a sky-high contract

Go ahead and double when you know that the opponents have just gotten beyond their depth. For example, suppose that you pick up the hand shown in Figure 15-1.

Figure 15-1:
Doubling can turn a sorry hand into mucho points.

♠ A K   ♥ 10 8 7 6   ♦ 6 5 4   ♣ 8 4 3 2
(7 HCP)

This hand is not very promising because you don't have many high-card points (HCP). However, the opponents bid back and forth, and lo and behold, they wind up in a contract of 6♠! The opponents have to take 12 tricks. You look at your hand and see that you have two sure spade tricks (see Chapter 2 to find out how to count sure tricks). Unless your opponents have a few cards up their sleeve and then some, they can't possibly take 12 tricks because your ♠A and ♠K will take two tricks, leaving them 11 at most.

Double! They can't make 6♠. You have just made a penalty double telling your partner that good things are about to happen, so please pass.

Passing when you have five or more cards in the suit bid to your right

Like everything else, you can get carried away with too much success. You double a few contracts, you defeat (or *set*) the contracts, and suddenly you think that you created the game of bridge. Be careful. Don't double unless you have the proper hand. The worst possible moment to double a contract for penalties is when your partner expects a completely different hand type than the one you have. Does that sound absurd? A prime example appears in Figure 15-2.

Figure 15-2:
When you have five or more cards in your opponents' suit, proceed with caution.

♠5 ♥A K Q 9 8 ♦A Q 8 7 ♣10 8 7
(15 HCP)

You hear the following as the bidding progresses:

East	South (You)	West	North (Your Partner)
1♥	?		

The person to your right has actually opened 1♥, your longest and strongest suit. In addition, you have 15 HCP. How can you show your partner all these hearts? You can't . . . just yet. Pass! If you double 1♥, it's not a penalty double; it's a takeout double showing short hearts with support for the other suits, plus at least 11 HCP (see "Taking a Chance on a Takeout Double," later in this chapter, for details). Your partner, relying on you for spades, will bid spades for all eternity — until the opponents double you!

When the person to your right opens the bidding and you have five or more cards in that suit, just pass! You may be able to make a penalty double later. You can't double right now because a first-round double is a takeout double showing shortness in the suit they bid, plus support for the other suits. You're asking your partner to bid!

For example, suppose you have the cards shown in Figure 15-3.

Figure 15-3:
Beware of doubling at your first chance.

♠A 4 3 2 ♥4 3 ♦5 4 ♣A K J 10 8
(12 HCP)

The bidding for this hand is humming right along:

West	North (Your Partner)	East	South (You)
1♠	Pass	2♣	?

Are you going to teach your opponents a lesson by doubling? Better watch out. Again, you're doubling at your first opportunity (your partner passing); you're making a takeout double showing the other two suits. Your partner thinks that you have diamonds and hearts, and you actually have clubs and spades. If you double now, I don't know you.

Talking Back: Redoubling

Some opponents don't like to be doubled. For some, doubling has the same effect as waving a red flag at a bull. Your opponents may think that your assessment is wrong. They may think that they can make their contract, double or no double.

Your opponents have an equally impressive way of telling you that they think that your penalty double was a colossal mistake. One of your opponents can *redouble*. If three passes follow the redouble, the deal is sealed — the side that made the last bid is playing a redoubled contract.

If the redoubled contract is defeated, the doubling side scores at least four times their normal score; if the contract is made, the redoubling side gets at least four times their normal score. (See Chapter 20 for details on scoring.) Because the stakes are so high, redoubled contracts tend to be played very slowly.

The following bidding sequence shows a redouble in action:

South (You)	West	North (Your Partner)	East
1♠	2♥	4♠	5♥
Double	Redouble	Pass	Pass
Pass			

The final contract is 5♥, redoubled. (Wow!) To get to this point, each player's bid has broadcast some pretty clear messages.

> ✔ When you doubled, you said, "I don't think you guys can make 5♥."
>
> ✔ West's redouble said, "Oh, yeah? Well, I think that we can, and you're going to pay big time for your double!"
>
> ✔ Your partner then passed, which told West, "I trust my partner. Go ahead. We want to see you make 5♥."
>
> ✔ East is content, in effect saying, "I trust my partner."
>
> ✔ Your final pass said, "Okay, bring it on — let's see who has made the last mistake."

With so many points at stake, blood flow has been known to increase. Keep your cool in one of these redoubled contracts and try to think clearly.

Of course, what's good for the goose is good for the gander; if the opponents double you in *your* contract and you think that you have a very good chance of making your contract, you can redouble them.

In addition to the rare redouble that follows a penalty double, bridge features a far more common use of the redouble. It occurs after your partner opens the bidding, the next hand makes a takeout double (see "Taking a Chance on a Takeout Double," later in this chapter, for details), and you have 11 HCP or more. This situation usually spells big trouble for your opponents. An example of this form of redouble appears in Figure 15-4.

Figure 15-4:
You have
the power
to redouble
a takeout
double.

♠ A J 5 4   ♥ 4   ♦ K Q 9 4   ♣ Q 9 4 3
(12 HCP)

The bidding for this hand goes like this:

North (Your Partner)	East	South (You)	West
1♥	Double	Redouble	

What exactly does this bidding sequence say so far?

- North's bid says, "I have 12 or more HCP with at least five hearts."

- East chimes in with a takeout double, saying, "I also have 11 or more HCP, plus support for the other suits."

- You counter with a redouble, saying, "Partner, don't worry about their takeout double. I have 11 or more HCP and we have the opponents outgunned point-wise. They could be in heaps of trouble if they don't have an eight-card fit. After all, they have to bid something, or let you play 1 ♥ redoubled, which you should make easily. You have hearts, and I have everything else. They may not have a home. Maybe we can lash them with a penalty double when they try to squirm out of this."

A start like this usually winds up with a happy ending for the opener's side.

Taking a Chance on a Takeout Double

What in the world do you do when the opponents open the bidding and you have a singleton or a doubleton in their suit, enough points to join in the action, but no long suit to overcall? You have an out. Open your mouth and say one word: "Double!"

You may think that you double only when you don't think that the opponents can make their contract (see "Putting Your Money Where Your Mouth Is: The Penalty Double," earlier in this chapter). However, far more often you use that one word, *double,* to show your partner that you have 11 or more HCP, along with three- or four-card support for each of the unbid suits. This double, called a *takeout double,* is often made directly after your right-hand opponent opens the bidding. The takeout double is by far the most flexible weapon in your entire armory of defensive bids. (I cover defensive bidding, including overcalls, in Chapter 14.)

A takeout double asks your partner to bid his longest unbid suit if the next hand passes. Any suit that your partner bids will be just fine with you because you have promised support for each of the unbid suits. Basically, a takeout double avoids guessing which of your two or three four-card suits to bid. By doubling, you are, in effect, bidding all your suits at once!

In the following sections, I show you a variety of instances in which you may want to make a takeout double.

Knowing when to make a takeout double

How do you know when to make a takeout double? Consider making a take-out double when your hand looks like this:

- 11 or more HCP — no upper limit; you can have 20 HCP
- Shortness (void, singleton, or doubleton) in the suit that your opponent has bid
- Three or four cards in each of the unbid suits

Making a takeout double after an opening bid

Figure 15-5 gives you a look at the most common takeout-double sequence of all, the double of an opening bid.

Figure 15-5: You can make a takeout double after an opening bid.

♠ A J 5 4   ♥ 5   ♦ A Q 6 5   ♣ Q 10 6 5
(13 HCP)

The bidding starts like this:

East	South (You)
1♥	Double

Figure 15-5 shows the ideal distribution for a takeout double: a singleton in the opponent's suit, an opening bid of your own, and four-card support for each of the unbid suits. In fact, this distribution is so ideal that you can make a takeout double with as few as 11 HCP. About 90 percent of the time, a take-out double shows 12 or more HCP. Now, assuming that the next hand (West) passes, your partner must bid, regardless of strength, and you find your fit; it works like a charm.

Making a takeout double after each opponent bids

Takeout doubles can also be made after each opponent bids a different suit. You would consider making a takeout double if you want to show length in the two unbid suits. Figure 15-6 gives you a look at such a takeout double.

Figure 15-6: Double with this hand to show both unbid suits.

♠A43 ♥KQ54 ♦54 ♣AQ98
(15 HCP)

The bidding has progressed as follows:

West	North (Your Partner)	East	South (You)
1♦	Pass	1♠	Double

This time your double says that you have opening bid strength with at least four-card support for each of the two unbid suits, clubs and hearts. You're basically bidding both suits at once! If your partner has four or more clubs or four or more hearts, he has an easy response, knowing of an assured eight-card fit.

Making a takeout double after you pass

If you pass originally, you can't have an opening bid, but you can still make a takeout double. If you make a takeout double after you pass, you show 10 to 11 HCP, with shortness in the opponent's suit(s). Figure 15-7 shows you a hand in which you can make a takeout double after you pass.

Figure 15-7:
You can pass and then come to life with a takeout double.

> ♠ A J 4 3   ♥ K Q 4 3   ♦ 10 9 4 3 2
> (10 HCP)

The bidding for this hand takes this interesting turn:

South (You)	West	North (Your Partner)	East
Pass	Pass	Pass	1♣
Double			

Perfect! You have support for any suit that your partner cares to bid. Even though you passed originally, this hand has big trick-taking potential for any suit that your partner bids. Your hand will make a great dummy.

Notice you wouldn't make a takeout double in Figure 15-7 if your opponent had opened the bidding in another suit because you wouldn't have support for the other three suits. Takeout doubles work best when your opponent opens the bidding in your short suit.

Passing after your partner's takeout double

When your partner makes a takeout double and the next hand passes, you have to bid, right? Not if you have five cards in the opponent's suit topped by four honors, or six cards in the opponent's suit topped by three honors. Just pass and let the opener suffer dealing with your basketful of powerful trumps.

Figure 15-8 shows you an example of how to stick it to your opponents.

The bidding has progressed as follows:

West	North (Your Partner)	East	South (You)
1♠	Double	Pass	Pass

Figure 15-8:
Pass after your partner's takeout double when you have serious length and strength in your opponents' suit.

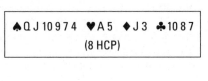

♠ Q J 10 9 7 4   ♥ A 5   ♦ J 3   ♣ 10 8 7
(8 HCP)

If West passes, how much fun do you think that West will have dealing with your spades when spades are trump and your partner has a strong hand? Answer: Not much.

How do you tell a double from a double?

With two kinds of doubles, takeout and penalty, how can your partner know which double you mean? It would be nice if you could say, "This is a penalty double, partner! Don't bid!" Or, "This is a takeout double, partner — bid something!" In lieu of such illegal communication, use the following guidelines to help you recognize a takeout double:

✔ If you double any opening bid lower than 4♠, it's a takeout double.

✔ If you double at your first opportunity and your partner hasn't bid yet, it's a takeout double.

✔ If you pass originally and then double at your first opportunity, and your partner hasn't bid yet ("pass" is not considered a bid), it's a takeout double.

✔ If you double after the opponents have agreed on a suit at the two level or three level, it's a takeout double.

On the other hand, the following situations indicate the other kind of double:

✔ If you double a game or slam contract, it's a penalty double.

✔ If you double the opponents' 1NT opening bid, it's a penalty double.

✔ If you double after your partner bids any number of notrump, it's a penalty double.

✔ If you open the bidding, the next hand doubles (takeout), and your partner redoubles showing 11 or more points, any subsequent double by either you or your partner is a penalty double.

Remember not to say "Double!" louder when you're making a penalty double, no matter how enthusiastic you are about the possibility of making your opponents pay through the nose. Changes in your voice are considered illegal. Shouting "Double!" isn't the ethical way to tell your partner what your double means. One guy once got so excited that he stood up on his chair to scream, "Double!" What kind of a double do you think that was?

Responding to a takeout double after your right-hand opponent passes

When your partner makes a takeout double and the next player passes, your partner expects you to respond even though you may, and often will, have a very weak hand. Whatever you do, don't pass (unless you have five or six cards in the opener's suit headed by multiple honor cards; see the previous section). You can't be too weak to respond to a takeout double.

Because you almost always must answer a takeout double if the next hand passes, how will your partner know whether you're broke (and just coughed up a response because you were afraid your partner would ax you if you didn't) or whether you really have a few goodies?

When your partner makes a takeout double and the next hand passes, use the following scale of responses when you plan to bid a suit:

- **With 0 to 8 HCP:** Bid your longest unbid suit. Your partner assumes 4 to 5 HCP when you make a minimum response to a takeout double, but you could have 0 HCP!

- **With 9 to 11 HCP:** Jump the bidding one level higher than necessary in your longest unbid suit. This bid lets your partner know that you aren't broke.

- **With 12 or more HCP:** You may be so thrilled to have an opening bid of your own facing a takeout double that you almost have to control yourself from cheering out loud. If you have a five- or six-card major, one option is to leap straight to game; however, you have another option.

Are you ready for this? You bid the opponents' suit! You read right. When you bid the opponents' suit, called a *cue bid,* you tell your partner that you have a whale of a hand and that you're sure that a game — maybe even a slam — is hiding in the hand someplace. Your cue bid asks your partner to further describe her hand. It also buys time to arrive at the best contract. When you make your first cue bid, you know that you have arrived.

Figure 15-9 gives you a chance to practice your responses to a takeout double.

The bidding has gone as follows:

West	North (Your Partner)	East	South (You)
1♠	Double	Pass	?

On the first hand, respond 2♥. Just do it! Your spades are not nearly strong enough to pass the double. On the second hand, jump to 3♥ to show 9 to 11 HCP. On the third hand, respond 2♠, a cue bid, showing 12 or more HCP. This bid tells your partner that the sky's the limit and the two of you should start looking for an eight-card trump fit or perhaps a 3NT resting place.

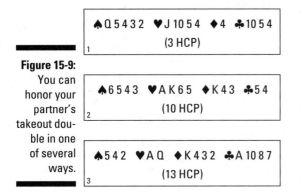

Figure 15-9:
You can honor your partner's takeout double in one of several ways.

> ♠Q5432 ♥J1054 ♦4 ♣1054
> (3 HCP)
>
> 1
>
> ♠6543 ♥AK65 ♦K43 ♣54
> (10 HCP)
>
> 2
>
> ♠542 ♥AQ ♦K432 ♣A1087
> (13 HCP)
>
> 3

Responding to a takeout double when you have strength in the opener's suit

You may have strength in the opponents' suit but not enough length or strength in the suit to pass your partner's takeout double. When this situation happens, try responding 1NT, 2NT, or 3NT. You don't have to worry about having strength in the other suits; your partner has promised length and strength in those suits with the takeout double.

When you have strength in the opponent's suit, respond in notrump to your partner's takeout double according to this scale:

✔ **With 6 to 10 HCP:** Respond 1NT.

✔ **With 11 to 12 HCP:** Respond 2NT.

✔ **With 13 to 16 HCP:** Respond 3NT.

Figure 15-10 shows you how to handle responding hands to a takeout double when you have strength in the opponents' suit.

Pretend that the bidding has gone as follows:

West	North (Your Partner)	East	South (You)
1♥	Double	Pass	?

With the first hand, respond 1NT, which is more descriptive than 2♣. With the second hand, respond 2NT, which is more descriptive than responding 3♦. (You have to jump the bidding in your suit when you have between 9 and 11 HCP.) With the third hand, leap to 3NT in preference to showing your clubs. Minor suits are for peasants when notrump is an option. It takes only 9 tricks to make game in notrump, but it takes 11 tricks to make game in either clubs or diamonds. Who doesn't like shortcuts?

Figure 15-10:
You have strength in your opponents' suit, so try responding in notrump.

1	♠A J 4 ♥Q 10 7 3 ♦5 4 ♣10 5 4 3 (7 HCP)
2	♠6 3 ♥A K J 2 ♦Q J 4 2 ♣9 4 3 (11 HCP)
3	♠J 5 ♥A Q 8 ♦5 4 3 ♣A Q 8 7 4 (13 HCP)

Responding to a takeout double after your right-hand opponent bids

When your partner makes a takeout double and the next hand bids, you're off the hook. You no longer have to bid, because your partner has another chance to bid and with a strong hand will make further noises.

Nevertheless, it's bidder's game. Excluding jacks and queens in the suits they have bid, you need five to eight HCP to introduce a four-card suit and four to eight HCP to show a five-card suit. If you're stronger, jump in your suit one level higher than necessary.

Figure 15-11 shows you that the game is all about courage.

The bidding has gone as follows:

West	North (Your Partner)	East	South (You)
1♦	Double	1♥	?

In the first hand, you have enough to bid 1♠. In the second hand, you have enough (barely) to bid 2♣. In the third hand, pass and thank East for taking you off the hook.

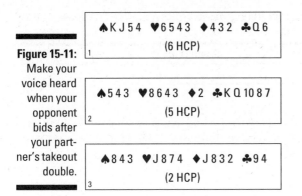

Figure 15-11:
Make your voice heard when your opponent bids after your partner's takeout double.

1 ♠ K J 5 4   ♥ 6 5 4 3   ♦ 4 3 2   ♣ Q 6
(6 HCP)

2 ♠ 5 4 3   ♥ 8 6 4 3   ♦ 2   ♣ K Q 10 8 7
(5 HCP)

3 ♠ 8 4 3   ♥ J 8 7 4   ♦ J 8 3 2   ♣ 9 4
(2 HCP)

Communicating Length: The Negative Double

As if you don't have enough double trouble already, I want to introduce you to yet another form of takeout double, the *negative double*.

You bid a negative double when you want to tell the opener, your partner, about four- or five-card length in the *unbid* major(s). You use this bid when, for one reason or another, you can't just bid the major. Only the responder can make a negative double (but you just say the one word, "Double") after his partner opens the bidding and an intervening overcall takes place.

In the following sections, I show you when to make and avoid negative doubles. See Chapter 14 for full details on overcalls.

Making a negative double when you have hearts and the opponents have spades

When your partner opens the bidding and second hand overcalls 1♠, you may have enough to respond, and you may have four or five hearts. Why not just bid 2♥? Because a 2♥ response shows at least five hearts with 11 or more HCP. You may have five hearts with fewer than 11 HCP or you may have four hearts. In neither case can you bid 2♥, so enter the negative double. (Remember, just say, "Double," not "Negative double.") This double of 1♠ tells your partner that you either have four hearts with eight or more HCP (an unlimited bid) or five hearts with specifically seven to ten HCP, a limited bid. The subsequent bidding will clarify which type of hand you have.

Assume that the bidding sequence has gone as follows:

North (Your Partner)	East	South (You)	West
1♣ or 1♦	1♠	?	

Consider the responding hands in Figure 15-12. Hearts is your longest suit (you have five in each hand), and keep in mind that a 2♥ response promises five hearts with 11 or more HCP.

Figure 15-12:
You may not need to make a negative double when you hold five hearts.

♠853 ♥A K J 7 4 ♦K 3 2 ♣4 3
(11 HCP)

1

♠853 ♥K Q 8 7 4 ♦K 3 2 ♣4 3
(8 HCP)

2

The first hand in Figure 15-12 fills the bill: five hearts and 11 HCP. Respond 2♥. The second hand has five hearts but only eight HCP. It's not strong enough to respond 2♥, but it is strong enough to make a negative double, which shows seven to ten HCP.

In Figure 15-13, it's time to deal with responding hands that have four hearts, the more common length. For openers, you can't respond 2♥ with four hearts, no matter how strong you are, so forget that. However, you can make a negative double with eight or more HCP.

Both hands in Figure 15-13 have four hearts with eight or more HCP. Double with both hands. But how will your partner know that you have 8 HCP in one hand and 14 HCP in the other? She won't — until you make your next bid. When you make a negative double with 11 or more HCP, you come out of the bushes on your next bid perhaps by raising your partner's suit or bidding some number of notrump. In the meantime, your partner, the opener, rebids as if you had responded 1♥.

Figure 15-13:
Holding
four hearts
instead of
five is more
common
when you
make a neg-
ative double
after a 1♠
overcall.

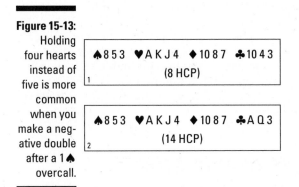

♠853 ♥A K J 4 ♦10 8 7 ♣10 4 3
(8 HCP)
1

♠853 ♥A K J 4 ♦10 8 7 ♣A Q 3
(14 HCP)
2

Making a negative double when you have spades and the opponents have hearts

When your partner opens the bidding with 1♣ or 1♦ and the second hand overcalls 1♥, you have a neat way of differentiating whether you have four or five spades. Assuming you have enough points (six or more) to respond, double with four spades and bid 1♠ with five (or more) spades. How sweet it is.

Assume that the bidding sequence has gone as follows:

North (Your Partner)	East	South (You)	West
1♣ or 1♦	1♥	?	

Consider the responding hands in Figure 15-14. Spades is your longest suit, and keep in mind that a 1♠ response promises five spades.

Figure 15-14:
Double with
four; bid 1♠
with more.

♠K J 5 4 ♥10 4 ♦Q J 4 ♣A 8 7 6
(11 HCP)
1

♠K J 5 4 3 ♥10 4 ♦Q J 4 ♣8 7 6
(7 HCP)
2

With the first hand in 15-14, double 1♠ to show exactly four spades with six or more HCP. But how will partner know you have such a nice hand? She won't until you make your next bid. With the second hand, respond 1♠ to show five spades with six or more HCP. This way, your partner knows how many spades you have; how great is that?

Sometimes your opponent will overcall 1♥, say, and you may have five or even six strong hearts! You'll face a strong temptation to double to show your partner that you have strong hearts. Quench that temptation! You will be showing your partner four spades, not hearts! Your best bet, by far, is to pass for the time being. Your day will come.

Making a negative double after a weak jump overcall

In case you think the opponents are always friendly enough to overcall at the one level, think again. Opponents are forever making weak jump overcalls to screw you up. And what is your defense? Usually a negative double. And what does a negative double mean at the three level? It means that you have a good hand, ten or more HCP, without a really long suit to bid. It says to your partner, "We have the majority of the high-card points and they're trying to screw us big time, and I'm not about to let it happen!"

The hand in Figure 15-15 shows a classic case of using a negative double after a weak jump overcall.

Figure 15-15:
Combat a weak jump overcall with a negative double.

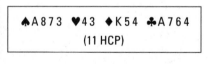

♠A873 ♥43 ♦K54 ♣A764
(11 HCP)

For the hand in Figure 15-15, assume that the bidding has proceeded like so:

North (Your Partner)	East	South (You)	West
1♦	3♥	?	

You can't let your opponents steal the pot right out from under you when you have two aces and a king, your partner has opened the bidding, and you have no long suit of your own to bid. The answer is to make a negative double telling your partner that you have ten or more HCP, usually a hand without a long suit, and let your partner decide what to do. Who knows? Your partner may have four spades to match up with your four spades, may be able to bid 3NT with heart strength, may have long suit of his own to repeat, or may pass at this level with a defensive hand, converting your lovely negative double into a penalty double!

Chapter 16

Hitting Hard: Slam Bidding

. . . .

In This Chapter

▶ Understanding what slams are all about

▶ Slam bidding at a notrump contract

▶ Slam bidding with a trump suit

▶ Asking for aces and kings with the Blackwood convention

. . . .

*O*nce in a while, you and your partner have so much strength between your two hands that you can try for a slam, which means bidding to a high level — all the way to the six or seven level. You may feel uncertain about making such a bold bid, but never fear: In this chapter I show you what you need to know to climb to such heights.

Getting to Know Your Slams

BRIDGE TALK

"What is a slam?" you may justifiably ask. "First Kantar has me trying to get to game, and now he wants me to bid even higher?" Calm yourself; a *slam* comes in two varieties, small and grand.

✔ A *small slam* involves bidding to the six level and taking 12 of the 13 tricks.

✔ A *grand slam* requires you to successfully contract for all 13 tricks, a seven-level contract. Grand slams are exciting . . . and scary.

Ninety-five percent of all the slam contracts you bid will be small slams (six-level contracts). Bidding a grand slam means going for all 13 tricks, so you really need to have a lot of confidence that you and your partner have the World's Fair between you before you attempt one.

When you bid a small slam, you have a little breathing room. You can afford to lose one trick. Besides, bidding a grand slam and taking only 12 tricks is such a downer — you score nothing and the opponents score points! Had you bid for 12 tricks, you would have scored in the neighborhood of 1,000 points. (See Chapter 20 for more information on scoring.)

Slam bidding falls into two groups: notrump slams and trump (or suit) slams. I give you a look at both types in this chapter.

Bidding Notrump Slams

Typically, you need the following two common ingredients to bid all the way up to 6NT:

- ✔ A balanced hand facing a balanced hand
- ✔ 33 high-card points (HCP) between the two hands

In the following sections, I give you examples of when to bid notrump slams immediately, when to ask for more information, and when to forget the whole thing.

Moving quickly when you have the information you need

Wouldn't you like to see a hand in which you have the combined power to make a small slam at notrump? Look no further than Figure 16-1.

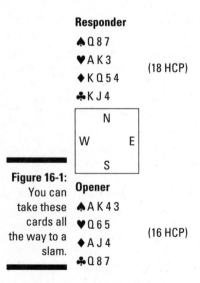

Responder

♠ Q 8 7
♥ A K 3
♦ K Q 5 4   (18 HCP)
♣ K J 4

```
      N
   W     E
      S
```

Figure 16-1:
You can
take these
cards all
the way to a
slam.

Opener

♠ A K 4 3
♥ Q 6 5
♦ A J 4   (16 HCP)
♣ Q 8 7

With your eyes on the prize (a small slam), the bidding goes as follows:

Opener (Your Partner)	Responder (You)
1NT	6NT

The responder (you) can't always get such a quick fix on partner's values, but in this case, you can count enough points between the two hands to go for the gold at an early juncture. You have 18 HCP with a balanced hand, and your partner has 15 to 17 HCP also with a balanced hand, because she opened with 1NT. (See Chapter 10 for more about this and other opening bids.) Therefore, the two hands add up to at least 33 HCP.

Five- and six-card suits headed by honor cards (such as the ace, king, queen, and jack) increase in value facing a balanced hand. See Chapter 11 for more on responding to 1NT with long, strong suits. Translation: You don't need 33 HCP to bid 6NT when one or both hands have long, strong suits, but it helps!

As soon as you have gathered enough information from the bidding to know that you have at least 33 HCP between the two hands and both hands are reasonably balanced, don't waste any time. Just bid 6NT. Practice saying, "6NT" in front of a mirror if you think you'll freak out by jumping all the way from the one level to the six level.

Bidding 6NT after the responder shows limited HCP

After you bid 6NT, you don't have to worry about further bidding; you are the captain because your partner made the first limit bid, 1NT. You make the final decision and your partner obeys. (See Chapter 13 for more about the captaincy.)

Sometimes the opener becomes the captain because the responder limits her hand first. Take the cards in Figure 16-2 as an example, where you are the opener and your partner's response shows a limited number of HCP.

The bidding for this hand should go all the way to a slam, as in the following sequence:

Opener (You)	Responder (Your Partner)
1♠	2NT
6NT	Pass

Responder

♠ Q 3

♥ K 10 3 2   (13 HCP)

♦ A 10 8

♣ A 7 5 4

```
      N
  W       E
      S
```

Figure 16-2:
The opener
adds up
the points
between the
two hands
and goes for
a slam.

Opener

♠ A K J 6 5

♥ A J 4

♦ K 5   (19 HCP)

♣ K 6 5

First things first. This time you are the captain because your partner has made the first limited bid, 2NT, showing 13 to 15 HCP with a balanced hand. Second, knowing your partner has a balanced hand, add two extra points for your strong five-card spade suit headed by three honors. (This happens to be the same revaluation scale that the responder uses when responding to a 1NT opening bid with a strong five-card suit. See Chapter 11 for more about responding to a 1NT opening bid.)

The opener's hand is now worth 21 points. With a count of 21 facing a minimum of 13 HCP, the magic 33 HCP exists and the opener bids 6NT.

Inviting a slam with a 4NT bid

Sometimes the captain (who can be either the opener or the responder, depending on who makes the first limit bid) can't be sure of 33 HCP between the two hands. Instead of guessing, the captain invites a slam by bidding 4NT, as she would with the hand in Figure 16-3.

The responder invites a slam in the following bidding sequence:

Opener	Responder
1♣	1♥
1NT	4NT
Pass	

Responder

♠ A K 9 3

♥ A Q 5 2   (19 HCP)

♦ A Q 10

♣ 3 2

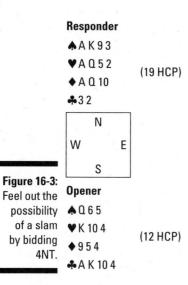

Figure 16-3:
Feel out the
possibility
of a slam
by bidding
4NT.

Opener

♠ Q 6 5

♥ K 10 4   (12 HCP)

♦ 9 5 4

♣ A K 10 4

The opener has a balanced hand with 12 HCP but scrapes the bottom of the barrel and comes up with a 1♣ opening bid. The responder, with 19 HCP, has visions of a slam — but first looks for an eight-card major-suit fit.

If your side has an eight-card fit (or longer), you no longer need 33 HCP between the two hands to make a slam. You can often make a slam with two or three fewer HCP.

The 1♥ response in Figure 16-3, the lower ranking of two four-card suits, gives the opener a chance to raise hearts or rebid 1♠, bringing either fit to light. (The 1♥ response is unlimited; it shows six or more HCP, so the opener must bid again. Must!)

The opener's 1NT rebid shows 12 to 14 HCP plus a balanced hand. The 1NT rebid denies holding four hearts and is unlikely to hold four spades. Now the responder knows that no eight-card major suit fit exists. Nevertheless, with 19 HCP, a slam may be in the works if partner has a maximum of 14 points, or even 13 with a strong five-card suit. Therefore, the responder invites a slam by bidding 4NT. The opener has no trouble whatsoever declining this invitation by passing with his abject minimum.

When your previous bid is 1NT, 2NT, or 3NT, an immediate raise to 4NT is invitational and asks you to bid 6NT with a maximum but to pass with a minimum. Every notrump bid you make has a range, frequently a three-point range. For example, a 1NT opening shows a range of 15 to 17 HCP. If your partner bids 4NT, an invitational raise, check to see whether you're at the top or at the bottom of your range and bid accordingly.

When your partner invites you to a slam by raising to 4NT after you open with 1NT, revalue your hand, taking into account that strong five-card suits should be upgraded. Make a rebid according to the following scale:

- ✔ **With 15 revalued points:** Pass.
- ✔ **With 17 revalued points:** Bid 6NT.
- ✔ **With 16 revalued points:** Pass with any 4-3-3-3 pattern (the pits), but bid on with any other pattern.

Bidding Slams at a Trump Contract

When you bid a slam at notrump, you do it with power. You overwhelm your opponents with aces, kings, queens, and jacks. When you bid a slam at a trump contract, whether it's a small slam or a grand slam, you do it with a little finesse. You don't need quite so many HCP. What works best is when you have a good trump fit and each player has a different short suit. Unbalanced hands take more tricks at a trump contract than balanced hands.

Here's a list of what you need to bid a slam at a trump contract:

- ✔ **A strong combined trump suit:** If you have any doubts about bidding a slam, particularly because of a mangy trump suit, sack the whole idea and play the hand in game.

- ✔ **33 or more revalued points between the two hands:** Both hands revalue after an eight-card fit or longer has been located. Don't even think about bidding a slam unless you have a good trump fit and the two hands total at least 33 points after revaluation.

- ✔ **At least three of the four aces between you:** Any one ace can be missing, but bidding a slam missing two aces is definitely not healthy!

- ✔ **No two immediate losers in any one suit:** You don't want your opponents rattling off the ace and king of the same suit, defeating your slam before you even get started! (See Chapter 5 for details on recognizing immediate losers.)

Say your partnership gets the hands in Figure 16-4. I know that you can't see your partner's hands while you're actually bidding — I just want you to see the building blocks that go into making a slam at a suit contract.

Go over the checklist and see whether you have the power you need between the two hands to make 6♠:

✔ Strong combined trump suit? Yes, in spades.

✔ 33 or more revalued points? Yes, you have 33 points before revaluation.

✔ At least three aces between the two hands? Yes.

✔ Two immediate losers in any suit? Yes — and that's the wrong answer if you want to bid and make a slam. Look at the hearts in each hand. You don't have the ace or king, which means that the bad guys have them and they may lead that suit.

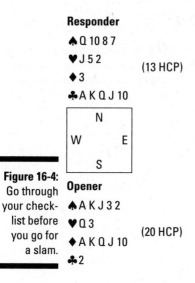

Responder

♠ Q 10 8 7

♥ J 5 2   (13 HCP)

♦ 3

♣ A K Q J 10

	N	
W		E
	S	

Opener

♠ A K J 3 2

♥ Q 3   (20 HCP)

♦ A K Q J 10

♣ 2

Figure 16-4: Go through your checklist before you go for a slam.

You don't want to be in a slam contract with these two hands.

In the following sections, I give you pointers on tallying revalued points and figuring out how many aces and kings you and your partner have.

Revaluating hands

When an eight-card or longer trump fit has been uncovered, both hands revaluate upward, tacking on extra points for side-suit shortness. (See Chapters 11 and 12 for the scales to use.)

You may start with 25 to 26 HCP between the two hands, but after revaluation, you may cross into the 32 to 33 HCP zone. You may have a slam staring you in the face — provided that the hand passes the previous checklist test.

So be awake; when you find your fit, start the revaluation. A quiet game hand can rip off its shirt and, beneath its mild-mannered exterior, be . . . a slam.

After you discover a fit, the wilder the distribution of the two hands, the better. If both hands are balanced, more losers have to be taken care of and both hands tack on fewer revalued points.

Solving the ace problem with the Blackwood convention

Bidding a slam only to see the opponents take the first two tricks with aces is just too embarrassing. That should not happen. You should have a way, and you do, to determine how many aces your partner has. Consider the hands shown in Figure 16-5.

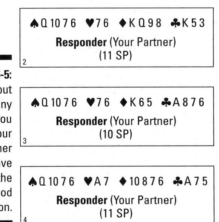

Figure 16-5: Find out how many aces you and your partner have with the Blackwood convention.

```
♠ A K 8 5 4 3   ♥ K Q J 10 2   ♦ A   ♣ 4
            Opener (You)
              (17 HCP)
1
```

```
♠ Q 10 7 6   ♥ 7 6   ♦ K Q 9 8   ♣ K 5 3
       Responder (Your Partner)
              (11 SP)
2
```

```
♠ Q 10 7 6   ♥ 7 6   ♦ K 6 5   ♣ A 8 7 6
       Responder (Your Partner)
              (10 SP)
3
```

```
♠ Q 10 7 6   ♥ A 7   ♦ 10 8 7 6   ♣ A 7 5
       Responder (Your Partner)
              (11 SP)
4
```

For each of the hands in Figure 16-5, the bidding has gone as follows:

Opener (You)	Responder (Your Partner)
1 ♠	3 ♠ (10 to 12 support points)

You are the opener, and your partner may have each of the three responding hands. On each hand, your partner makes the same response of 3♠. Are you in the slam zone? You know that your partner has four spades and about ten support points (SP; see Chapter 11 for more details), but what about you? You have 17 HCP plus two singletons, each worth three points. Your hand is worth a whopping 23 points.

More important, just look at your hand. What tricks can you possibly lose? Certainly, you are a huge favorite to have no spade losers with ten spades between the two hands, including the ♠A and ♠K. Certainly, you have no diamond losers. The only possible losers you can have are one in hearts and one in clubs.

However, if your partner has the ace in either of those suits, you have only one loser. If your partner has the ace in both of those suits, you have no losers. If your partner has neither ace, you have two losers. You must find out how many aces your partner has so you know whether you can make a slam! It would be nice to say, "Hey, partner, how many aces do you have? That's all I need to know." Unfortunately, the rules forbid such direct questions. But bridge offers a very popular bidding convention that allows you to ask that burning question about missing aces legally.

A bid of 4NT (as long as the previous bid is not 1NT, 2NT, or 3NT) asks your partner how many aces she has. This handy little convention is called *Blackwood,* named after Easley Blackwood of Indianapolis, Indiana. Way back in 1933, Blackwood had a hand in which he wanted to know how many aces his partner had. So he invented a bid of 4NT, called it the Blackwood convention, and turned himself into a legend. With this simple bid, he invented one of the most beloved conventions of all time.

When you play the Blackwood convention, you use the following responses to 4NT to tell your partner how many aces you have:

- ✔ **5♣:** Zero or all four aces
- ✔ **5♦:** One ace
- ✔ **5♥:** Two aces
- ✔ **5♠:** Three aces

If your response to 4NT is 5♣ and your partner can't tell from your previous bidding and her own hand whether you have zero or all four aces, change partners — quickly!

The following bidding sequence shows you how the Blackwood convention would play out facing the first hand in Figure 16-5:

Opener (You)	Responder (Your Partner)
1♠	3♠
4NT	5♣
5♠	Pass

Blackwood is a great convention for staying out of slams if you are missing two aces. On this hand, you have to give up on the slam because your partner's bid of 5♣ showing zero aces tells you that you're missing two aces.

In the second hand in Figure 16-5, the bidding would go like this:

Opener (You)	Responder (Your Partner)
1♠	3♠
4NT	5♦
6♠	Pass

In this hand, your partner's 5♦ response shows one ace, so you can bid 6♠ knowing that you are missing only one ace. Well done!

In the third hand in Figure 16-5, the bidding progresses as follows:

Opener (You)	Responder (Your Partner)
1♠	3♠
4NT	5♥
7NT	Pass

Your partner has two aces and responds 5♥. Bingo. You bid 7NT because you don't have any losers. You can count 13 notrump tricks: six spades, five hearts, and two minor-suit aces. As easy as pie!

A contract of 7NT with 13 top tricks is safer than 7♠ because every so often the opening lead is trumped, leaving the declarer in shock.

Just because you have all the aces doesn't mean that you can take all the tricks. You have to be able to count 13 tricks (which may include trumping your losers in the short hand or setting up the dummy's long suit; see Chapters 7 and 8) before you bid a grand slam. Blackwood should carry a government health warning, really — aces on their own are not enough to ensure a slam.

Asking for kings

After you ask for aces and you find that you have all four, you may suddenly be thinking about a grand slam! But first you may need to check on the number of kings your partner holds. Not to worry, Easley Blackwood thought of everything. If the Blackwood bidder follows up a 4NT ace-ask with 5NT, he promises his partner that all four aces are held jointly and asks his partner for kings. If you have your eyes on a grand slam, you may also need to locate any missing kings.

Use the following responses to tell your partner about the number of kings you have, after the king-ask of 5NT:

- ✔ **6♣:** One or all four kings
- ✔ **6♦:** One king
- ✔ **6♥:** Two kings
- ✔ **6♠:** Three kings

Look at Figure 16-6 to see the Blackwood convention for kings in action.

Responder

♠ K Q 2
♥ A 8 7 6   (22 HCP)
♦ A K Q
♣ A 5 4

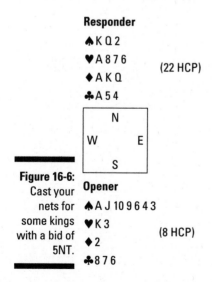

Figure 16-6:
Cast your
nets for
some kings
with a bid of
5NT.

Opener

♠ A J 10 9 6 4 3
♥ K 3   (8 HCP)
♦ 2
♣ 8 7 6

The bidding for this hand could proceed as follows:

Opener (Your Partner)	Responder (You)
3♠	4NT
5♦	5NT
6♦	7NT
Pass	

As the responder, you use the Blackwood convention and find one ace and one king in the opener's hand. Armed with this information, the responder can actually count 13 tricks:

- **Spades:** Seven tricks (your partner shows a seven-card suit for the 3♠ opening bid)

- **Hearts:** One trick — your ♥A

- **Diamonds:** Three tricks — your ♦AKQ

- **Clubs:** One trick — your ♣A

- **Kings:** One trick — your partner has either the ♥K or the ♣K

Add 'em up — your total number of tricks comes to 13! When one suit (spades) produces seven tricks, a slam can be made with fewer HCP than are needed when both hands are balanced.

Part V

Playing a Strong Defense and Keeping Score

The 5th Wave   By Rich Tennant

"...and do you promise to love, honor, and always lead the highest card from the short side?"

In this part . . .

After you play bridge for a while, you discover that you're playing defense about half the time. Many of the contracts that the opponents reach can be defeated by accurate defense (provided that neither you nor your partner makes a major goof). In this part, I show you how to take all your defensive tricks so the declarer doesn't get away with murder during the play of the hand.

After each hand is over, it's time to tally up the score. In this part, I explain how to keep score and show you why knowing the score as the game progresses is so very important.

Chapter 17

Defending against Notrump Contracts

· ·

In This Chapter

▶ Making the best opening lead

▶ Playing third hand like a pro

· ·

Defensive play is partnership play. Together with your partner, you can work to keep your opponents from making their contract. As you read this chapter on defensive play against notrump contracts, you may notice how similar defensive play is to the play of the hand. Both sides are trying to take tricks by using the same techniques.

However, one significant compelling difference distinguishes declarer play from defensive play. When you play as the declarer, you have full access to your partner's cards — you can see your own hand and your partner's hand, the dummy. As the declarer, you can plan your plays. When you play defense, planning your plays becomes much harder because you can't see your partner's hand. Obviously, more intuition and deduction have to go into defense.

In this chapter, I cover opening leads and third-hand play in a notrump contract. See Chapter 18 for details about defending against trump contracts.

Making the Opening Lead against a Notrump Contract

Even a strong defensive player can get lost without a little help from his partner. One way to pass information across the table legally is with the card(s) you lead. Your opening lead tells your partner quite a lot about what you have in the suit you are leading. That information, in turn, helps your partner plan the defense.

When you defend a notrump contract, your side and your opponent (the declarer) both try to accomplish the same things:

- ✔ You both want to establish tricks in strong suits. With the KQJ10, for example, you both want to drive out the ace and establish three tricks.

- ✔ You both want to take tricks with small cards in long suits by relentlessly playing the suit until your opponents run out of cards in the suit. After you get rid of their cards, your remaining cards in that suit are winning tricks.

The defense has one big advantage: tempo. By virtue of the opening lead, the defense gets a vital opportunity to take the lead in the race to establish its suit. As the saying goes, "Thrice armed is he who gets his blow in first." Starting with the opening lead, the defense hopes to strike at the declarer's weak point. Then the defense goes for the soft underbelly.

In the following sections, I explain the importance of the opening lead and show you how to use the bidding to help plan your opening-lead strategy.

Appreciating the importance of the opening lead

The defenders make the first lead, called the *opening lead*. At times, an opening lead is pure guesswork. After all, you can't see your partner's hand, and you may not have a clear-cut lead.

On the other hand, you may be able to work out what to lead from your own hand; you may have a strong suit of your own to lead, for example. Your partner may have helped you with the opening lead by making a bid — particularly an overcall to show a strong suit (see Chapter 14 for details on overcalls) — or you may have an inkling of the best lead by listening to your opponents' bidding. From their bidding you may be able to work out the suits in which they are well heeled and in which they may have little or nothing.

For these reasons, the opening lead gives the defense an overwhelming advantage. Sometimes the declarer can't overcome the head start that the defense gets with the opening lead. As a defender, if you can find the declarer's Achilles' heel, you may find yourself working wonders and taking tricks from nowhere.

Statistically, the opening lead is far and away the most important single card the defense plays. An average player would be a world champion if he or she made the best opening lead on every hand! There wouldn't even be any competition for the title.

Listening to the bidding to create a plan of attack

Before you make your opening lead, you have to listen to the bidding. Sometimes the bidding provides enough information about the hand to fill a library, and sometimes the bidding doesn't provide enough information to fill the surface of a postage stamp. However, most of the time the bidding furnishes you with some clues to the best opening lead.

During the bidding, the opponents frequently tell you how strong they are and in which suits they do and don't have strength. The clearer the picture you get of both their hands, the more likely you are to find the most lethal lead. If you watch TV, text, or otherwise zone out during the bidding, don't expect to make a killer opening lead.

Just to show you how much you can find out from keeping a keen ear on the bidding, take a peek at the following bidding sequence. You're West, and South is the declarer:

West (You)	North	East (Your Partner)	South
Pass	Pass	Pass	1NT
Pass	3NT	Pass	Pass
Pass			

These cats have told you nothing. No suits have been bid. All you know is that South has a balanced hand in the 15 to 17 high-card points (HCP) range, and North, a *passed hand* (who couldn't open the bidding), has enough to raise to game, presumably 10 to 11 HCP. However, you do know that North didn't bother to use the Stayman convention (see Chapter 11 for information on using Stayman when responding to 1NT), so North probably doesn't have a four-card major.

Now check out this sequence:

South	West (You)	North	East (Your Partner)
1♣	Pass	1♦	Pass
3♣	Pass	3♦	Pass
3NT	Pass	Pass	Pass

Again, South is playing a contract of 3NT, but in the process of arriving at this contract, the opponents showed you two suits, clubs and diamonds. South has long and strong clubs, and North has the same sort of holding in diamonds. The declarer will use these two suits to take tricks. You also know a little about your partner's hand, albeit through negative inferences; your partner didn't have enough points or a good enough suit to come into the bidding even at the one level at his first turn. Don't expect the moon from him.

So which suit should you lead? Unless you are a close relative of the declarer, lead a heart or a spade. Which one? Try the longer suit. If they're both the same length, lead the stronger.

Before selecting your opening lead, listen to the bidding and then decide which suit to lead and pick the right card in that suit. More often than not, you will lead either your *fourth-highest card* or the *top of a sequence in your longest suit.* I go into more detail on your lead choices in the following sections.

Don't expect to make the winning lead on every hand. Nobody does. First of all, you can't always trust the opponents' bidding. And even if you weigh all the information perfectly, you can still be unlucky — everyone's favorite excuse.

Leading from length

Because your goal is to establish tricks, and because tricks come from long suits, your best shot is usually to lead from your longest suit. The hand in Figure 17-1 gives you a chance to kick off with your longest suit.

Figure 17-1:
Your best chance for establishing tricks is to start with your longest suit.

♠ K J 7 4 2   ♥ J 9 8 2   ♦ 5 4   ♣ J 7
(6 HCP)

The bidding for this hand has gone as follows:

South	West (You)	North	East (Your Partner)
1NT	Pass	3NT	Pass
Pass	Pass		

Because neither opponent has bid a suit, you have no clues to help you sniff out their weakness. When the opponents haven't given you any tips on their favorite suits, try to take tricks by establishing winners in your long suit. You want to lead from your longest suit, spades. But which spade?

After you choose a suit to lead, you need to determine whether that suit is headed by three consecutive cards, where the highest of the three must be an honor. If your suit is headed by the AKQ, KQJ, QJ10, J109, or 1098, you've been blessed with a perfect three-card sequence. When you have such a sequence, lead the top honor. For example, if you have the ♥QJ1032, lead the ♥Q. If the *third-highest* card in your treasured honor sequence is missing by just one place, like the AKJ, KQ10, QJ9, J108, or 1097, that is also considered a sequence and the top card is led. You can never have too many sequences!

If your longest suit doesn't sport any consecutive honor cards, just lead the fourth-highest card in the suit. Start from the highest card in the suit, count down four places, and throw that fourth-highest card face up on the table. In Figure 17-1, where your longest suit doesn't have any consecutive honor cards, you lead the ♠4, the fourth-highest card in your suit. Leading your fourth highest often tells your partner how many cards you have in the suit, which can be very helpful.

Suppose for a moment that you have the cards in Figure 17-1 again and the bidding has gone as follows:

South	West (You)	North	East (Your Partner)
1♠	Pass	2♣	Pass
2NT	Pass	3NT	Pass
Pass	Pass		

You must make the opening lead, and you have plenty of information from the bidding to help you decide which card to lead. The opponents have bid spades and clubs. Because you don't want to lead suits that the opponents have bid, lead a diamond or a heart, whichever suit is longer. In this case, you lead the ♥2, your fourth-highest heart.

If your opponents bid both of your long suits, consider a short-suit lead hoping you lead partner's strongest suit. If the opponents bid all four suits, you're on your own! You may treat the auction as if they had bid none of the suits and fall back on old faithful: your longest suit.

Leading your partner's suit

You may not always want to lead your longest suit. For example, you may not want to lead it if

- ✔ An opponent bids your longest suit
- ✔ Your partner bids another suit

In the interest of partnership harmony (particularly marital partnership harmony), lead your partner's suit, especially if your partner has overcalled (see Chapter 14 for more on overcalls). Overcalls show strong five- or six-card suits. Your partner uses overcalls to tell you what to lead. Of course, if your partner bids two suits, you must choose between the suits. If you don't lead either of your partner's suits, the suit you lead had better be pretty strong, or you'd better be a pretty fast runner.

Say that you have the hand shown in Figure 17-2.

Figure 17-2:
You may have to lead a short suit if your partner overcalls it.

♠ 10 4   ♥ Q 7 4 3 2   ♦ K 6 5   ♣ 9 8 7
(5 HCP)

For Figure 17-2, the bidding has gone as follows:

North	East (Your Partner)	South	West (You)
1♣	1♠	2NT	Pass
3NT	Pass	Pass	Pass

Had your partner not bid, your lead would be the ♥3, fourth highest from your longest suit. However, because your partner overcalled, by all means lead a spade — but which one?

- ✔ Anytime you have two cards in the suit that you want to lead, lead the higher card, period. In Figure 17-2, lead the ♠10.

✔ With three cards headed by one honor card, lead your lowest card. For example, from A83, lead the 3; from K72, lead the 2; and from Q65, lead the 5.

✔ If you have three cards headed by two honors, lead low unless the honors are of equal value. If the honors are equals, called *touching honors,* lead the higher honor. For example, from QJ4, lead the Q because the two honors are equals. However, from the Q103, lead the 3 because the two honors aren't equals.

✔ If your suit has no honor card in it but is topped by three or four spot cards (meaning anything below a 10), lead the top of the spot cards. This play is called *leading top of nothing.* That is to say, from the 853 or the 8532, lead the 8. When you have four worthless cards, you don't lead the fourth-best card. The lead of a low spot card promises at least one honor card in the suit.

Use top-of-nothing leads as a last resort. You may decide to lead top of nothing if it is the only unbid suit, for example.

If your partner bids a suit, you tend to lead that suit. However, if you have a suit of your own headed by a strong honor sequence, you can overrule your partner and lead your suit. Leading partner's suit keeps partner happy, but at times you have to go with what you think is best and let the chips fall where they may.

If the opponents bid your longest suit, you usually look elsewhere for another lead. However, if your suit is headed by a strong honor sequence (AKJ, KQJ, or QJ10), lead it anyway.

Leading unbid major suits versus unbid minor suits

When you lead against a notrump contract and the choice of leads is between an unbid major suit (hearts or spades) and an unbid minor suit (clubs or diamonds), tend to lead the unbid major. Opponents go out of their way to bid major suits. If they don't bid them, they usually don't have them. On the other hand, opponents routinely conceal minor suits.

For example, suppose you have the cards shown in Figure 17-3.

Figure 17-3:
When choosing between an unbid major and unbid minor suit, stick with the major.

♠ Q 10 7 4   ♥ A 6 5   ♦ 5 4   ♣ Q 10 7 4
(8 HCP)

The bidding has gone as follows:

West (You)	North	East (Your Partner)	South
Pass	Pass	Pass	1NT
Pass	3NT	Pass	Pass
Pass			

Should you lead the ♠4 or the ♣4? Because your opponents haven't bid spades and North didn't use Stayman (indicating no four-card major), the dummy's length figures to be in the minors. So try the ♠4 — it's your best shot in the dark.

However, if your choice of leads is between an unbid major and an unbid minor and you have a sequence of honor cards in the minor suit, lead the top of the sequence in the minor.

Playing Third Hand against a Notrump Contract

Your partner makes an opening lead. The dummy comes down, the declarer plays a card from the dummy, and now it's your turn to play, making you *third hand*. By the time you have to play, you've heard the bidding, you've seen your partner's opening lead, and you've seen the dummy. Now you need to digest and try to process all this information. Are you still having fun?

Your partner will lead either a low card, typically fourth highest from her longest suit showing some strength in the suit, or an honor card, top of a sequence. Your play depends on whether your partner leads a low spot card or an honor card and what you see in the dummy.

Your play to the first trick and to the next trick, if you win the first one, are the two most important cards you play during the entire defense. They set the tone for the whole hand; if you start off on the right foot, you may deal the declarer a blow from which he can't recover. If you mess up . . . but you won't, will you? Just stick to the pointers in the following sections. I show you the proper card to play as third hand and the proper card to return in your partner's suit if you take the trick.

In the following sections, I use spades as the example suit in most of the figures. Dig up a deck of cards, remove the spade suit, lay the cards out on the table, and use those spades to follow the description of the play throughout the sections. The play relates equivalently to the play in any suit. Don't think that you always have to lead spades (although I know some players who would be better off if they did just that!).

When your partner leads a low card and the dummy has only low cards

When your partner leads a low card and the dummy has only low cards, play your highest card. *Third hand high* is an easy term to remember, and playing third hand high is a great defensive rule.

To understand the idea behind playing third hand high, think about your partner's opening lead. You know that your partner has an honor in the suit because she led a small card. Therefore, you play third hand high to protect your partner's strength and to prevent the declarer from winning a cheap trick.

Figure 17-4 shows you a hand in which you'd better play third hand high.

Figure 17-4:
Play third hand high when your partner and the dummy have low cards.

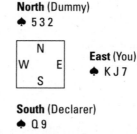

North (Dummy)
♠ 5 3 2

West (Your Partner)
♠ A 10 8 6 4

East (You)
♠ K J 7

South (Declarer)
♠ Q 9

Your partner leads the ♠6, his fourth-highest spade, the dummy plays low, and you hold the ♠KJ7. Which spade should you play? In Figure 17-4, you play the ♠K because it's your highest spade. The ♠K takes the trick.

In Figure 17-4, if you had played the ♠J on the first trick, an ugly play, the declarer would have taken the trick with her ♠Q, a trick to which she is not entitled. You would play the ♠J only if you were playing against a good friend or close relative. If you play the ♠K and then the ♠J, the higher of your two remaining spades, you take the first five spade tricks.

If your partner leads a low card and the dummy has small cards, play third hand high. If you remain with two cards in the suit, play the higher of the two cards.

When you have two or three equal honor cards

When you have equal high cards (such as the AK, AKQ, KQ, KQJ, QJ, QJ10, J10, or J109) in the third seat, play the lower or the lowest equal. This method of playing the lower or lowest equal in the third seat is a universal agreement. The whole world does it this way! By playing the lower or lowest equal, your partner can often tell what cards you don't have! For example, if you play the king, you can't have the queen. If you play the queen, you can't have the jack; if you play the ten, you can't have the nine, and so on.

The cards in Figure 17-5 give you a chance to choose between two equal honor cards in the suit your partner leads.

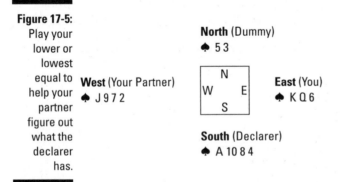

Figure 17-5:
Play your lower or lowest equal to help your partner figure out what the declarer has.

North (Dummy)
♠ 5 3

West (Your Partner)
♠ J 9 7 2

N
W   E
S

East (You)
♠ K Q 6

South (Declarer)
♠ A 10 8 4

Your partner leads the ♠2, his fourth-highest spade, the dummy plays low, and you expertly play the ♠Q, the lower of your equal honors (you intend to play the ♠K, the higher of your two remaining cards, the next time you get a chance).

Had you played the ♠K to the first trick, your partner would be fooled. Your partner would assume that the declarer has the ♠Q on the premise that you would have played the ♠Q if you had both the ♠K and ♠Q.

TIP

When third hand plays by the rules, the opening leader can deduce who holds certain cards. For example, knowing that third hand will play the lower of equals allows the opening leader to figure out who has the missing ♠K in Figure 17-6.

Figure 17-6:
Playing the lower equal in third seat can help your partner determine where the king is.

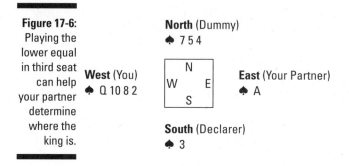

North (Dummy)
♠ 7 5 4

West (You)
♠ Q 10 8 2

East (Your Partner)
♠ A

South (Declarer)
♠ 3

You (as West) lead the ♠2, the dummy plays low, and your partner, East, plays the ♠A. Who has the ♠K? Well, you don't have the ♠K, partner doesn't have it, and the dummy doesn't have it. The right answer must be South, or else the ♠K has fallen on the floor and no one has it.

Remembering the rules of playing third hand, you know immediately that South has the ♠K. If your partner has the ♠AK, the proper play is the ♠K, the lower equal. When she plays the ♠A, East is practically shouting that she doesn't have the ♠K. Elementary, my dear Watson.

As an aside, I once showed the cards in Figure 17-6 to a class and asked who had the ♠K. Some said South and some said East. One of my students decided she wasn't taking any chances, so she answered, "Southeast!"

When you have both a lower and a higher honor card than the dummy

The dummy doesn't always have just low cards. Sometimes the dummy comes down with an honor (or two) in the suit your partner leads, but you may happen to have a higher and a lower honor than the dummy's honor. In the following sections, I show you how to handle this when it comes up.

Seeing when holding back your high honor works

REMEMBER

Say that your partner leads a low spade and the dummy tables with an honor in spades. You, third hand, have a higher and a lower spade honor than the dummy. What to do? It's simple:

✔ **If the dummy plays low, play your lower honor.** When the dummy plays low, you keep the honor that is higher than the dummy's honor to zap it later. It's like you're keeping guard over the dummy's honor.

✔ **If the honor is played from the dummy, cover that honor with your higher honor.**

The cards in Figure 17-7 provide a prime example of when you should hold back your high honor when the dummy has a lower honor.

Figure 17-7:
Have a higher honor waiting in the wings when the dummy plays an honor.

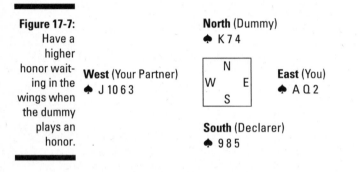

North (Dummy)
♠ K 7 4

West (Your Partner)
♠ J 10 6 3

N
W   E
S

East (You)
♠ A Q 2

South (Declarer)
♠ 9 8 5

Your partner leads the ♠3, her lowest spade (you know that the ♠3 is her lowest spade because you are looking smack at the ♠2) and the dummy plays low, saving the ♠K for later. You have an honor that is higher than the dummy's honor, the ace, and an honor that is lower, the queen. Play the lower honor. In this case, you know that the queen will take the trick. But don't play the ace next and turn that king into a trick. Save the ace to smack the king dead the next time the suit is played.

Finding out when holding back your high honor doesn't work

Holding back your higher honor doesn't always win the trick for you. Sometimes the declarer has a higher honor than your honor. Take a peek at Figure 17-8 to see what I mean.

In Figure 17-8, your partner leads the ♠2, the dummy plays low, and you correctly play the ♠J. (Big Brother is still watching!) But this time, the declarer (South) takes the trick with the ♠K. Don't despair — despite this momentary setback, you've made a good play.

If you had erred by playing the ♠A, the declarer would have taken two later tricks with the ♠Q in the dummy and the ♠K. This way declarer takes only one trick, the ♠K. You are still hovering over the dummy's ♠Q with your ♠A, making it impossible for the declarer to take a second trick with the ♠Q. If you patiently wait for your partner to lead the ♠10 the next time on lead, your neat play at trick one will pay dividends. At that point, when the ♠Q is played from the dummy, you zero in on it with your ♠A so the declarer takes only one spade trick, not two.

Figure 17-8:
Sneak
attack:
South steals
your thun-
der with
a higher
honor in this
hand.

North (Dummy)
♠ Q 8 3

```
    N
W       E
    S
```

West (Your Partner)
♠ 10 9 4 2

East (You)
♠ A J 5

South (Declarer)
♠ K 7 6

When your partner leads an honor card

The lead of an honor card shows a sequence of three equal (consecutive) honors, or a sequence with the third card missing by one link. For example, the KQJ and the KQ10 are considered sequences; the KQ963 is not considered a suit headed by a sequence.

In the following sections, I show you how to read your partner's honor card lead and how to respond appropriately.

Deducing what sequence your partner has

Your partner can lead five possible honor cards: the ace through the 10. Each honor card lead suggests a different holding.

After your partner leads an honor, assume that your partner has one of the following sequences:

- ✔ **The ace:** The lead of an ace, the strongest honor lead, shows a suit headed by the AKJ or the AKQ.

- ✔ **The king:** The lead of a king shows a suit headed by the KQJ or the KQ10.

- ✔ **The queen:** The lead of a queen shows a suit headed by the QJ10 or the QJ9.

- ✔ **The jack:** This lead is a little tricky. The lead of a jack can show a suit headed by the J109 or the J108, or a suit headed by the AJ10 or the KJ10.

- ✔ **The 10:** The lead of the 10 can show suits headed by the 1098 and the 1097, as well as suits headed by the A109, K109, or the Q109.

When your partner leads an honor card, you may have one of the following holdings in your partner's suit:

> ✔ An honor equal to the one your partner has led
>
> ✔ A higher unequal honor
>
> ✔ Any doubleton honor (two cards headed by one honor card)
>
> ✔ No honors (bummer)

Your job is to tell your partner which of these holdings you have. And exactly how do you do that? Keep reading.

Showing an equal honor

If your partner leads an honor card and you have an equal (touching) honor card, you want to let your partner in on the secret. In Figure 17-9, you want to tell your partner all about your equal honor. No, you can't do it by smiling; that's illegal.

Figure 17-9:
Tell your partner that you have an equal honor with an encouraging (high) spot card.

North (Dummy)
♠ 6 5 3

West (Your Partner)
♠ Q J 10 9 2

```
    N
W       E
    S
```

East (You)
♠ K 8 4

South (Declarer)
♠ A 7

Your partner leads the ♠Q, the dummy plays low, and you come out of your shell with an encouraging equal-honor signal by playing the highest spot card you can afford: in this case, the ♠8. Now your partner assumes that you have a high honor. If you play the ♠4, your lowest spade, a discouraging signal, your partner assumes that you have no honors in spades. See Chapter 18 for more details on when your partner leads an honor card.

Showing a higher unequal honor

When your partner leads a 10 or jack, it may not be the top of a sequence — your partner may have higher honors in the suit. You must play third hand high if you have a higher unequal honor and the dummy has low cards, as in Figure 17-10.

Your partner leads the ♠J. Play the ♠A and then the ♠9, the higher of your two remaining spades. South's ♠Q is caught in a vise and can't take a trick.

Figure 17-10:
Don't let
your partner
down — go
up with
a higher
unequal
honor.

North (Dummy)
♠ 6 4

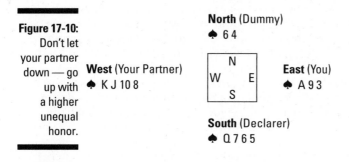

West (Your Partner)
♠ K J 10 8

East (You)
♠ A 9 3

South (Declarer)
♠ Q 7 6 5

Play the same when your partner leads the 10 and the dummy has small cards.
Play any higher unequal honor that you may have to protect your partner's
lead.

Showing a doubleton honor

When your partner leads an honor and you have a doubleton honor, play it!
It only hurts for a little while. Although this sacrifice of a high card may look
unnecessary, just do it. It is called *unblocking,* and it helps set up your partner's suit.

If you don't unblock, you will be stuck on lead the second time the suit is
played and won't be able to return partner's suit. Remember playing the high
card from the short side? That's what the declarer does and that's what the
defenders do. (See the discussion of notrump play in Chapter 3.)

Figure 17-11 shows you a case in which you need to play high, called *overtaking,* if your honor is higher than your partner's.

Figure 17-11:
Clear the
decks;
unblock your
doubleton
honor for
the greater
good.

North (Dummy)
♠ 6 5 4

West (Your Partner)
♠ K Q J 9 2

East (You)
♠ A 7

South (Declarer)
♠ 10 8 3

Your partner leads the ♠K; you have just two spades, but you do have a doubleton honor. Play your honor; play that ♠A, even if you have to overtake your partner's trick. Just do it! After you win the trick and return a spade, your partner takes four more spade tricks, or five in all.

If you wimp out and play your seven on the first trick, you win the second round of spades with the ♠A. But then what? You have no more spades. You blew it one trick earlier when you didn't overtake your partner's spade lead with your ♠A. It's almost too tragic for words.

Overtaking a king with the ace is not as awful as it looks if you consider that your partner usually has the KQJ or the KQ10 in that suit. You're actually doing your partner a favor by overtaking the king — you're clearing the decks for partner to take a bundle of tricks!

Showing no honors

When your partner leads an honor and you don't have any honors, play your lowest card, a discouraging signal. Your partner will get the picture — you don't have an honor in the suit.

When your partner leads an honor and you have a higher honor than the dummy

Frequently, when your partner makes the opening lead of an honor card, the dummy also has an honor card, but on a good day, you have a higher honor than the dummy's honor. Take the cards in Figure 17-12 as an example.

Figure 17-12:
The dummy has an honor, but you have a higher honor.

North (Dummy)
♠ J 6 5

West (Your Partner)
♠ Q 10 9 8

```
    N
 W     E
    S
```

East (You)
♠ K 7 3

South (Declarer)
♠ A 4 2

In Figure 17-12, your partner leads the ♠10 (top of an interior sequence), the dummy plays low, and you have a higher honor than the dummy but no lower honor. No matter: Your partner is leading an honor, so you need to save your higher honor to zap the dummy's honor later.

Your proper play is the ♠7, your highest spot card, to say that you have an honor in your partner's suit. Let your partner's honor card do the dirty work of driving out the declarer's honor card.

If you play the ♠7, the declarer takes the trick with the ♠A, his only trick, and you and your partner remain with the ♠K and ♠Q. If you play the ♠K at the first trick, the declarer wins the ♠A and later can lead a low spade toward dummy's ♠J. Your partner wins the ♠Q, but the declarer gets a second undeserved trick with the ♠J.

When your partner leads an honor card in your suit

During the bidding, you may have mentioned a suit, and your partner may lead that suit. If your partner leads an honor card that's going to take the trick, give her either an encouraging signal (play a high spot card), if you want the suit continued, or a discouraging signal (play your lowest spot card), if you want your partner to lead another suit. Even if your partner's honor card isn't going to take the trick, signal the same so your partner will know whether to continue the suit or try something else when she regains the lead.

Figure 17-13 allows you to explore your options when your partner leads an honor in a suit that you mentioned during the bidding.

North (Dummy)
- ♠ 4 3
- ♥ Q 6 4
- ♦ Q J 10 9
- ♣ K Q 10 9

West (Your Partner)
- ♠ K 6
- ♥ 9 8 5
- ♦ 9 7 5 2
- ♣ 7 6 5 2

	N	
W		E
	S	

East (You)
- ♠ A 9 8 7 2
- ♥ A K J 10
- ♦ 8 3
- ♣ 4 3

South (Declarer)
- ♠ Q J 10 5
- ♥ 7 3 2
- ♦ A K 6
- ♣ A J 8

Figure 17-13: Your partner leads an honor in the suit that you bid.

The bidding for this hand has gone as follows:

East (You)	South	West (Your Partner)	North
1♠	1NT	Pass	3NT
Pass	Pass	Pass	

Your partner dutifully leads the ♠K, and now you can make either an encouraging or a discouraging signal. Do you want a spade continuation, or do you want another suit played even more? Better take a good look at your hand and then make a quarter turn to the right with your neck (always a good idea) to look at the dummy.

See the ♥AKJ10 in your hand and the ♥Q in the dummy? If somehow your partner can be persuaded to lead a heart, your side can take four heart tricks, not to mention the two tricks from the ♠AK. Play the ♠2 to tell your partner to lead something else. How will your partner know that "something else" means to lead a heart? (Remember, you can't beat on your chest or stare at the hearts in the dummy to help your partner!)

Your partner, being very observant, notices that your ♠2 is a discouraging signal and that you're asking for another suit. But which other suit? Your partner makes a quarter turn of his neck to the left (another good idea) and looks at the dummy, trying to figure out what you have in mind.

Your partner sees strong clubs and strong diamonds in the dummy. If you don't want spades, and the clubs and diamonds in the dummy are strong, the logical conclusion is that you want a heart shift. If your partner "reads" your signal and plays a heart, you can take four heart tricks along with two spade tricks to defeat this contract by two tricks. If your partner plays anything else, the declarer makes the 3NT contract by establishing a ninth trick in spades.

As the player who makes the lead, pay very close attention to your partner's signal. Even though your partner has bid a suit and you lead a winning card in that suit, your partner will tell you whether to continue the suit or whether to switch to something else. You can do it!

Chapter 18

Defending against Trump Contracts

After your opponents arrive at a trump (or suit) contract, you need to swing into defense. You may need to make the opening lead, or you may need to play third hand (your partner leads, dummy plays a card, and you're in third seat). Both positions, which I cover in this chapter, offer you a chance to stop your opponents' contract dead in its tracks. (Head to Chapter 17 for defensive tips against a notrump contract.)

Opening Leads against a Trump Contract

When you defend a notrump contract, you tend to lead from your long suit, trying to establish small cards in that suit. This strategy doesn't always work against a trump contract. If either the declarer or the dummy is short in that suit, your good trick will be trumped. Bummer. To retaliate, at times you can return the favor and trump the declarer's or the dummy's winning tricks if you or your partner are void in the suit that's led.

Because you have the advantage of the opening lead, you can map out your defensive strategy depending on the bidding and your hand. In the following sections, I spell out your options for opening leads when defending against a trump contract. The opening lead is critical, so you really don't want to blow it!

When you have a sequence of three honor cards

Sequences of honor cards (three adjacent honors or the third card in the sequence missing by one place) make such strong leads that you must have a good reason not to lead one if you are lucky enough to have one. The stronger the sequence, the better. Suits headed by the AKQ, AKJ, KQJ, KQ10, QJ10, QJ9, J109, or J108 are particularly attractive.

When you're blessed with such a sequence, lead the top (or highest) card in the sequence.

When you have two touching honor cards

Almost as good as three touching honors at the head of your suit are suits headed by two touching honors. Suits that have two touching honors, such as the AK632, KQ6, QJ82, or J1053, also warrant leading the top card.

Versus trump contracts, you can lead the top of two touching honors, whereas at a notrump contract, you need three touching honors (or the third card missing by one place) to lead the top card.

To see the power of leading the top card in a suit headed by two touching honors, look at Figure 18-1.

Figure 18-1:
Make the opening lead of the top card with touching honors.

♠ A K 6 5   ♥ 4 3   ◆ Q 6 5 4   ♣ 10 7 6

The bidding for this hand has gone as follows:

South	West (You)	North	East (Your Partner)
1♥	Pass	3♥	Pass
Pass	Pass		

You must make the opening lead, and you know that the dummy has heart support for South and a moderate hand; South has a minimum opening bid because he passed an invitational bid from North. What should you lead?

Ah, look no further than that ♠A. The lead of the ace from the ♠AK is one of the strongest of all opening leads, for three reasons:

- ✔ You take the trick (South and North are 99 percent sure to have at least one spade each).

- ✔ You can study the dummy while retaining the lead to plan what to do next.

- ✔ You see your partner's signal advising you what to do next.

It doesn't get much better than that.

I advise you to lead the *ace* from suits headed by the AK at trick one only. After trick one, the *king,* not the ace, is lead from suits headed by the AK. Why? Because you seldom lead an ace at trick one without the king to back it up, but you *often* lead an ace without the king later in the hand to see if your partner has the king. You don't want your partner to think that you have the king when you lead an ace after trick one. Trust me.

When you have a short suit

Leading a short suit — a singleton (one card) or a doubleton (two cards) — against a trump contract is a very tempting lead. If your lead works out, you can trump one or two of the declarer's tricks before the declarer can draw trumps. (*Drawing trumps* means extracting your opponents' trump cards before taking your sure tricks; see Chapter 5 for details.)

But don't rush to judgment every time you have a short suit lead available. At least glance at your trump suit first. You may not want to trump anything — your trump holding may be too strong. For example, if you have the QJ10 of the trump suit, trumping with one of these honor cards doesn't gain you a trick and it often costs a trick; you have a certain trump trick anyway.

Figure 18-2 shows an example of when you don't want to lead a short suit.

Figure 18-2:
Don't make
a short suit
lead with
this strong
trump
holding.

♠ A K ♥ 3 ♦ K Q 5 4 ♣ 10 8 7 4 3 2

The bidding for this hand has gone as follows:

West (You)	North	East (Your Partner)	South
1♣	Double	Pass	2♠
Pass	4♠	Pass	Pass
Pass			

What is your opening lead? Listen to the opponents' bids. You expect South to have nine or ten high-card points (HCP) with four or five spades, and North has a good hand, probably short in clubs. Most takeout doubles are made with shortness in the opener's suit; the shorter, the better.

Because you have the ♠AK, the two highest cards in the trump suit, you have two sure trump tricks. It doesn't benefit you to trump a heart (your short suit) with either the ♠A or the ♠K. You will be trumping with a sure spade trick anyway. So a heart lead doesn't look like such a great idea. But if your spades are something like ♠AK7, ♠A7, ♠A72, or ♠842, trumping a heart with a small spade is a great idea.

When you have certain trump tricks (KQJ, QJ10, or J1092), don't bother leading a short suit; you don't want, or need, to trump anything. Lead something else. The proper opening lead for Figure 18-2 is the ♦K because you want to build up a trick. After the ♦A is driven out, the ♦Q is a trick. And if partner happens to have the ♦J, maybe two tricks can be taken. A good partner will have the jack of diamonds, or perhaps a doubleton diamond, and be able to trump the third round of the suit.

When your partner bids a suit

When your partner bids a suit, you tend to lead that suit. One of the reasons your partner bids a suit is to help you out on the opening lead. Unless you can find a strong alternative lead, look no further than your partner's suit.

For example, take a look at the hand in Figure 18-3.

Figure 18-3:
Lead your
partner's
suit when
you can.

♠ A 7 6 2   ♥ 8 4 3   ♦ J 10 5 4   ♣ 9 3

The bidding for this hand is:

South	West (You)	North	East (Your Partner)
1♥	Pass	2♦	3♣
3♥	Pass	4♥	Pass
Pass	Pass		

A good card to put on the table, assuming that you value your life, is the ♣9 (top of a doubleton) because your partner bid clubs.

When you lead your partner's *unsupported suit* (you have never raised or helped the suit), lead the top of doubleton and low from any three or four cards. A high-card lead in an unsupported suit indicates shortness.

If you have *supported* (or raised) your partner's suit, indicating that you have at least three cards in the suit, lead low if your highest card is an honor. If it isn't an honor, lead your highest card. Your partner can usually tell by looking at the size of card whether or not you have an honor in the suit.

Finally, if you have the ace in your partner's suit, supported or not, lead the ace.

After you play with different people, you may notice that at every table sits at least one self-designated teacher. Conservative estimates say that the advice given by these "teachers" is on target about 23 percent of the time. Be forewarned. You may hear one of these self-appointed teachers tell you to lead the highest card in your partner's suit no matter what you have. Don't believe it. You lead low when you have three or four cards headed by an honor in your partner's suit (or any suit for that matter).

The cards in Figure 18-4 show you why you should disregard unsolicited advice.

Figure 18-4:
Walk the other way when someone tells you to always lead the highest card in your partner's suit.

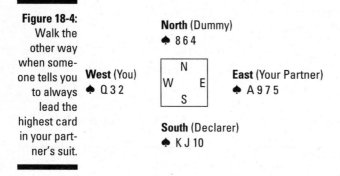

North (Dummy)
♠ 8 6 4

West (You)
♠ Q 3 2

East (Your Partner)
♠ A 9 7 5

South (Declarer)
♠ K J 10

Say that your partner has bid spades. If you lead the ♠Q (ugliness!), the declarer must wind up taking two tricks with the ♠KJ10. However, if you lead the ♠2, your partner wins with the ♠A (third hand high when dummy has low cards) and then plays a low spade. The declarer can take only one trick. If the declarer plays the ♠K, your ♠Q is the highest outstanding spade. If the declarer finesses the ♠J, you win with the ♠Q.

When one suit hasn't been bid

During the bidding, your opponents may mention three out of the four suits. When the opponents bid three suits, consider leading the unbid suit. That advice doesn't mean that you should never lead a suit that the opponents have bid; your own hand may tell you that it's right to lead one of their suits. If you have the AKQ or the KQJ in their suit, leading the suit could be right. But as a general rule, you tend to look for the opening lead in places where the opponents have not advertised strength, and the unbid suit is a likely candidate.

The cards in Figure 18-5 give you a chance to make the opening lead in the only suit that your opponents haven't mentioned during the bidding.

Figure 18-5:
Try leading the suit that your opponents don't mention during bidding.

♠ Q 10 4 2   ♥ K 8 3   ♦ J 8 3   ♣ 10 9 7

The bidding for this hand is as follows:

South	West (You)	North	East (Your Partner)
1♣	Pass	1♠	Pass
3♣	Pass	3♦	Pass
5♣	Pass	Pass	Pass

Even on Mars, they lead a heart on this bidding. When the opponents bid three suits and don't end up in notrump, the unbid suit is usually a good bet. Lead the ♥3, low from a suit headed by any honor other than the ace.

When two suits haven't been bid

When two suits have gone unmentioned during the bidding, you usually lead one of those suits, but which one? The right one! Just kidding.

When you need to choose between two unbid suits, lead from the stronger suit. However, if one of the suits is headed by an unsupported ace (no king attached), lead the other suit. The card you lead in the other suit depends on what you have in the suit. For example: top of a two- or three-card sequence; low from three cards headed by an honor; or fourth highest with four or more cards.

The cards in Figure 18-6 give you a chance to choose between two unbid suits.

Figure 18-6:
Choose carefully when you select an unbid suit to lead.

♠93 ♥K J 4 3 ♦A 8 7 5 ♣8 4 3

Just look at the exciting bidding for this hand:

South	West (You)	North	East (Your Partner)
1♠	Pass	2♣	Pass
2♠	Pass	4♠	Pass
Pass	Pass		

In general, eliminate clubs and spades as possible lead choices because the opponents have bid these suits. You can choose between hearts and diamonds. Because your diamonds are headed by the ♦A, lead the ♥3, fourth highest from a nonsequential suit

When you have four trumps

Long suit leads aren't quite as fashionable against trump contracts as they are against notrump contracts. However, leading from your longest suit makes good bridge sense when you're blessed with four trumps.

If you have four trumps, the idea is to try to run the declarer out of trumps by making him trump the suit you're leading. A good bet is to lead the fourth-highest card from your long suit unless the suit is headed by a sequence; then lead the top card.

When you pick up the hand in Figure 18-7, you may be able to force the declarer (with the longer trump hand) to give up a few of his beloved trumps.

Figure 18-7:
When you have four trumps, lead from your long suit.

♠A 9 4 3 ♥K 10 7 4 3 ♦6 5 ♣J 5

The bidding for this hand goes as follows:

South	West (You)	North	East (Your Partner)
1♠	Pass	2♠	Pass
3♠	Pass	Pass	Pass

Because you have four trumps, you decide to lead from your longest suit rather than from one of your doubletons (diamonds or clubs). The proper opening lead is the ♥4, your fourth-highest heart, and you're hoping you can make the declarer trump hearts a couple of times. If the declarer started with five spades and has to trump twice, you will have more spades than the declarer. Great news for you; terrible news for the declarer.

When you want to remove the dummy's trumps by leading a trump

Trump opening leads should be saved for specific occasions; the old advice of "When in doubt, lead a trump" really means that if you're too lazy to work out the right lead, lead a trump!

Kidding aside, sometimes leading a trump card can be a primo idea. For example, if the declarer bids two suits and you're very strong in one of those suits, but the opponents wind up in the other suit, then you usually lead a low trump.

In Figure 18-8, you get a chance to lead a trump.

Figure 18-8:
Steal the
opponents'
thunder by
opening with
a trump card.

♠ A Q 10 9   ♥ 6 4 3   ♦ K 5 4   ♣ J 8 3

The bidding has taken this interesting turn:

South	West (You)	North	East (Your Partner)
1♠	Pass	1NT	Pass
2♥	Pass	Pass	Pass

You can almost see the dummy's cards before they come down. The dummy has about seven points and is short in spades, perhaps a singleton spade, probably with three or maybe four hearts. The declarer, who bid spades first, has five spades and probably four hearts.

What is the declarer going to do with those five spades? She is going to try to trump as many of them as possible in the dummy (see Chapter 8 for more information on trumping losers in the dummy).

What can you do to stop the declarer from trumping those spades in the dummy? You can lead a trump. Each time you lead a trump, the dummy has one fewer heart for the declarer to use to trump a spade. After you get rid of the dummy's trumps, your remaining spades will all be winning tricks.

In the case of Figure 18-8, lead a low heart. You're so tough on defense, is it any wonder that your opponents are becoming intimidated?

When you have the ace of a suit

Yes, leading an ace and taking a trick is great fun. But don't forget that aces were put on this planet to capture kings and queens, not deuces and threes. If you wait to play your ace, you usually get more for your money.

Nevertheless, you may come across the following instances when you may need to bang down an ace on the opening lead:

- ✔ If your partner has bid the suit.
- ✔ If the opponents have bid every other suit.
- ✔ If the opponents have arrived at a six- or seven-level (slam) contract. (See Chapter 16 for more about slams.)
- ✔ If you have a singleton ace (the ace is the only card that you have in the suit).
- ✔ If you have a doubleton ace (the ace plus one low card), you may be lucky enough to find your partner with the king. Your partner wins the second lead of the suit and then plays the suit a third time, and you can trump this third round of the suit, generating an extra trick for your side. Whenever I try that lead, my partner seldom has the king; perhaps you will have better partners!

If you need to lead a suit that's headed by the ace, lead the ace. If you *underlead* the ace (lead a low card in the suit instead of the ace), you may lose your ace altogether! If one opponent has a singleton and the other has the king, you have just "gone to bed" with (or lost) your ace. The next time you play the ace, the opponent who started with a singleton will trump.

When you have a suit with no honor cards

Welcome to the pits. It doesn't get much worse than having to lead from an empty suit with no honors in it. You have three or four cards, but for some reason, every other suit is taboo. The right lead from this holding is the top card (called *the top of nothing*), but you don't have to like it.

When you lead the top of three or four small cards in an unbid suit, your partner may think that you're leading from a doubleton and, subsequently, misdefend. If instead you lead your lowest card, your partner may think that you have an honor and may also misdefend. No matter which card you lead, trouble may lurk. For that reason, leading anything from a pathetic-looking three- or four-card suit is near the bottom of the what-not-to-lead list. Leading the top card is slightly the lesser of the two evils, but I don't know you if it doesn't work out!

Selecting the proper card for any suit

After you select a suit to lead, you need to select the right card in the suit. For the most part, you lead the same card against a trump contract as you do against a notrump contract. When you decide on the suit, lead any of the following cards that apply to your suit:

- **Top of any doubleton:** For example, the 8 from the 83 or the queen from Q6

- **Top of three or four small cards:** For example, the 7 from the 764 or the 7643

- **Low from three cards headed by one honor:** For example, the 4 from the K64

- **Top of two touching honors:** For example, the queen from the QJ76 or the jack from the J106

- **Top of a three-card sequence of honors:** For example, the king from the KQJ4

- **Fourth highest from any four-card suit or longer that's not headed by a sequence or two touching honors:** For example, the 3 from the Q1063 or the Q10632

- **The ace from any suit that includes the ace:** For example, the ace from the A8743

The lead of least resistance

I like to tell the story of a successful married bridge partnership, a near impossibility: Lew and Eugenie Mathe.

Lew, a great player, was one of the toughest of all partners to play with. If anything went wrong, you heard about it! Nobody could understand how Eugenie, a very fine player in her own right, could deal with this or how they could do so well. Finally, someone asked her how she did it. She said it was worth it because she liked to win tournaments. "For example, on opening lead, Lew told me (and all of his partners,

for that matter) never to lead a trump, never to lead from Kx because it was too dangerous a lead, and never to lead from a jack, a lead he detested." In any case, "Everything was going just fine until I picked up the one hand that I had always dreaded: ♠ xxx ♥ Jxxx ♦ Jxxx ♣ Kx. The opponents wound up in 4♠ and it was my lead, but every lead was barred! As I stewed over my opening lead seemingly forever, Lew said, 'Eugenie lead whatever you want; I know what you have anyway!'"

Third-Hand Play against a Trump Contract

Versus a notrump contract, your partner typically leads a low card, fourth highest from his longest suit. Versus a trump contract, more often than not, your partner leads an honor card or from shortness.

You see more honor-card leads against trump contracts because the requirements for leading an honor are less restrictive than against a notrump contract. Against a trump contract, you need *two,* not three, touching honors to lead an honor. As a result, the lead of the ace from the AK and the lead of the king from the KQ are regular customers versus a trump contract.

Regardless of your partner's opening lead, you want to be prepared for your turn to play *third hand,* which means that you're the third person to play to the trick. In the following sections, I show you what to do when your partner leads an honor card or leads from a short suit. I also explain how to avoid some common third-hand errors.

When your partner leads an honor card

When your partner leads an honor card (the ace, king, queen, or jack), she expects a little help from you in the form of an *attitude signal.* An attitude signal is a play that tells your partner whether you like the suit she has led.

You can make two types of attitude signals to convey your feelings about your partner's lead (and neither involves glaring across the table!):

- **An encouraging signal:** By playing the highest *spot card* (any card that isn't an honor) you can afford, you indicate that you want your partner to continue the suit.

- **A discouraging signal:** By playing your lowest spot card, you tell your partner that you have no interest in that suit.

What determines which signal you use? Broadly speaking, if you have an equal honor in the suit that your partner has led, you give an encouraging signal. If you have three or more worthless cards in the suit, you give a discouraging signal. Your partner will watch your attitude signal and proceed accordingly.

Sometimes the spot card that you play may not be all that easy for your partner to read; a 9 is a big card and a 2 a small one, but what about a 5 or a 6? Sometimes your partner has to wait to see the second card you play in the suit.

- ✔ If the second card is lower than the first (a *high-low signal*), the signal is considered encouraging and asks your partner to continue the suit.
- ✔ If the second card is higher than the first (a *low-high signal*), the signal is considered discouraging.

The following sections cover both high-low and low-high signals.

The high-low signal

Versus a notrump contract, the high-low signal (or simply playing a high spot card) shows an honor, usually an equal honor. However, versus a trump contract, a high-low signal can also show a doubleton. The high-low doubleton signal is given primarily when your partner leads the ace, typically from the AK*x*.

A high-low signal in a trump contract suggests that your partner play the suit a third time. When you give a high-low signal, you either produce an equal honor or trump the third round, both of which are winning scenarios.

The hand in Figure 18-9 shows an encouraging signal in action.

North (Dummy)
- ♠ Q 6 5
- ♥ K Q 9 8
- ♦ A Q J 2
- ♣ 4 3

West (Your Partner)
- ♠ A K 9 8 2
- ♥ 4 3
- ♦ 10 9 8
- ♣ Q J 2

```
      N
  W       E
      S
```

East (You)
- ♠ 9 3
- ♥ 5 2
- ♦ K 7 6 5
- ♣ 10 9 7 6 5

Figure 18-9: Go full steam ahead by giving an encouraging high-low signal.

South (Declarer)
- ♠ J 10 4
- ♥ A J 10 7 6
- ♦ 4 3
- ♣ A K 8

Your opponents have landed in a 4♥ contract, which means that hearts are trump and they need to win ten tricks.

Your partner leads the ♠A, which almost always means that your partner has the king as well. If your partner has the ♠AK and you have a doubleton, you can trump the third round of spades. Obviously, a good defensive move is to trump your opponents' tricks as soon as possible — after all, you need to take only four tricks to defeat their contract. Start by playing the ♠9, and then play the ♠3 when your partner continues with the ♠K, a high-low signal showing a doubleton. Nice signal.

When your partner sees that ♠9, she clearly recognizes the start of a high-low signal showing either an equal honor or a doubleton. Because the only equal honor is the ♠Q, and because the dummy has it, your partner brilliantly deduces that your high-low signal must be showing a doubleton.

Your partner continues with the ♠K and then a third spade, allowing you to trump the dummy's ♠Q. Now you have the lead. Make a quarter turn to the right, and what do you see in the dummy? You see weak clubs and strong diamonds. I don't generally stoop to verse, but "When the dummy is to your right, lead the weakest suit in sight." Lead the ♣10, top of a sequence.

The declarer wins the trick, plays the ♥K and the ♥A to draw trumps, ending in his hand, and leads a low diamond to the ♦J in the dummy, taking a finesse (see Chapter 4 for more about finesses). He hopes to find your partner with the ♦K, in which case he will make his contract by avoiding a diamond loser altogether.

No luck. You have the ♦K, and you end up defeating the contract by one trick. You have actually taken two defensive tricks with that meatball hand of yours!

The low-high signal

When your partner leads a high honor card and you have worthless cards in that suit, waste no time in telling your partner to cease and desist by playing your lowest card. The next time the suit is played, play a higher card confirming weakness (low-high). Keep in mind that the 3 followed by the 2 is a high-low signal (strength), but a 3 followed by a 4 is a low-high signal (weakness).

Figure 18-10 shows a hand in which you need to give a low-high signal to turn your partner off.

Again, the opponents wind up in a contract of 4♥; hearts are trump and your opponents need to win ten tricks to make their contract. Your mission: to defeat the contract by winning four tricks. Your partner leads the ♠A.

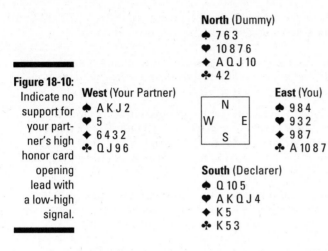

North (Dummy)
♠ 7 6 3
♥ 10 8 7 6
♦ A Q J 10
♣ 4 2

West (Your Partner)
♠ A K J 2
♥ 5
♦ 6 4 3 2
♣ Q J 9 6

East (You)
♠ 9 8 4
♥ 9 3 2
♦ 9 8 7
♣ A 10 8 7

```
    N
W       E
    S
```

South (Declarer)
♠ Q 10 5
♥ A K Q J 4
♦ K 5
♣ K 5 3

You have zilch in spades, so you pass that message across the table to your partner by playing your lowest spade, the ♠4. When your partner determines that the ♠4 is your lowest spade (your partner has the ♠2 and can see the ♠3 in the dummy), your partner knows that you can't have a doubleton spade or even the ♠Q, or else you would have started a high-low encouraging signal.

Instead of plunking down the ♠K and setting up a trick for the ♠Q that the declarer surely has, your partner smartly shifts to the ♣Q, the top of the sequence. When you see the ♣Q, you know that the declarer has the ♣K, so you take the trick with the ♣A (the declarer may have a singleton king!). Now you return a spade, the suit that your partner has led. When the declarer plays the ♠10, your partner wins the trick with the ♠J, and continues with the ♠K, capturing South's ♠Q for the fourth and setting trick.

If your partner makes the Nervous Nellie play of the ♠K at the second trick, establishing a trick for declarer's queen, the declarer winds up losing two instead of three spade tricks and makes her 4♥ contract. Because of accurate defensive signaling, the declarer loses three spades and one club, and winds up going down one trick. Nice defense.

When your partner leads a short suit

The most common leads versus trump contracts are the ace from suits headed by the AK and the king from suits headed by the KQ. And don't forget short-suit leads. The first two are easy to spot because the size of the card hits you in the face. You have to be a bit more of a detective to spot a short-suit lead.

When your partner leads something like the 5, you may have to wait until you see whether your partner's second card is higher or lower than the 5.

✔ If his second card is a 3, a high-low, there's a good chance that partner has led high from a doubleton, so you try your darnedest to make your partner happy by leading the suit a third time so he can trump.

If your partner has bid the suit and then leads high-low, he can't be showing a doubleton; he's showing you a five-card suit. For example, from the Q10653, your partner leads the 5, fourth highest, and then plays the 3 next, if possible. As third hand, you're expected to play third hand high when your partner leads low.

✔ If your partner leads a 5 followed by a 6, a low-high, your partner can't have a doubleton; your partner is leading low from an honor. Keep that fact in your memory bank in case you want to return the suit.

The trick is to watch the first card closely so you know whether the next one is higher or lower.

Avoiding common errors

In this section I cover two errors in third-hand play against a trump contract that surface so frequently. Here they are; forewarned is forearmed.

Being sure to play the ace when the declarer has the king

When your partner leads the queen, you have the ace, and the king isn't in the dummy, the declarer must have the king. At times, that king will be a singleton, such as in Figure 18-11. In such cases, it behooves you to overtake the ♠Q with the ♠A. If you don't and the declarer has a singleton king, you will never hear the end of it. Later, when you do play your ace, declarer will trump it. Guess what? You'll have gone to bed with an ace!

North (Dummy)
♠ 7 5 4 3 2

Figure 18-11:
If you don't
play the
ace, you'll
lose it.

West (Your Partner)
♠ Q J 10 9

East (You)
♠ A 8 6

South (Declarer)
♠ K

When your partner leads the ♠Q, play the ♠A. If you don't, you may have to kiss your ♠A goodbye. Maybe you can use it on the next hand.

Staying safe by unblocking the suit with ace doubleton

When your partner leads the king and you have ace doubleton (A*x*), overtake with the ace to unblock the suit, just as you would at notrump. Just do it; the eyes of Texas (and your partner) are upon you. The cards in Figure 18-12 show you how vital this overtake can be.

Figure 18-12: Avert disaster by overtaking your partner's king with your ace.

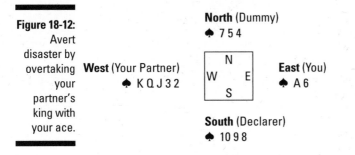

North (Dummy)
♠ 7 5 4

West (Your Partner)
♠ K Q J 3 2

East (You)
♠ A 6

South (Declarer)
♠ 10 9 8

Your partner leads the ♠K, showing that he also has the ♠Q. When you have an ace doubleton, overtake the ♠K with the ♠A and return the suit! By doing so, you give yourself a surefire way of taking three tricks in the suit.

How you take these three tricks dependspon one of these two scenarios:

✔ Your partner has led from a KQJ combination, as in Figure 18-12, in which case your side takes the first three spade tricks.

✔ Your partner has led from the KQ without the jack and the declarer has the J109. No sweat. Your partner wins the second spade with the queen and then leads a third spade, which you trump. You've got them coming and going.

Chapter 19

Playing Second Hand

· ·

In This Chapter

▶ Formulating your strategy when the dummy is to your right

▶ Figuring out what to do when the dummy is to your left

· ·

*W*hen you make an opening lead, you play first to the trick. When your partner makes an opening lead, you play third to the trick and are called *third hand*. When you're the last player to play to a trick, you're *fourth hand*.

This chapter discusses your strategy for defending when you play second to a trick, or *second hand*. The strategies outlined in this chapter apply to both notrump or any *side suit*. (Side suits are suits that aren't trump.) Second-hand play in the trump suit is discussed separately.

Haul out the spades from some handy deck. You can help yourself follow the explanations in this chapter if you have the cards in front of you.

Playing Second Hand with Vision

Whenever you play second hand, either the declarer or the dummy has led the suit initially. Your plays are governed by which opponent leads the suit first and whether a low card or an honor card is led. I show you how to react in each situation.

Blind man's bluff: When the dummy's on your right

If during the course of play some suit is led from the dummy, the North hand, then you, East, are second to play, as shown in Figure 19-1. In this scenario, you can't see the hand that plays after you, the declarer's hand. Basically, you play second hand blind, meaning that you may have to guess what declarer has in his hand.

```
┌────────────────────────────────────────────────┐
│                                                 │
│                  North (Dummy)                  │
│                                                 │
│    West (Your Partner)          East (You)      │
│                                                 │
│                 South (Declarer)                │
│                                                 │
└────────────────────────────────────────────────┘
```

Figure 19-1: The dummy is to your right.

You can see! When the dummy's on your left

When the declarer (South) leads the suit first, then you (West) are second hand, as shown in Figure 19-2. But this time you can see the dummy, the hand that plays after you, which helps because the declarer's options from the dummy are limited by the cards that you can see in the dummy. After all, if the dummy has only small cards, you can take the trick cheaply.

```
┌────────────────────────────────────────────────┐
│                                                 │
│                  North (Dummy)                  │
│                                                 │
│    West (You)              East (Your Partner)  │
│                                                 │
│                 South (Declarer)                │
│                                                 │
└────────────────────────────────────────────────┘
```

Figure 19-2: The dummy ends up on your left.

Because playing second hand blind (the declarer plays after you do) differs from playing second hand sighted (the dummy plays after you do), I divide the rest of this chapter into two sections that cover your course of action in each of these scenarios.

Defending with the Dummy on Your Right

When the dummy is on your right and the lead comes from the dummy, you are second to play. In the following sections, you pick up some clever strategies for playing a smart second-hand defense. Obviously, following these general guidelines doesn't guarantee that you'll play the right card every time. But you'll usually be right, and at least you won't slow the game to a crawl every time you play second hand.

Following a low-card lead with a low card

When the dummy leads a low card, you normally play the lowest card you have, which is called playing _second hand low._

You play second hand low most of the time. In fact, it is an exception not to play second hand low when the dummy leads a low card. You don't give away any secrets when you play second hand low.

Figure 19-3 shows you one good reason to play second hand low.

In this hand, hearts are trump and the dummy leads a low spade, ♠3. You play a low spade, ♠2, giving your partner a chance to take a trick, perhaps with a lower honor card. Had you played your ♠A, you would have brought your partner's ♠K down to earth with a sickening crash. Ugh.

Figure 19-3:
Avoid a crash landing by playing second hand low.

North (Dummy)
♠ 6 4 3

West (Your Partner)
♠ K

	N	
W		E
	S	

East (You)
♠ A 8 7 5 2

South (Declarer)
♠ Q J 10 9

Exceptions to playing low occur if you have a sequence of three or more equal cards headed by an honor, such as the QJ10 or the J1098. If you do, play your highest equal, the same card you would have led had you been on lead. Your partner now has a good read as to what you have in the suit.

However, when the dummy leads a low card and you have two consecutive honors, such as the QJ4 or the J1042, you usually play low.

A different sort of exception occurs in a side suit at a trump contract only. If the dummy leads a singleton (a one-card holding in a suit) and you have the ace, play it; you may lose it if the declarer has the king and can trump his other losers in the suit. If the dummy has a doubleton (two cards) and you have the AKxx (the x's stand for unimportant small cards in the suit), take the trick with the king.

If you decide not to play second hand low and you blow a trick, at least tell your partner that you meant to play low but the wrong card fell out of your hand. It's called saving face. Use the same excuse when you play second hand low and you blow a trick when you should have played high.

Covering an honor with a higher honor

When the dummy has one honor card (10 or higher), it is led, and you have a higher honor card, gently place your honor right on top of the dummy's honor. By so doing, you force the declarer to play yet another honor to that trick. After at least three honor cards are played to the same trick, lower spot cards have a way of becoming winning tricks; it's called *promotion* — the reason you cover.

The cards in Figure 19-4 give you a chance to do a little promoting. If the dummy leads the ♠Q, play the ♠K, covering an honor with a higher honor. If you see the declarer take the trick with the ♠A, don't think that you have wasted your ♠K — think that you have promoted your ♠10. After ♠AKQ have been played, the ♠J becomes top dog in the suit. But after the ♠J is played, the ♠10 moves up a notch to top rank. You have the ♠10. Long live the 10!

Figure 19-4:
Take that:
Your honor
is bigger
than the
dummy's
honor.

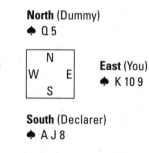

North (Dummy)
♠ Q 5

West (Your Partner)
♠ 7 6 4 3 2

East (You)
♠ K 10 9

South (Declarer)
♠ A J 8

If you stubbornly refuse to play your ♠K, the ♠Q takes the trick and the declarer remains with the ♠AJ. The declarer then takes the next two tricks by leading the ♠5 to the ♠J. You wind up with nothing.

Covering an honor with a higher honor can work in strange and wonderful ways that save you from losing tricks. Take a look at Figure 19-5 to see what I mean.

If the dummy leads the ♠5, play the ♠6 (playing second hand low; see the previous section for more details). However, if the dummy leads the ♠J, play the ♠Q. If you play the ♠Q, the declarer wins the ♠A. The ♠K and then the ♠10 are also high, but eventually your partner's ♠9 tops the declarer's ♠8. If you cover an honor with a higher honor, the declarer takes only three spade tricks.

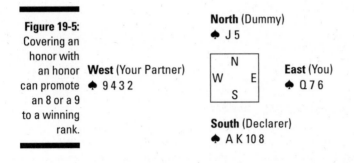

Figure 19-5:
Covering an honor with an honor can promote an 8 or a 9 to a winning rank.

North (Dummy)
♠ J 5

West (Your Partner)
♠ 9 4 3 2

East (You)
♠ Q 7 6

South (Declarer)
♠ A K 10 8

If you don't cover, the ♠J wins the trick, and later your queen drops and declarer takes three more tricks with the AK10. Your side gets zilch. By not playing the queen and allowing her to promote your partner's 9, you have not done her majesty justice.

If you cover an honor with an honor and the declarer takes the trick with yet another honor, three of the top five honors vanish on one trick. Suddenly the lower honors and the 8s and 9s sit up and take notice, because they may soon become winning tricks. You cover an honor with an honor to promote lower honors (not to mention 8s and 9s) for either you or your partner.

Covering the last of equal honors in the dummy

When the dummy leads one of several equal (consecutive) honors, do not cover the first honor; instead, cover the last equal honor. For example, if the dummy has two equal honors, such as the QJ6 or the J103, cover the second honor led. If the dummy has three equal honors, such as the QJ10 or the J109, cover the last equal led from the dummy. I explain why in the following sections.

When the dummy has two equal honors

In Figure 19-6, the dummy has two equal honors. Which one should you cover? If either honor (♠Q or ♠J) is led from the dummy, play low. When the second honor is then led from the dummy, cover that one with your ♠K. Even though your ♠K loses to the ♠A, your partner's ♠10 becomes the highest remaining spade. If you cover the first honor, the declarer wins the ♠A and can lead a low spade, finessing the dummy's ♠9, and take all three tricks.

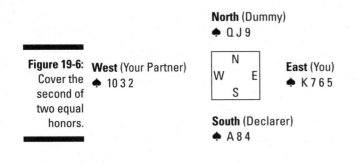

Figure 19-6: Cover the second of two equal honors.

North (Dummy)
♠ Q J 9

West (Your Partner)
♠ 10 3 2

East (You)
♠ K 7 6 5

South (Declarer)
♠ A 8 4

When the dummy has three equal honors

Figure 19-7 gives you a look at a dummy that has three equal honors. Whichever honor is led from the dummy (say the ♠Q), don't cover. When a second honor is played, don't cover again. Now you can see how your patience pays off. If you play low twice, the declarer takes the first trick with the ♠Q and the second trick with the ♠A, and winds up taking only two spade tricks. If you mistakenly cover the first or second honor, the declarer takes three tricks because dummy's remaining spade is a winning trick.

Figure 19-7: Cover the last of three equal honors led from the dummy.

North (Dummy)
♠ Q J 10

West (Your Partner)
♠ 9 7 4 3

East (You)
♠ K 8 5 2

South (Declarer)
♠ A 6

Defending with the Dummy on Your Left

When the dummy is on your left, you can see what's in the hand that plays after you do. When the dummy is visible, you usually know what the declarer is planning to play from the dummy. In the following sections, I show you a variety of strategies for playing second hand when the dummy is to your left.

Using common sense

When the dummy is on your left, you can often just let common sense take over. The cards in Figure 19-8 show you a case in which you can very easily think through your defense because you can see the dummy.

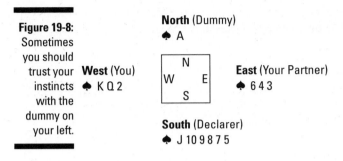

Figure 19-8:
Sometimes you should trust your instincts with the dummy on your left.

North (Dummy)
♠ A

West (You)
♠ K Q 2

East (Your Partner)
♠ 6 4 3

South (Declarer)
♠ J 10 9 8 7 5

In Figure 19-8, no matter which spade South leads, play the ♠2 because you can see that the ♠A must be played on this trick. By playing the ♠2 first, you conserve your ♠K and ♠Q for taking later tricks.

Letting the declarer take a losing finesse

When the dummy is on your left, give the declarer a chance to take a losing finesse when the suit has a hole (broken honor strength) in it. How do you do that? Play low! Figure 19-9 shows a dummy that's missing the ♠Q between the ♠K and the ♠J.

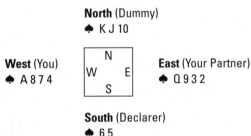

North (Dummy)
♠ K J 10

Figure 19-9:
Give the declarer a chance to take a losing finesse.

West (You)
♠ A 8 7 4

East (Your Partner)
♠ Q 9 3 2

South (Declarer)
♠ 6 5

Suppose that the declarer leads a low spade, ♠5. When you can see broken honor strength, play low, ♠4, and give the declarer a chance to take a losing finesse. If the declarer finesses the ♠10, your partner wins with the ♠Q, and you can take another trick with your ♠A the next time you get a chance. (Check out Chapter 4 for details on finesses.)

Leaving the dummy's honors alone

When the declarer leads a low card toward the dummy, you generally don't waste a 9, 10, or jack to force a higher honor out of the dummy; those higher honors will be played anyway. The cards in Figure 19-10 show you what to do when the declarer leads up to an ace in the dummy.

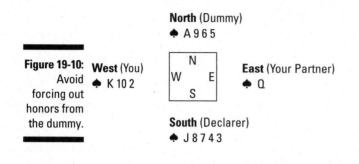

North (Dummy)
♠ A 9 6 5

Figure 19-10: Avoid forcing out honors from the dummy.

West (You)
♠ K 10 2

East (Your Partner)
♠ Q

South (Declarer)
♠ J 8 7 4 3

If the declarer leads a low spade, the ♠3, *don't* (do not, not, not) play the ♠10 to force the ♠A out of the dummy. The declarer intends to play the ♠A anyway, and the card you play to force out the ♠A may be a card that can take a later trick if you keep it.

If you play low, the ♠2, the declarer plays the ♠A, dropping your partner's ♠Q, but you remain with the ♠K10 over the declarer's ♠J for two tricks. If you play the ♠10, the declarer plays the ♠A, which he was going to do anyway; you get only one trick, the ♠K.

Use your ace to capture something worthwhile — such as an honor card. Don't use your ace on a low card unless you need just one more trick to defeat the contract. If so, take it! You don't want to go to bed with the setting trick!

Figure 19-11 gives you a chance to make good use of your ace.

North (Dummy)
♠ K 7 5

Figure 19-11: Use your aces wisely when the dummy is on your left.

West (You)
♠ A 3 2

East (Your Partner)
♠ J 10 9 8

South (Declarer)
♠ Q 6 4

Suppose that the declarer leads a low spade, ♠4. If you play low, ♠2, the dummy takes the trick with the ♠K. Big deal. If you play your ♠A, not only does the dummy take a later trick with the ♠K, but the declarer also takes a trick with the ♠Q. By playing your ♠A, you capture air: You get the declarer's ♠4 and the dummy's ♠5. If you play low, later you capture declarer's ♠Q with your ♠A and the declarer takes only one trick. Aces were bred to capture kings and queens, not fours and fives!

Dealing with higher honors in the dummy

Your real problem arises when the declarer leads an honor, you have a higher honor, and the dummy has a higher honor yet.

If the declarer leads an honor in a side suit (any suit other than the trump suit) and you have one higher honor, follow these guidelines:

- ✔ If the dummy has one higher honor than you, don't play your honor.
- ✔ If the dummy has two higher honors than your honor, play your honor.

I cover both of these scenarios in more detail in the following sections.

When the dummy has one higher honor

In Figure 19-12, spades are trump and South leads the ♠J. Don't cover when the dummy has one higher honor. In this instance, you have ♠Q, but the dummy has ♠A.

Figure 19-12:
The dummy has one higher honor than you have.

North (Dummy)
♠ A 8 7 4

West (You)
♠ Q 3 2

```
    N
W       E
    S
```

East (Your Partner)
♠ 6

South (Declarer)
♠ K J 10 9 5

Sometimes the declarer leads an honor just to coax you into covering. In this case, for example, the declarer almost surely doesn't intend to take a finesse — the declarer intends to play the ♠AK. He's just offering you a little bait — don't bite! Play low.

When the dummy has two higher honors

In Figure 19-13, South leads the ♠J. If you cover with the ♠K, the declarer takes only one trick, the ♠A. If you play low and the dummy plays low, your partner wins the ♠Q, but next time the declarer leads low to the ♠10 and takes two tricks: the ♠10 and the ♠A.

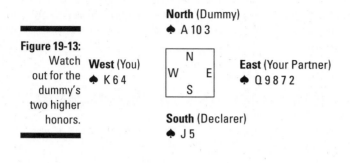

Figure 19-13:
Watch
out for the
dummy's
two higher
honors.

North (Dummy)
♠ A 10 3

West (You)
♠ K 6 4

East (Your Partner)
♠ Q 9 8 7 2

South (Declarer)
♠ J 5

You cover an honor to promote 9s and 10s for either you or your partner. However, if you can see both of those cards in the dummy (A109, AQ109), no promotion is possible, so don't cover. (See "Covering an honor with a higher honor," earlier in this chapter, for more information about promotion.)

Overpowering the opponents' honor cards with your honor cards

If the declarer leads an honor and you have two higher honors, cover the declarer's honor with your lower honor. You need to play one of your honors in Figure 19-14.

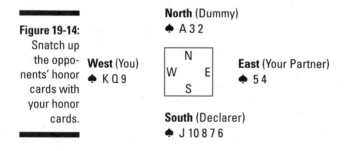

Figure 19-14:
Snatch up
the oppo-
nents' honor
cards with
your honor
cards.

North (Dummy)
♠ A 3 2

West (You)
♠ K Q 9

East (Your Partner)
♠ 5 4

South (Declarer)
♠ J 10 8 7 6

If the declarer leads the ♠J or ♠10, cover with the ♠Q, your lower equal. If you do, you will take two tricks with your ♠K and ♠9. In the world of promotion, a 9 is a big card, a very big card.

In general, whether you decide to cover or not to cover, do it nonchalantly, as though you couldn't care less about what's going on. If you start hemming and hawing, sweat starts appearing, and you finally play low, a declarer who isn't comatose will pick up on your strange behavior and work out that you must have the missing honor. If you play low quickly, you can fool even the best declarer.

Knowing when you're beat

When the dummy's cards are higher than your cards, don't fight it — just play low. For example, you need to play low when you have the cards shown in Figure 19-15.

Figure 19-15:
You can't fight City Hall when the dummy has higher cards than you do.

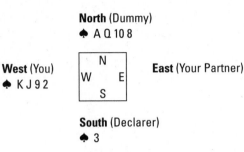

North (Dummy)

♠ A Q 10 8

West (You)

♠ K J 9 2

East (Your Partner)

South (Declarer)

♠ 3

South leads a low spade, ♠3. You see that whichever spade you play, the dummy has a higher one, so play low. Don't waste an honor. For all you know, the declarer may intend to play the ♠A.

Chapter 20

Wrapping Up with Scorekeeping

. . . .

In This Chapter

▶ Scoring up partscores, games, and slams

▶ Walking through the scoring of a Chicago wheel

▶ Racking up penalty points when a contract bites the dust

▶ Scoring doubled and redoubled contracts

. . . .

Can you imagine playing a game without knowing how to keep score? It's unthinkable. You wouldn't know who was winning, how many points you needed to win, or when to stop playing.

Bridge is no different. The bidding is intertwined with scoring. You can't bid effectively, play, or defend intelligently unless you know how to keep score.

Over the years, bridge scoring has undergone some minor revisions, and what I present here is a current method of scoring, called *Chicago* (also known as *four-deal bridge*). This form of scoring is exactly the way duplicate-bridge tournaments are scored the world over. In this chapter you discover what you need to know about this important aspect of the game.

Understanding How Bidding and Scoring Are Intertwined

During the bidding, you hope to end up in a reasonable contract that you can make. If you make your contract, you score points; if you don't make your contract, you lose points. Final contracts come wrapped in three packages: *game, partscore,* and *slam.* In this section I explain the basic aspects of scoring and then tell you how to score up the result of each hand depending on the final contract and how many tricks were taken by the side that bought the contract.

Tallying up your trick score

You earn a certain number of points for each trick you take after the sixth one. The first six tricks, which are unspoken during the bidding, do not count in the scoring of any contract.

- ✔ When hearts or spades winds up as the trump suit, each trick taken is worth 30 points.
- ✔ When clubs or diamonds winds up as the trump suit, each trick is worth 20 points.
- ✔ The first trick in notrump is worth 40 points, but each subsequent trick is worth 30 points.

Table 20-1 saves you time figuring out scores for each contract. Because the first six tricks don't count, the tricks taken in Table 20-1 start with seven tricks.

Table 20-1			Charting Your Score				
Tricks Taken	*7*	*8*	*9*	*10*	*11*	*12*	*13*
Notrump	40	70	100	130	160	190	220
Spades	30	60	90	120	150	180	210
Hearts	30	60	90	120	150	180	210
Diamonds	20	40	60	80	100	120	140
Clubs	20	40	60	80	100	120	140

As an example, say your final contract was 2♥ and you took nine tricks; you made an *overtrick* (one more trick than you contracted for). Start on the left where you see *Hearts* and follow the row across until you come to the *9* column. You can see that you made 90 points.

Your goal on every hand is to make your contract; making overtricks is icing on the cake. They count, of course, but do not entitle you to any bonus points. If you don't make your contract, you don't have to worry about this table, because you don't score any points — your opponents do! (See "Scoring up undertricks, vulnerable and not vulnerable" later in this chapter for more information about how to score when you don't make your contract.)

Adding up game-contract bonus points

Bridge has five special contracts called *game contracts:* 3NT, 4♥, 4♠, 5♣, and 5♦. They all give you a trick score of at least 100 points. If you arrive at any of these game contracts and make them, bonus points await.

By far the most common game contract is 3NT. Because six assumed tricks are always added to any bid, you need to take nine tricks to make this contract. The other game contracts require 10 or 11 tricks: 4♥ and 4♠ require 10 tricks, and 5♣ and 5♦ need 11 tricks.

After making your game contract and seeing your trick score (refer to Table 20-1), here come the bonus points!

If you bid and make a game contract, you get either 300 or 500 bonus points. Why two different bonuses? The amount of the game bonus (or penalty) depends on whether you are *not vulnerable* or *vulnerable.* There is no mystery to being vulnerable. It means you score a bigger bonus for making a game contract, but you also concede more points if you don't make a game or slam contract.

When we get to keeping score (see "Keeping Track of the Score in Four-Deal Chicago"), I further explain the terms and how you know whether your side is vulnerable or not. Fortunately, vulnerability is preordained when playing Chicago. In other words, everyone knows before the hand is dealt who is vulnerable and who is not, which makes the scoring easier.

The formula for scoring up any game contract is the trick score + 300 for bidding and making a not-vulnerable game and + 500 for bidding and making a vulnerable game.

Let's say you bid and make 3NT, not vulnerable. Your trick score is 100 points + 300 bonus points = 400 points. If you were vulnerable, your trick score would still be 100 points, but you'd add 500 bonus points, making 600 points total.

If you bid and make 4♥ or 4♠, not vulnerable, your trick score is 120 points + 300 bonus points = 420 points. Vulnerable, your trick score would be 120 points + 500 bonus points = 620 points.

If you bid and make 5♣ or 5♦, not vulnerable, your trick score is 100 points + 300 bonus points = 400 points. Vulnerable, your trick score would be 100 points + 500 bonus points = 600 points.

Earning points for a partscore contract

Any final contract lower than a game contract is called a *partscore contract*. When you and your partner feel that the combined strength of the two hands doesn't warrant bidding game, just settle in for a partscore contract. After all, making a partscore contract is better than going down in a game contract!

Scoring up a partscore contract that has been made is rather simple. You simply add 50 bonus points to your trick score (which you can find in Table 20-1). For example, say your contract is 2♥ and you make it by taking your needed eight tricks. Table 20-1 shows that 60 is your trick score. To this amount you add the automatic 50 bonus points for making any partscore contract, and voilà, your total score on this hand is 110 points.

In other versions of Chicago bridge (most often used when playing for money or by many veteran players), completed partscore contract points are carried over to the next deal with no 50-point bonus. In some instances those partscore points can be used as a stepping stone to a game contract on the next hand. The Chicago version championed here simplifies that approach by scoring each hand *separately* with no carryover of successful partscore contracts, which is exactly what you will encounter when you play in your first novice game or in any tournament level event played throughout the world.

Scoring up a small slam

Sometimes you have enough strength between the two hands and are courageous enough to bid a *small slam,* meaning you have to take 12 of the 13 possible tricks to make your contract. This contract is exciting and perilous because if you come up short, penalties are involved: Your opponents get penalty points while you get nada. But I don't focus on the negative here (I save that for a later section "Not Making Your Contract: Handling Penalties"). Suppose you take those 12 tricks and you do make your contract. Read on to see how many points you have just piled up making a small slam.

When you bid and make a small slam, you earn a bonus of 500 or 750 on top of your game bonus. Follow this formula:

- **Not vulnerable:** Trick score + 300 (game bonus) + 500 (small-slam bonus)
- **Vulnerable:** Trick score + 500 (game bonus) + 750 (small-slam bonus)

Say you bid and make 6♠, not vulnerable. Hooray for your side! Your trick score is 180 points. (Refer to Table 20-1.) You get to tack on your game bonus of 300 points, plus your not-vulnerable small-slam bonus of 500 points. It all comes to 980 points!

Had you been vulnerable, your trick score would still be 180, your game bonus would be 500, and your small-slam bonus would be 750. If you add it all up, it comes to a four-digit number: 1,430!

Cashing in on a grand slam

The granddaddy of all slams is the *grand slam*. You have to bid all the way up to the seven level, the very top of the elevator, which means contracting for all 13 tricks and then taking that many! If you do it, your score will be enormous, but if you take fewer tricks, you get nothing and the opponents get penalty points. It's unbearable.

Scoring up a grand slam is similar to scoring up a small slam, only with larger slam bonuses and more tension!

The formula remains the same: Trick score + game bonus + grand-slam bonus. As usual, vulnerability enters into the bonus points. It works like this:

✔ **Not vulnerable grand slam** = 1,000 bonus points

✔ **Vulnerable grand slam** = 1,500 bonus points

Pretend your contract is 7NT, not vulnerable, meaning you have to take all 13 tricks, and you do! Your trick score is 220 (refer to Table 20-1), which you add to a 300 game bonus and a 1,000 grand-slam bonus. Add it all up and it comes to 1,520. Not bad.

More good news. If you make a vulnerable 7NT grand slam (you're going to like this), you get a trick score of 220 + the game bonus of 500 + the grand-slam bonus of 1,500! The grand total this time is 2,220 points! You could play for a week and not score that many points.

Incidentally, after you bid and make a grand slam and you want to see happiness, glance at your partner's face. If you want to see abject misery, glance at your opponents' faces!

A not-vulnerable grand-slam bonus (1,000) is double that of a small-slam bonus (500). A vulnerable grand slam bonus (1,500) is double that of a small-slam bonus (750).

Keeping Track of the Score in Four-Deal Chicago

You and your partner are about to give it a go against a hopefully congenial twosome. The game can last as long as all four players want to continue playing.

In any home game, including Chicago, of course, you may agree to play the whole session with the same partner, which is called a *set game*. Not all bridge games are set games, because some people like to rotate partners. In any case, the scoring is the same.

Setting up the score sheet and bridge wheel

In this section I introduce you to the easiest and most popular form of bridge scoring. But first, someone has to step up to the plate and be the official score-keeper for your game, and you have been elected!

Dig up a sheet of paper to be your score sheet. Take a look at Figure 20-1 to see what your score sheet looks like, and be sure to include a *We* and a *They*. From now on, any plus score your team makes goes under *We,* and any plus score your opponents make goes under *They*.

Figure 20-1:
Draw a few
lines on
your score
sheet to
start the
scoring
process.

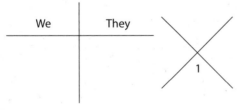

You're almost ready. Now all you have to do is draw a *wheel,* which is the indicator of whose turn it is to deal the cards. Most people wouldn't know it was a wheel unless you told them! Check out Figure 20-1 again to see that all you have to do is draw a large vertical X and call it a wheel. Think of this diagram as four open triangles, each representing a hand you are about to play.

You start by writing a "1" in the triangle directly in front of you. This mark indicates that you are the dealer on the first hand. In fact, you will be the dealer on the first hand of each new wheel. The deal and follow-up deals always rotate to the left in a clockwise manner.

When playing Chicago, as well as when playing in a bridge tournament, the vulnerability is arbitrarily assigned to you in advance. Yes, in advance!

- **On deal #1:** Neither side is vulnerable.
- **On deal #2:** The dealer's side only is vulnerable.
- **On deal #3:** The dealer's side only is vulnerable.
- **On deal #4:** Both sides are vulnerable.

Keep in mind that the bonuses are different for making not-vulnerable game contracts and slams, as opposed to making vulnerable game and slam contracts. However, the 50-point bonus for making any partscore contract remains constant irrespective of vulnerability.

Scoring a Chicago wheel

Fun and games are over. Now it's time to experience playing and scoring your first Chicago wheel! Can you stand all this excitement?

On the very first hand, you're the dealer and your side winds up playing a contract of 2♥. By sheer brilliance, you fulfill your contract and take exactly eight tricks. Your trick score is $30 \times 2 = 60$ + an automatic 50 for bidding and making a partscore contract (review the first half of this chapter for basic and partscore scoring). Drum roll, if you please: Chalk up 110 points and enter them so your score sheet looks like the one in Figure 20-2.

Figure 20-2: Enter your trick score on the first deal.

We	They
110	

1

Now you're on to the second hand, in which the dealer's side is vulnerable. The person to your left deals the second hand. Before the cards are dealt, put a "2" in the triangle to your left, just as in Figure 20-3.

Figure 20-3:
On the
second
deal, they
hit you with
a vulnerable
game!

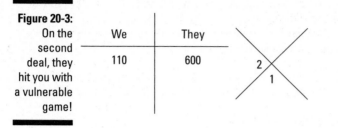

We	They
110	600

This time, your opponents get most of the high cards and wind up in 3NT, vulnerable, and make it. They get a 100-point trick score + 500 bonus points for bidding a vulnerable game. Enter 600 points under *They,* as in Figure 20-3. Oh well, life goes on. In fact it goes on to hand #3, as shown scored up in Figure 20-4.

Figure 20-4:
Make a
partscore
with an
overtrick
on the third
deal.

We	They
110	600
	170

On hand #3, the dealer's side (your team) is vulnerable. With both sides bidding, the opponents eventually outbid you buying the contract at 3♠. They need nine tricks but actually take ten! They make an *overtrick* (an extra trick). Their trick score is $4 \times 30 = 120 + 50$ (the partscore bonus) = 170. Stick it on the *They* side, as in Figure 20-4.

Hand #4 is the last hand of the wheel. This time both sides are vulnerable, and your side is behind! You have 110 points on your side and they have 670 on theirs. Not to worry, I'm rooting for you to win. On this last hand your side bids 6♠, which is a small slam. You make it — with an overtrick! Remember the formula: the trick score ($7 \times 30 = 210$) + the game bonus (500, because you were vulnerable) + the small-slam bonus (750; again, because you were vulnerable), and in one fell swoop you have just made 1,460 points. Put them on the *We* side as in Figure 20-5. Why did I have a strong inkling that you were going to win this wheel?

Figure 20-5:
Slamming
your way
to victory!

We	They
110	600
1,460	170

After entering the 1,460 points on your side, the first wheel is history. Add up the scores under *We* (1,570) and under *They* (770) and calculate the difference, in this case 800. After you have that total, draw a double line under all scores and put 800 directly under the double line on the 'We' side of the ledger. This score represents your carryover going into the next wheel. Further scores go under the double line on either the *We* or the *They* side and the process is repeated every four deals until quitting time.

Figure 20-6:
Carry over
the differ-
ence, ready
for the next
wheel.

We	They
110	600
1,460	170
1,570	770
800 (carryover)	

The carryover method of scoring is far easier than waiting until the session is over and then adding up all the scores, needing a calculator to see who has actually won! Most bridge players like to know how they are doing as the play progresses by simply looking at the latest carryover number.

Not Making the Contract: Handling Penalties

In some wheels, neither side can make a contract even if their lives depend on it. When you don't make your contract, you're penalized when it comes to reckoning time at the end of the hand. Welcome to the sad world of *going set, going down,* or *failing*. All these terms mean the same thing: You didn't take enough tricks and didn't make your contract. When you come up short, the missing tricks are called *undertricks,* and in this section I tell you the ugly truth about the points they'll cost you.

Don't despair when you don't make your contract. The fact is that about one-third of all contracts bite the dust. You may not have done anything wrong. You may have run into a ghastly suit division in their hands making the contract impossible to realize. In fact, sometimes you get an advantage by bidding more than you think you can make because your loss is less than the number of points they could have made in the contract they were in. This move is called making a *sacrifice* bid — a big part of the game.

Scoring up undertricks, vulnerable and not vulnerable

When you don't make your contract, opponents score penalty points on the *They* side of the score sheet.

- ✔ **Not vulnerable:** 50 points per trick
- ✔ **Vulnerable:** 100 points per trick

As an example, say your contract is 4♠ and you need ten tricks to make it. Alas, you wind up with only nine. The normal way to describe this scenario is *4♠ down one.* Because you've gone down in a contract, their side gets the penalty points. If you aren't vulnerable, they get 50 points; if you are vulnerable, they score 100 points.

Scoring doubled contracts that bite the dust (go down)

The final contract has been doubled. The stakes have just been raised, and excitement and terror now loom on the horizon. In this section, I show you how to score up doubled contracts (see Chapter 15 for more on doubling and redoubling).

Your opponents may arrive at a final contract that either you or your partner thinks is just too high. For example, if the opponents wind up in 7NT, contracting for all 13 tricks, and you are on lead holding an ace, you know that they can't take all 13 tricks. You have a weapon (a bid) at your disposal to let the opponents know that they have made a big mistake. You say, "Double," the equivalent of saying "I dare you" when you bid. If you defeat the contract, as you will, I show you how to score doubled undertricks.

Not-vulnerable undertricks in doubled contracts carry the following penalties (awarded to the opposing team):

- ✔ **Down 1:** 100 points
- ✔ **Down 2:** 300 points
- ✔ **Down 3:** 500 points
- ✔ **Down 4:** 800 points

Each subsequent undertrick results in an additional 300 penalty points awarded to your opponents.

Vulnerable undertricks in doubled contracts carry the following penalties:

- ✔ **Down 1:** 200 points
- ✔ **Down 2:** 500 points
- ✔ **Down 3:** 800 points
- ✔ **Down 4:** 1,100 points

Each subsequent undertrick results in an additional 300 penalty points. It can get pretty wild.

Scoring Doubled Contracts That Make

The reality is that you don't defeat a contract every time you double it. When you double and your opponents make their contract, points go up on their side of the line. As it happens most doubled contracts are game contracts: 3NT, 4♥, 4♠, 5♣, or 5♦. Here is the formula for scoring doubled contracts that make:

1. **Double the trick score.**
2. **Add the game bonus points of either 300 or 500, depending on the vulnerability.**
3. **Add *the insult:* another 50 points for making a doubled contract!**

Suppose you wield the ax and double 3NT, not vulnerable, and they make three on the nose, taking nine tricks.

1. Double the trick score. The trick score for 3NT is 100, so it becomes 200.

2. Add 300 for the not-vulnerable game bonus, and they're up to 500. (If they had been vulnerable, the bonus would be 500, giving a score of 700 at this point.)

3. Then add that aggravating automatic 50 points for making any doubled contract. When the smoke clears, they have 550 on their side.

You may think that hand went badly for you, but it could be worse! Read on.

When a doubled contract makes overtricks

Sometimes the doubling side really miscalculates. Not only does the declarer make the contract, but he also makes an overtrick or two!

- **Each doubled overtrick, not vulnerable:** 100 points
- **Each doubled overtrick, vulnerable:** 200 points

To calculate the score in this ugly situation, follow these steps:

1. **Double the trick score of the contract.**

2. **Add the game bonus.**

3. **Add the overtrick score.**

4. **Add 50 for making a doubled contract.**

It's so depressing if you're the doubling side, and it's so exhilarating if you're the declaring side.

Doubling your opponents into game

Doubling a game or even a slam contract that makes is not healthy of course, but doubling a partscore contract that makes, thus turning it into a game contract, is serious misery. The following scoring conventions show you why:

1. **Double their trick score (refer to Table 20-1). If the total comes to more than 100, you have just doubled them into game — without their having to bid a game contract.**

2. **Add in the game bonus, depending on vulnerability, of course.**

3. **Give them an additional 50 points for making a doubled contract.**

For example, say you double a 2♠ contract, vulnerable, and they make it on the nose. Their trick score of 60 is now doubled into 120. It's as if they bid a game! Add 500 for the vulnerable game bonus and an additional 50 points for making a doubled contract. It all comes to 670 points. Had you not doubled, they would have scored a modest 110 points!

Some doubled partscore contracts don't earn a *trick* score of 100 points even if the opponents make the contract. As a result, they earn no game bonus. For example, a doubled one-level contract, as well as doubled contracts of 2♣ or 2♦, even if made, don't total 100 points for the trick score (refer to Table 20-1).

A contract of 2♣ doubled, making two on the nose, works out like this: The trick score for 2♣ is 40. Doubling that makes it a trick score of 80. Then add 50 points for making a doubled contract, equaling 130 points in all.

Be careful about doubling a partscore contract that puts the opponents into game if they make it.

A wise man once said: "If you defeat every contract you double, you are not doubling enough!" In other words, you can be too timid. If your hand screams for a penalty double, make it! If they make a doubled contract once in a while, so be it. In the long run, you will come out way ahead of the game.

Do you know who I am?

This is one of my favorite doubling stories. I have a good friend named Erik Paulsen who lives in Downey, California. Erik is a terrific bridge player and one year was on a team that represented the United States in the World Championship. That year, the U.S. won and Erik came home a World Champion!

People who played at the local club that Erik used to frequent despaired of ever seeing him at the club again, but lo and behold, one evening Erik showed up to play. Early on, Erik found himself playing against two young men. The bidding was competitive, with the opponents bidding hearts and Erik and his partner competing in spades. Finally a bid of 3♥ came

around to Erik, who knew he should pass but didn't think either of these fellows would dare double a World Champion if he bid 3♠. Erik bid 3♠ in a confident voice, hoping to discourage even the thought of being doubled.

The next word out of the young man to his left was, "Double."

Erik looked at the young man and said, "Do you know who I am?"

"Yes, Mr. Paulsen, I know who you are."

"Do you know how many master points I have?"

"No, Mr. Paulsen, but do you know how many spades *I* have?"

Scoring Redoubled Contracts

Some players treat a penalty double as a personal insult. Those players are prone to say, "Redouble" ("I double dare you"), actually quadrupling the stakes! When a redoubled contract is either made or not made, the scores grow to behemoth proportions. Prepare yourself.

Redoubled undertricks

The following list shows how you to score not-vulnerable undertricks in a redoubled contract. If you're the declarer, your opponent wins these penalty points for your undertricks:

- ✔ **Down 1:** 200 points
- ✔ **Down 2:** 600 points
- ✔ **Down 3:** 1,000 points

The redoubled score for undertricks, not vulnerable, is twice the score it would be in a doubled contract, not vulnerable.

Following are the scores for vulnerable undertricks in redoubled contracts:

- ✔ **Down 1:** 400 points
- ✔ **Down 2:** 1,000 points
- ✔ **Down 3:** 1,600 points

The redoubled score for undertricks, vulnerable, is twice the score it would be in a doubled contract, vulnerable.

Redoubled contracts that make: Complete joy!

In bridge there is always the other side of the coin. They double you, you teach them a lesson by lashing them with a redouble, and then you make your contract!

When the contract is made, the lucky declarer and his partner get *four* times the trick score, plus normal game and slam bonuses and an extra bonus of

100 on top of that for the insult. For example, say you make a contract of 5♦ doubled and redoubled, vulnerable:

1. The trick score of 5♦ is 100, so that becomes 400 (because it's quadrupled).

2. You add the game bonus of 500 (because you're vulnerable).

3. The insult grows from 50 to 100 points.

Their little adventure in doubling your contract (Don't they know who you are?) has cost them 1,000 points!

You get an extra bonus of 100 points for making a redoubled contract, twice the bonus of 50 for making a doubled contract.

Redoubled overtricks

Sometimes the redoubling side makes overtricks. When this earth-shattering event happens, each overtrick score is quadrupled:

- ✔ **Each non-vulnerable redoubled overtrick:** 200 points
- ✔ **Each vulnerable redoubled overtrick:** 400 points

In real life, *very* few contracts end up doubled and redoubled; many players just can't stand the stress, so you can put away your calculator.

Part VI
Feeding Your Addiction to Bridge

The 5th Wave   By Rich Tennant

" On the other hand, he could be a fourth
for bridge."

In this part . . .

After you play a few hands, you may find that you can't stop playing bridge. If this happens, call a doctor — you may be a bridgeaholic. The only cure for your addiction is play, play, play.

To satisfy your craving for bridge, you can turn to this part to read about playing in bridge clubs (where other fanatics like you can be found), in tournaments (where the serious bridgeaholics hang out), on the computer, and on the Internet (where you can get support from fellow bridgeaholics as far away as China and, of course, play some bridge).

Chapter 21

Joining Bridge Clubs and the Tournament World

The title of this chapter may make you feel like you're being pushed out the door before you're ready, but that's not so. Although bridge clubs and tournaments often cater to more-advanced players, both also offer services for novice players, both give you a chance to meet other newcomers to the game, and both give you the chance to play bridge against players of your own skill level.

Connecting with Your Local Bridge Club

Depending on where you live, you're likely to be able to find a bridge club within striking distance. If you can't find the address and phone number for a bridge club in your local telephone directory, call the American Contract Bridge League (ACBL) at 662-253-300, or check out www.acbl.org to obtain a club directory or a referral to the nearest club. Incidentally, the ACBL has free apps for iPhones, iPads, and for Android smartphones to locate clubs just about anywhere. (See Chapter 24 for more information on the ACBL.)

After you find your local bridge club, call to see what it has to offer. Most clubs have beginner's lessons as well as supervised play sessions — right up your alley. The club managers will treat you royally; beginners are the life-blood of the game. The clubs need you!

Some services, such as the lessons and supervised play offered by local clubs, may have fees attached, but they are minimal and well worth the expense.

Playing in Novice Tournaments

After you gain some confidence with your play, you may consider the next big step: playing in a novice tournament. You can find these novice tournaments staged at your local bridge club.

In many of these games, you can ask questions as you're playing. In short, you don't have to sweat bullets playing in novice tournaments — you can ask a more advanced player if you aren't sure about your next move.

You may really enjoy the novice tournaments. Most people begin to have fun at these tournaments after they see that they're going to survive.

In the following sections, I give you a few pointers on preparing to play in a novice tournament and explain how you gather masterpoints.

Preparing to play with others

Before you play in a novice tournament, you'll probably be nervous. It's normal, so don't sweat it. And don't worry about making mistakes; they're inevitable. Keep in mind that everyone else is in the same boat you are, with the same thoughts and feelings. If you treat the tournament as a fun learning experience, you'll do just fine.

When you begin playing in novice tournaments, you'll find that 99 percent of the people whom you meet and play against are pleasant and eager to learn, and you're bound to make many friends who share bridge as a common interest.

Of course, you can also expect to find the one percent who can't control themselves when something goes awry. These types like to lay the blame for their mistakes on their partner. Don't worry about these jokers. If they get out of line once too often, the club owner will bar them for a month or two — an eternity to a bridge player.

Accruing masterpoints

The American Contract Bridge League (ACBL) records the successes of its members in tournament play by awarding *masterpoints*. If you join the ACBL, the League tracks your masterpoints and sends you a point-count summary with your monthly copy of the ACBL *Bulletin* so you can see your progress.

You don't have to win (or even come in second) in tournaments to win points. You can garner fractional points by placing third, fourth, or even fifth (sometimes lower), depending on the number of players who are competing.

Masterpoints come in colors. You can win black, silver, red, or gold points, depending on the importance of the event. At first, you will probably be winning black points, the color you pick up in club games. When you start playing in the larger tournaments (see "Advancing in the Tournament World," later in this chapter, for details), you can win the prettier-colored points. The points you win are all of equal value, but you must win a minimum number of each color to attain the ultimate goal — Life Master.

The ACBL gives you a title according to how many masterpoints you rack up. Table 21-1 shows how many masterpoints you need to achieve each title.

Table 21-1	Racking Up the Masterpoints
ACBL Title	**Masterpoint Requirement**
Rookie	0–4.99
Junior Master	5–19.99
Club Master	20–49.99
Sectional Master	50–99.99
Regional Master	100–199.99
NABC Master	200–299.99
Advanced NABC Master	300–499.99
Life Master	500 or more

To reach the upper plateaus, some of your points must be in particular colors. In other words, you have to win some of your masterpoints in larger tournaments, which means leaving the safety net of your local bridge club to get them.

When you play through enough blood, sweat, and tears to amass 500 of these coveted masterpoints, the ACBL makes you a *Life Master* and rewards you by sending you a gold card with your name emblazoned on it. You get the following benefits from being a Life Master:

✔ Bragging rights for the rest of your life

✔ Eligibility to play in certain restricted events

✔ Respect from the bridge community

Hooked on bridge at an early age

I started playing in local bridge tournaments when I was 14 years old. I was so hooked by the time I entered high school that I hid bridge books inside my regular schoolbooks so I could study bridge during class. Once when the rest of the class was being raucous, my teacher pointed me out to the class as a shining example of good behavior, saying, "Why can't you have study habits like Eddie? Look how quiet he is!" Thank goodness the teacher wasn't closer to my desk.

I got my gold card when I was 24 years old. Some players don't even have to wait as long as I did — some child phenoms have become Life Masters at the age of 10! Of course, their parents taught them to play as soon as they uttered their first word.

When you start playing in novice tournaments, you will eventually start to win masterpoints. When you get your first masterpoint, you'll be hooked, baby.

Because everyone wants to get to that magic 500 points needed to become a Life Master, most everyone knows to the fraction of a point just where they stand. Of course, they act as though it's not important to them. I once played with a lady who was approaching Life Masterdom (one only needed 300 points at that time) and I asked her, "How many masterpoints do you have?" She said, "Oh, I don't know — who cares? About 278.63."

Advancing in the Tournament World

Tournaments come in many sizes, shapes, and locations, offering a variety of skill levels and prizes. One day you may find yourself ascending in the tournament world. But when you first begin to play bridge, you may want to attend the tournaments to meet other players and watch some of the best players in action. All the tournaments are ACBL affiliated, and anyone can play in most of them (although some events may require a minimum number of masterpoints to enter). I describe the different tournament levels in the following sections.

How can you find out when and where these tournaments are so you can do a little planning? Join the ACBL. Joining is your second good move — reading this book was your first. After you join the ACBL, you get the League's monthly magazine ("It's great — I write two articles each month," he added modestly) that gives you all the details on tournaments, instructional material, and much, much more. For more information on joining the ACBL, see Chapter 24.

Getting started: Club tournaments

When you screw together your last ounce of courage and charge off to play in your first club tournament, there's no turning back. You'll soon be ringing the phone off the hook down at the club, asking for the latest tournament information. Of course, you can also check the ACBL website (www.acbl.org) for all sanctioned events.

Working up to the next level: Sectional tournaments

You may see many of the same people from your club tournaments when you enter a sectional tournament. Sectionals mostly draw their competitors from the immediate area. *Card fees* (the fees for entering the tournament) are a little higher at sectional tournaments because you're playing in a larger venue and somebody has to pay the rent. The higher card fees may be worth your while if you're trying to accrue masterpoints: You receive more masterpoints for placing in sectional tournaments than in club tournaments.

Sectional tournaments usually last three days: Friday, Saturday, and Sunday. Most tournaments offer events for everyone, including novices, and you can play as much or as little as you like.

Really testing your stuff: Regional tournaments

You're moving up in the world when you enter a regional event. Regional tournaments usually take place in a classy hotel or a convention center (the extra space is necessary because of the larger number of participants). Regionals offer the players an opportunity to win a substantial number of gold and red points, awards that are necessary to achieve the rank of Life Master. Experts often come out of the woodwork from other states to play in regional tournaments. Masterpoints flow like champagne at these events.

Regional tournaments generally last one week, sometimes longer. Anyone can play, and often the tournaments offer events for players with any number of masterpoints — from 0 to 60,000!

Playing in the big leagues: National Championship tournaments

The Nationals take place three times a year in the United States or Canada, and thousands of people descend from nowhere and everywhere to attend. If you get a chance to attend a National Championship, by all means do it. I went to 93 of them in a row before I finally missed one!

National tournaments are 11 days of fun and/or hard work, depending which way you want to go. Although the Nationals do feature some big-time players doing what they do best, the tournaments also boast novice events every morning, afternoon, and evening.

If you don't feel quite up to playing at that level, you can *kibitz* (that is, watch for free!) some of the best players in the world, not to mention celebrities such as Bill Gates and Warren Buffet, two real bridge aficionados. International stars are now coming in droves to the National Championships and earning a living by playing on sponsored teams. Certain important National events decide qualification for the United States in both team and pair events in the next World Championship.

Nothing matches the feeling of winning a National tournament. True, you don't play for money, but the glory and ego gratification can't be discounted! The great Paul Soloway and I once played on a team that won a National event. The event ended one day before the tournament was officially over, so I decided to head home. On the way out of the hotel, I saw Paul in the lobby and asked him why he wasn't going home. He said that he wanted to stay for an extra day of adulation.

Keeping your cool

Winning a World Championship is the ultimate high for a bridge player — it's an experience that never fades from memory. The play is always exciting. For example, in Rio de Janeiro in 1979, the U.S. team played the mighty Italians in the finals of the World Championships. On the very last hand of the match, my partner, Billy Eisenberg, and I just managed to defeat the opponents' contract by one trick. Had the Italians made that contract, they would have walked away with the prize. To this day, that hand still sends shivers down my spine.

Of course, such high-stakes play can get to your nervous system. In another Championship, I made a costly bidding decision. Billy saw how upset I was and tried to calm me down by saying all the right things, such as "You couldn't be sure," "Don't let it get to you," and "It's only one hand." Then, to show me how calm he was about the situation, he picked up a gum wrapper on the table and lit it, thinking it was a cigarette. Sure, Billy, we were both cool.

Going global: International tournaments

International tournaments are glamorous affairs, usually held in phenomenal locales such as on the French or Italian Riviera. The tournaments often take place in lush casinos, with large cash prizes going to the top finishers. The casino owners hope that after you win in the tournament, you want to put some of your prize money into the casino slot machines or baccarat tables.

International tournaments differ from the United States National Championships in several ways:

- ✔ You compete for cash prizes, not masterpoints. (The ACBL is toying with the idea of initiating cash prize tournaments in the United States. Right now, you play only for glory and masterpoints when you play in U.S. sanctioned tournaments.)

- ✔ You get to play in exotic locales.

- ✔ You play one long session per day, usually from 3 p.m. to 8 p.m., rather than two 3½-hour sessions per day.

- ✔ You have a better chance of meeting and playing against many international stars.

Enjoying the Major Tournaments

What are you going to do at major tournaments, where everyone looks like a bridge shark ready to eat you alive? Well, you have several neat options, which I describe in the following sections.

The bottom line is that you have to get your feet wet by attending a tournament. Even if you only watch until you gather up your courage to play, you won't be sorry. When you give tournament play a whirl, you'll be hooked like the rest of us. Furthermore, if I see you playing in the midnight game, I'll understand.

Playing

The major tournaments offer players a chance to play in four sessions a day. (A session usually consists of 26 hands, played against 13 different pairs of opponents.) Of course, you need the endurance of a marathon runner to even think about playing this much. Major tournaments offer a morning, an afternoon, an evening, and a midnight session. Each session lasts about 3½ hours. Would you believe that some people play three sessions a day and think nothing of it? A few nut cases (who are addicted beyond repair) play all four sessions. One tournament now offers five sessions a day. Give me a break!

I once played in a tournament that lasted nine days (meaning that I could have conceivably played in 36 sessions if I had decided to forgo sleeping entirely). At the end of the tournament, they awarded a prize to the only person who played in all 36 sessions. I expected to see a weight lifter come up and get the award — but, no, it was a little old lady in her 70s!

Big tournaments have novice events for players with 0 to 5 masterpoints as well as events for players who have many more masterpoints. The bottom line is that you wind up playing against people who play like you do.

You are charged by the session — card fees currently range from $8 to $10 a session at most Sectionals, $12 to $15 at most Regionals, and about $5 more per session at national tournaments. Novice events are a bit cheaper, and at the National Championships, they even set aside one "free day" for novices and junior players.

When the session is over, you get a printout, called a *hand record,* of the hands you have just played. You get to review all your mistakes ("accidents" is what you call them), if your partner hasn't already reminded you of them. Hand records are great for discussing hands with your partner or even with your opponents. If you have a guru, you can go over your bids and plays (if you can remember them) with him or her. Everyone likes hand records.

Suppose that you come to a tournament and you don't have a partner. Not to worry, most tournaments have professional matchmakers just waiting for you at the partnership desk. Just tell the people at the partnership desk your vital statistics (how many masterpoints you have), and they will find someone with about the same number of masterpoints as you have. If they can, the match-makers will even try to pair you up with someone of the same or opposite sex, depending on your preference. I'm going to let you in on a little secret: When some people arrive at the partnership desk, they inflate their masterpoint total a bit so they can be fixed up with a player who has more masterpoints and therefore presumably is a better player. Now I'll let you in another little secret: It's even money that the player who gets matched up with the "inflator" has also inflated his or her masterpoint total! What goes around comes around.

The greatest bridge stories of all come from pairings at the partnership desk. Don't be afraid to try it.

Watching

Bridge is a strange game. The people who watch don't pay a cent to attend the tournaments. Only the performers, the players themselves, pay the card fee to participate — sort of a role-reversal of most events. If you get lucky, you can pull up a chair behind some of the best players in the world and watch them perform. But you have to be quiet — very, very quiet.

Pulling a late-nighter

Once at a National Championship, I was on a late-night question-and-answer panel flanked by three panelists and a moderator. We were being peppered with questions from people who never wanted to go to bed. Finally, mercifully, the moderator asked for just one more question. He recognized a player who asked, "Does anyone want to form a quorum for a membership meeting after the panel?" (A few people actually raised their hands.) The moderator said that this wasn't the kind of question he was looking for, and he asked for one more question. A man in the back raised his hand and asked about a bid he had made (which some of his friends had criticized). The late Jim Jacoby, one of the panelists, offered to field the question. He said that anyone who would make such a bid would also vote to attend the quorum.

Attending free lectures

All National Championship tournaments offer at least two free lectures a day, one before the afternoon session and one before the evening session. In addition, the Nationals offer two novice lectures each day. You don't even have to play in the tournament to attend the lectures. The lecturers are often world-renowned players who zero in on a practical topic, and many speakers have quite humorous stories to tell. When I lecture, I go over instructive hands that I was involved in. These hands usually have a humorous ending where someone has goofed big time. The audience gets a big kick out of hearing that experts can go wrong too. I try to work in some really good bidding, play, and defensive tips, along with telling them the crazy things that have happened in my classes. I see smiles on most people's faces when they leave the lecture.

Eating, dancing, and partying

After many evening sessions at a National tournament, free food is offered — and it's good stuff. After the game, everybody is starving, but they seldom run out of food until you get to the front of the line. Just kidding.

Starting at about 11:30 p.m., the tournament organizers offer the players either dancing, professional entertainment, or both. Sometimes the local unit may put on a well-known musical with accompanying bridge lyrics. Again, it's all free. Of course, not everyone sticks around to enjoy it — some people actually choose to go home and go to bed, even though it means missing the midnight games. Keep in mind that some of these loonies have *only* played for 10 or 11 hours by the time the midnight session rolls around.

It seems that most bridge players hate to go to sleep. In truth, you have to unwind a bit. Each night at national tournaments, you can find parties all over the place. If you have social-butterfly instincts and don't mind going to bed at about 3 or 4 in the morning, bridge tournaments are really for you.

Chapter 22

Playing Bridge on Your Computer and Online

In This Chapter
- ▶ Practicing bridge with computer software
- ▶ Making use of bridge games and resources online

*Y*our computer offers you the opportunity to play bridge, no matter who's around, no matter what time of day or night it is, and no matter where you are. In addition, with Internet access, you can tap into the online bridge world and play with bridge fanatics from all over the planet.

Learning Bridge from Software Programs

Sorry to break the news to you, but as yet no one has come up with software that can play bridge at an expert level. However, the quality of the software has improved immensely over the years. The beginner bridge programs in the following sections give you a chance to practice your bidding, card play, and defense without risking the embarrassment of an angry partner. A computer program allows an additional benefit: You can always have the last word by simply quitting the program!

Computer bridge programs, like everything else to do with computers, change fast enough to make your head spin. You can find many new bridge programs wherever you buy software online or from local bridge-supply houses (see Chapter 24 for details on these houses). You probably won't find bridge software at regular computer stores.

Learn to Play Bridge with Audrey Grant

Learn to Play Bridge with Audrey Grant is for the absolute beginner. Grant, a top international instructor, reads the lessons while you focus on the hands and the astounding graphics. The software includes 29 interactive quizzes and a progress screen to track your results.

Introduction to Bridge: Play & Learn with Pat Harrington

Pat Harrington offers two programs in easy-to-use interactive lessons, starting with the absolute basics in lessons 1 to 6 and progressing to topics such as rebids, takeout doubles, preempts, and more in lessons 7 to 13.

Learn Bridge CD

Learn Bridge uses video, sound, and animation to present 40 interactive lessons on basics, bidding, and defense. It comes with an unlimited number of practice quizzes for players at the beginner or intermediate level.

Learn to Play Bridge 1 & 11

The Learn to Play Bridge series includes two programs, and both are available as free downloads through the American Contract Bridge League (ACBL) at www.acbl.org.

- ✔ The first program is a comprehensive course in bridge, designed for people who have never played but want to learn the game.
- ✔ The second program takes the beginner to the intermediate level.

Both of the Learn to Play Bridge programs contain excellent graphics and hundreds of quizzes and other interactive exercises. These programs are a fun and effective way to study the game. They were written by Fred Gittelman, a world-class player and a world-class programmer. *Note:* The programs are available for Windows only.

Surfing Bridge Websites

The Internet provides a vital forum for bridge players all over the world. Currently, you can find hundreds of bridge-related websites that offer everything from bridge games to bridge instruction. Following are my picks for websites where you can play bridge and dig for bridge info.

Playing bridge (against humans)

The Internet allows players all over the world to play against each other online, keep abreast of the latest conventions, find out what's happening in the bridge world, and connect with suitable partners. One can also *kibitz* (or observe) famous experts, because bridge players from novices to experts all enjoy playing online. Here are some tempting options:

- **Bridge Base Online:** Bridge Base Online (BBO) (www.bridgebase. com) is a free online service through which more than 100,000 people (including many new players) from all over the world play bridge. BBO offers possibilities of playing 24/7 with your own partner or choosing a partner. It also has a number of internal clubs, such as the BIL (Beginner-Intermediate Lounge). It offers tournaments at all levels, and ACBL Masterpoints can be won in certain events. You can also match wits or kibitz some of the game's top players.

  BBO regularly produces live broadcasts of major tournaments, including trials for the United States team and the World Championships. You can learn a lot by watching the world's best players in action.

- **MSN Games:** MSN (www.zone.msn.com) is a free online service that offers the possibility to play many different games, including bridge. MSN is a portal to BBO that offers casual, low-pressure play with other bridge players.

- **Okbridge:** OKbridge (www.okbridge.com) bills itself as the original Internet bridge club. For a fee of $100 a year, OKbridge offers the possibility of playing 24/7 with your own foursome, playing with a partner of your own choice, or just digging up a partner if you don't have one. The graphics are top notch.

- **Swan Games:** You can join Swan Games (www.swangames.com), a friendly club with duplicate games, free lessons, and tournaments for all levels. It has an easy-to-use interface for 24/7 play with people around the world. You can also use individual chat boxes for managing private conversations. (*Note:* This club is Windows-compatible only.)

Finding bridge information

You can locate plenty of bridge-related info by doing an online search. For example, just by typing "bridge for beginners" into a search engine, you'll be amazed by what you'll find! In addition, the following websites have links and useful information for all kinds of bridge players:

- ✔ **The American Contract Bridge League:** This fabulous website (www. acbl.org) has loads of information for new players. Joining the ACBL is a very good idea. The ACBL is an excellent source of information of current events in the bridge community, bridge clubs all over the United States, and new conventions and techniques. Membership is $28 for the first year. After that, membership is $37 per year or $105 for three years. If you are 26 years old or younger, membership costs $15 per year.

  The *Bridge Bulletin* is the official monthly publication for members of the ACBL. The magazine includes a special section for new players as well as sections for intermediate and advanced players.

- ✔ **The Bridge World:** *The Bridge World,* the popular offline publication, puts a sampling of its content online at www.bridgeworld.com (see Chapter 24 for more on the offline version of the magazine). Here you find a brief introduction to the game, bridge practice hands and puzzles for intermediate-level players, and the obligatory plea for subscriptions to the offline magazine.

Be sure to check out the "Bridge Glossary" section at this website. Have you ever wondered what an Alcatraz Coup is? Check it out in the Glossary section so you don't wind up in jail!

Part VII
The Part of Tens

The 5th Wave   By Rich Tennant

"Some people just carry a lucky rabbit's foot, but Roger has resorted to the big Gods for his online bridge prowess."

In this part . . .

It wouldn't be a *For Dummies* book without a Part of Tens. I found it very hard to keep the chapters in this part limited to only ten items apiece. After all, I can think of more than ten ways to be kind to your partner. And it wasn't easy to hold down the ten best bridge resources, either. However, you can't go wrong with the ten that have been listed. "Nor can you go wrong reading this book," he added very immodestly.

Chapter 23

Ten Ways to Be a Better Bridge Partner

In This Chapter

▶ Improving your results by treating your partner with consideration

▶ Having fun at the bridge table

Most bridge players value a reliable, happy partner above anything else. Working together as a team is important for the success of your partnership. You both want to win, so you can't gain anything from getting upset when play doesn't go exactly as planned. It seldom does! In this chapter, I give you tips on keeping your partner one happy camper.

Treat Your Partner Like Your Best Friend

Even if you don't know your partner well, treating her with respect improves her play. Treat your partner like your best friend, and you'll be repaid in "spades." (And if you're a pleasant, courteous opponent, you'll win everyone's "hearts.")

Tolerate Your Partner's Errors

Don't keep harping on your partner's errors — just forgive and try to forget (at least until after the game). After all, do you want to be reminded of all the mistakes you've made? (*Everybody* makes mistakes, including you.) If you have constructive criticism, save it for after the session, when you'll both be calmer. Expect (demand) that your partner show you the same respect.

Keep a Poker Face

Never make any facial or body movements or use mannerisms that indicate whether you're pleased or displeased with a bid or play. You'll lose the table's respect. Facial expressions and body gestures can be construed as illegal signals.

Deal Well with Disaster

A truly good partnership handles the inevitable disaster with a touch of humor. If your partner doesn't have to worry that you'll have an apoplectic fit whenever something goes wrong, he'll play better.

Play Conventions You Both Want to Play

Don't force your partner to play your favorite conventions (such as artificial bids). A partner worried about a convention inevitably makes more errors in the bidding, play, and defense, not to mention screwing up the convention if it comes up.

Pick Up the Slack for the Weaker Player

The better player in a partnership should make the weaker player feel at ease. Make your bids, leads, and signals as simple and clear as possible, and don't give an inexperienced partner tough contracts to play. When you judge that partner is going to play the hand, bid somewhat conservatively.

Own Up to Your Own Errors

Avoid the human tendency to lay your own errors at your partner's doorstep. A weaker partner will feel good to know that you, the stronger player, make errors as well — and are a big enough person to admit them.

Offer Words of Encouragement

Give your partner a few words of support after the hand is over, particularly if she doesn't make her contract. "Tough luck" and "Nice try" go over better than "My great-grandmother could've made that hand in her sleep."

Treat Your Partner the Same Whether You Win or Lose

When the session is over, win or lose, tell your partner how much you enjoyed playing with him (no matter how you feel). Kind words mean the world to a player who knows that he hasn't played well. It also shows class.

Know When to Have Fun

When all is said and done, you play bridge to have fun, and so does your partner. You've done your job if your partner leaves the table happy.

Chapter 24

Ten Great Bridge Resources

*T*his book tells you everything you need to know to sit down and start playing bridge. When you get hooked on the game, you may want to reach out for bridge information that goes beyond this book. In this chapter I point out ten great references and resources that you may find handy.

The American Contract Bridge League

Joining the American Contract Bridge League (ACBL) is a "must do." The ACBL is an excellent source of information about current events in the bridge community. The League can help you find bridge clubs throughout the country as well as locate local and national tournaments all over America. At times they even offer sanctioned bridge cruises at sea. The ACBL also maintains a fabulous website (www.acbl.org) with a wealth of information for new players.

Bridge Bulletin is the official publication of the ACBL and is worth many times more than the yearly dues. The magazine includes a special "New Players Section" as well as sections for intermediate and advanced players with monthly articles by various bridge writers, including yours truly.

Membership is $28 for the first year. After that, membership runs $37 per year or $105 for three years. If you are 26 years old or younger, membership costs only $15 per year. (The ACBL encourages younger players as much as it can.) You can contact the ACBL by phone at 662-253-3100.

Your Local Bridge Club

The local bridge club is a great place to go when you're starting out with bridge. Clubs offer all kinds of enticements, but best of all you can get together and play with people who are at approximately your skill level. Nothing can supplant actual play for gaining experience. Suddenly the books you read, even this one, make more sense because you actually experience what you read about.

Visit the ACBL website for more information about how to contact bridge clubs in your area.

Adult Education Classes

Some adult schools offer bridge classes at modest prices and give you an opportunity to meet beginning bridge players like yourself. Check your local high school or parks and recreation department for adult education classes in your area. You may get lucky.

Your Local Library and Bookstore

Most libraries have a reasonable selection of bridge books, and borrowing a book is cheaper than buying one, especially if you're just starting out with the game. Of course, your local bookstore also may have the latest bridge books if you want one of your own.

The Daily Bridge Column in Your Newspaper

 Some people who don't even play bridge read the bridge columns because they're amusing. A good column is informative, instructive, and entertaining. The major bridge columnists usually come through on all three counts. Here are your five best bets, in no particular order (they're all good):

- ✔ "Bridge," by Frank Stewart
- ✔ "Goren on Bridge," by Tannah Hirsch

- ✔ "The Aces on Bridge," by Bobby Wolff
- ✔ *The New York Times* bridge column, by Phillip Alder
- ✔ "Bridge," by Steve Becker

Shop around in other major newspapers if you can't find the column you want to read in your regular newspaper. (Try finding additional newspapers at your local library or bookstore.)

Bridge Magazines

Some of the information in the following magazines may go a little over your head until you have played a little bridge, but all of them also offer articles for beginners.

Bridge Bulletin

See "The American Contract Bridge League," earlier in this chapter, for more information on the ACBL and its offerings, which include this fabulous magazine.

The Bridge World

The Bridge World is the granddaddy of all bridge publications and is the most respected bridge publication in the world. Unfortunately, the magazine is aimed primarily at advanced players. However, don't despair; *The Bridge World* offers information for players of all levels, including beginners, at its website (www.bridgeworld.com).

You can contact *The Bridge World* at the website or e-mail circulation@ bridgeworld.com for current subscription information.

Bridge Software Programs

Many excellent teaching programs are available for the computer. In Chapter 22 I mention some of the current programs available for beginning players.

The Internet

The Internet is such a great resource for bridge players, I devote most of Chapter 22 to the subject. You can take to the Net to find all kinds of bridge information and to play bridge online. By the way, my website, www. kantarbridge.com, is loaded with tips, quizzes, and even a section on bridge humor. Check it out.

Bridge Supply Houses

Want a bridge book, bridge software, or a bridge-related gift? You can get all of these items, plus a friendly voice, if you call one of these supply houses. You can ask for a free catalog before you make any truly momentous decisions.

American Contract Bridge League, Inc.
6575 Windchase Blvd.
Horn Lake, MS 38637-1523
Phone 662-253-3100
Fax 662-253-3187
Website www.acbl.org

Baron Barclay Bridge Supplies
3600 Chamberlain Ln., #206
Louisville, KY 40241
Phone 800-274-2221
Fax 502-426-2044
E-mail baronbarclay@baronbarclay.com
Website www.baronbarclay.com

Master Point Press Publishers
331 Douglas Ave.
Toronto, ON, Canada
M5M 1H2
Phone 416-781-0351
Fax 416-781-1831
E-mail info@masterpointpress.com
Website www.masterpointpress.com

Bridge Travel

Would you like to go on a bridge cruise? Would you like to spend a week at a beautiful five-star hotel and be surrounded with bridge activities? Read on.

Bridge instruction on cruise ships

Cruise ships offer an unequaled opportunity to immerse yourself in bridge activities. Many major cruise ships set sail with a bridge teacher on board. When the ship is at sea, you get a lesson in the morning and the chance to enter a friendly tournament in the afternoon. However, you can just play bridge in the card room, if you prefer. Check with the cruise line you're interested in to verify whether it offers a bridge program.

Bridge tours

Bridge tours offer great opportunities to play bridge to your heart's content at some really great places. I can unhesitatingly recommend several travel agencies that deal specifically with bridge groups, but you can type "contract bridge tours" into your favorite search engine for more options.

Finesse West Tours
Phone 800-548-8062 or 626-564-9327
Website www.finessewest.com

Bridge Holidays with Roberta and Arnold Salob
Phone 800-807-7009
Website www.bridgeholidays.com

The Cruise Professionals
Phone 800-265-3838
Website www.cruiseprofessionals.com

Alice Travel
Phone 800-229-2542
Website www.alicetravel.com

Appendix

Acol Bidding System

O ne great aspect of the game of bridge is that it's played the same way worldwide. However, many different countries use their own bidding system to arrive at the final contract (and naturally, every country thinks its system is best). The system I use in this book is called *Standard American*. Another system, called *Acol*, is played primarily in the United Kingdom, but it enjoys popularity in other parts of the world as well.

Nowadays, when so many people play in tournaments and play online with players around the globe, being aware of other popular bidding systems such as Acol is helpful. Standard American and Acol bidding methods have many similarities but many differences, too. In this appendix I explain the differences, and when similarities occur, I refer you to the chapter where the topic can be found.

Getting a Handle on Acol

Following are the two paramount features that differentiate Acol from many other bidding systems:

- ✔ The range of an opening 1NT bid is 12 to 14 high-card points (HCP), called the *weak* notrump (as opposed to 15 to 17 HCP, a *strong* notrump, in Standard American).
- ✔ Bidding is opened with a four-card major suit (instead of the mandatory five-card major suit opening in Standard American).

The underlying principles of Acol are to keep the bidding as simple and natural as possible, always looking for an eight-card major-suit fit or longer. It's a system based on the sound premise that the sooner you limit your hand (telling your partner your strength and distribution), the easier it is to arrive at the best final contract.

Of late, Acol in the U.K has seen a movement toward far more preemptive bidding with weak hands and long suits. The idea is to take away needed bidding space from the opponents who figure to have the balance of power.

Opponents don't like to be preempted. In fact, they hate it because they lose needed bidding space to describe their hands. If they hate it, it must be a good idea.

Opening 1NT (12 to 14 HCP)

Far and away, the most common opening bid is 1NT. With such a high frequency, you definitely need to know what strength and distribution is needed. In Acol, the strength is 12 to 14 HCP, and the distribution must be any 4-3-3-3 or 4-4-3-2 pattern or be a 5-3-3-2 pattern with clubs or diamonds as the five-card suit. Opening 1NT with a five-card major is not part of the system.

In this section I walk you through some bidding scenarios involved in the weak notrump so you can get a feel for this important part of the Acol system.

Responding to 1NT with a balanced hand

Your partner has opened 1NT; suppose the next player passes, and it's your turn. Don't look now, but you are the captain because your partner has limited his hand to both strength and distribution. Placing the contract is up to you.

As captain, your troubles are over if you have a balanced hand that doesn't have a four- or five-card major. A balanced hand facing a balanced hand thinks notrump — and bids notrump if strong enough to bid!

As responder, add your HCP to partner's. You need about 25 HCP between the two hands to make 3NT, your goal contract. As a bonus, add one point to your hand if you have a five-card suit headed by two of the top-three or three of the top-five honors. Here are the general rules for responding with a balanced hand:

- ✔ **With 0 to 10 HCP:** Pass.

- ✔ **With 11 to 12 HCP:** Bid 2NT (which invites your partner to bid 3NT with a maximum 14 points).

- ✔ **With 13 to 18 HCP:** Bid 3NT.

- ✔ **With 19 to 20 HCP:** Bid 4NT (which invites your partner to bid 6NT with a maximum 14 points).

- ✔ **With 21 to 24 HCP:** Close your eyes and bid 6NT. Okay, open them.

Responding to 1NT with one or two four-card majors

You know that a balanced hand facing a balanced hand plays best in notrump; however, a 4-4 major-suit fit usually plays at least one trick better in a trump contract. To discover whether a 4-4 major-suit fit exists, the responder has *Stayman,* a world famous convention, available. It is an artificial response of 2♣ made with 11+ HCP, asking the opener if he has a four-card major. (See Chapter 11 for more details on Stayman.) It works like this facing a 12 to 14 opening 1NT bid:

Opener (You)	Responder (Your Partner)
1NT (with 12–14 HCP)	2♣ (Do you have a four-card major?)
2♦ (Sorry, I don't)	2NT (with 11–12 HCP; an invitational bid)
	3NT (with 13–18 HCP)
2♥ or 2♠ (shows a four-card major)	

If the responder has four cards in the opener's major, the responder raises to the three level with 11 to 12 HCP, and to game with 13+ HCP. (To make game in a major with a 4-4 fit, the partnership needs 24 or 25 HCP.) If the responder has four cards in the other major, he bids 2NT with 11 to 12 HCP or 3NT with 13+ HCP.

With 4-3-3-3 distribution and the four-card suit a major, the responder does best *not* to use Stayman and just stick it out in notrump.

Responding to 1NT with a five- or six-card major: Using the Jacoby transfer

As the responder, your objective is to play in a major suit if you have an eight-card fit or longer. If you're lucky enough to have a five- or six-card major, your first move is to *transfer* the play to your partner's hand by bidding 2♦ with five or six hearts, forcing partner to bid 2♥; or by bidding 2♥ with five or six spades, forcing partner to bid 2♠. Check out Chapter 11 to find some examples of the Jacoby transfer.

Using the Jacoby transfer with a six-card major

When you have a six-card major suit facing a 1NT opening bid, you know you have at least an eight-card major-suit fit. By agreement, you respond in the suit directly in rank *beneath* your major suit. Holding six hearts, bid 2♦, forcing your partner to bid 2♥. Holding six spades, bid 2♥, forcing your partner to bid 2♠. You have transferred the play of the hand to your partner!

Opener (Your Partner)	Responder (You)
1NT (with 12–14 HCP)	2♦ (forces your partner to bid 2♥)
2♥	Pass (with 0–9 HCP)
	3♥ (with 10–11 HCP)
	4♥ (with 12+ HCP)

Use the same formula with six spades, but start with 2♥.

Using the Jacoby transfer with a five-card major

Remember, when you transfer with a five-card major, partner expects you to have at least five cards in that major. I show you a very common follow-up bid you will often make after you have transferred, assuming you're strong enough to bid again and have a balanced hand (with 11+ HCP).

Opener (Your Partner)	Responder (You)
1NT	2♥ (forces partner to bid 2♠)
2♠	Pass (with 0–10 HCP)
	2NT (with 11–12 HCP; invitational)
	3NT (with 13+ HCP)

Notice that you do *not* raise spades, a bid that shows six spades. Your partner *knows* you have five spades so if you rebid 2NT or 3NT or bid another suit, he will return to spades with three spades. Keep in mind, your partner may have only two spades!

If you have a five-card major and a five-card minor with 12+ HCP, transfer into your major (you know how) and then bid your minor at the three level, a game force. If you have 5-5 in the majors, start with 2♥, showing five spades, and then bid *3♥*, showing five hearts. Partner must have at least three cards in one of your majors. You've struck gold! When a 5-5 hand uncovers a 5-3 major-suit fit, as few as 23 HCP can be enough for game.

Opener (Your Partner)	Responder (You)
1NT (with 12–14 HCP)	2♦ or 2♥
2♥ or 2♠	3♣ or 3♦

When you have an eight-card fit or longer, the more distributional the two hands are, the fewer the HCP that are needed to take tricks. Five-card suits headed by two of the top three or three of the top five honors are worth an extra point. Six-card suits of similar strength are worth two extra points. Having opened 1NT, your partner has some length and likely some honor-card strength in these suits, making it easier to take tricks in the suit.

Opening the Bidding with a Suit at the One Level

Because you can't open one notrump with every hand that has 12 to 14 HCP, (it may not be balanced), you have to make do by opening in a suit with 12+ HCP. I show you the guidelines:

- **With 15 to 19 HCP:** Open with your *longest* suit (which has at least four cards). With any 4-3-3-3 pattern, open the four-card suit. With any 4-4-3-2 pattern, open with the *higher* ranking of the two suits; however, with 4-4 in the majors, open 1♥, giving partner a chance to respond 1♠.

- **With three four-card suits and a *red* singleton:** Open the suit beneath the singleton: 1♦ with a singleton heart, and 1♣ with a singleton diamond.

- **With three four-card suits and a *black* singleton:** Open the middle suit: 1♦ with a singleton spade, and 1♥ with a singleton club.

- **With two five-card suits and 11+ HCP:** Open the higher ranking suit.

- **With a six-card suit:** 11+ HCP is enough to open.

- **With a seven-card suit:** In this case, ten or more HCP will do.

Responding to a one-level opening bid

Your partner opens the bidding, second hand passes, and now it's your turn. Your duty is to try to tell partner your strength and distribution, limiting your hand as quickly as possible. You have six options:

1. **Pass (zero to five HCP).** This option is the one your partner hates to hear.

2. **Bid your longest suit at the one level, if possible, called *one over one* (six or more HCP).** At times, you may not be able to bid your longest suit at the one level. Say partner opens 1♥ and you have five diamonds and seven HCP. You aren't strong enough to bid 2♦, a *two-over-one* response (nine or more HCP). The solution is to respond 1NT.

3. **Make a two-over-one response showing nine or more HCP with a five-card suit, or ten or more HCP with a four-card minor suit.** A response of 2♥ promises a five-card suit or longer.

4. **Raise your partner's suit to the two, three, or four level.**

5. **Respond 1NT, 2NT, or 3NT.**

6. **Jump in another suit, called *a jump shift*.** This response, the strongest option, is the one your partner loves to hear.

Options 2, 3, and 6 are *unlimited* responses (no upper limit) and therefore *forcing*. Options 4 and 5 are *limited* responses because they have a narrow range and are *not forcing*. Assuming you have enough to respond, I give you the guidelines in the following sections.

Responding at the one level with two four- or five-card suits

When responding with two four-card suits, bid up the line. If partner opens 1♦ and you have four hearts and four spades, respond 1♥. If you have four clubs and four hearts, respond 1♥, a cheaper response than 2♣. With two five-card suits, respond in the *higher* ranking suit.

This response is called responding *up the line* with four-card suits and *down the line* with five card suits.

Responding at the two level, a two-over-one response

Holding a *five*-card minor that would have to be shown at the two level and a *four*-card major that can be shown at the one level, bid the minor first with 13+ HCP (intending to bid the major next); and bid the major first with less.

Responding in notrump

A common response to a one-level opening bid is some number of notrump. I describe these notrump responses, because you will be using them often.

> ✔ **1NT:** This response shows six to nine HCP, not necessarily balanced, and denies a four-card major. However, a 1NT response specifically to a 1♣ opening bid shows eight to ten HCP, balanced, and denies a four-card major, usually your first option.
>
> ✔ **2NT:** This response describes 10 to 12 HCP, balanced.
>
> ✔ **3NT:** This response describes 13 to 15 HCP, balanced.

Having support for partner's minor suit opening bid

The Acol responses when you have support for partner's minor-suit opening bid are almost identical to Standard American. You can check out Chapter 11 for more details on responding to a minor-suit opening bid.

Having support for partner's major-suit opening bid

When raising your partner's suit directly with *four*-card support, add extra points for side-suit shortness. A commonly used method is the one-three-five scale:

> ✔ **For each doubleton, add one point.**
>
> ✔ **For a singleton, add three points.**
>
> ✔ **For a void, add a whopping five points.**

Add your HCP to your short-suit points, and the grand total is considered the number of *support points* (SP) you have. Trump support with a short side suit translates to extra tricks in the play.

Opener (Your Partner)	Responder (You)
1♥	2♥ shows 6–9 SP.
	3♥ shows 10–12 SP. (This bid is called a *limit raise* and is invitational rather than forcing.)
	A direct jump to 4♥ shows a "weak freak" with 5+ trumps, a side-suit singleton or void, and 5–8 HCP. It is a preemptive response.

With 12+ HCP and four-card trump support, bid your longest side suit and then jump to *game* in partner's suit, a strong sequence.

Avoid raising partner's 1♥ or 1♠ opening bid with three-card support unless you have a side-suit singleton (or void) or three-card support to die for (AK*x*, AQ*x*, KQ*x*) plus a *small* doubleton on the side.

Jumping the bidding: A jump shift

When your partner opens the bidding and you have 17+ HCP, a slam may be just around the corner and your partner must be forewarned! The alert signal is a *jump shift,* jumping one level higher than needed to show this powerhouse responding hand.

Opener (Your Partner)	Responder (You)
1♦	2♥, 2♠, or 3♣ (the three possible jump shifts)

- ✔ **With a five-card suit:** 18+ HCP (or 17 HCP with strong intermediates in the long suit)
- ✔ **With a six-card suit:** 17+ HCP (or 16 HCP with strong intermediates)
- ✔ **With a seven-card suit:** 16+ HCP (or 15 HCP with strong intermediates)

More often than not, intermediate cards in long suits (9s and 10s)are the deciding factor when faced with a close bidding decision.

Opener's Second Bid: The All-Important Rebid

You have opened the bidding and your partner has responded at the one level, an unlimited response showing six or more HCP. Now it's your turn to further describe your hand, hopefully with a limit bid. It all begins by pigeon-holing the strength of your opening hand in three ranges:

- ✔ **12 to 15 HCP:** Minimum
- ✔ **16 to 18 HCP:** Intermediate
- ✔ **19+ HCP:** Powerhouse

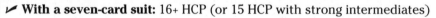

Limiting your hand by rebidding notrump

After your partner's first response in a new suit, your rebid is frequently some number of notrump. In the following table, I show you what you need for each of your three likely notrump rebids after a *one* level response.

Opener (You)	Responder (Your Partner)
1♦	1♠ (with 6+ HCP, one over one, with 4+ spades)
1NT (with 15–17 HCP, balanced)	
2NT (with 18–19 HCP, balanced) Any continuation by responder is a game force.	
3NT (with 6- or 7-card solid-suit plus stoppers in the unbid suits; 16–18 HCP)	

Limiting your hand by rebidding a five- or six-card suit

A weak five-card suit can be rebid if there are no alternatives, but a six-card suit is always rebid.

Opener (You)	Responder (Your Partner)
1♥	1♠, 1NT, 2♣, or 2♦ (the four possible responses lower than 2♥)
2♥ (with 12–15 HCP, 5+ hearts; minimum rebid)	
3♥ (with 16–18 HCP, 6+ hearts; a *jump* rebid)	
4♥ (with 18–20 HCP, 6+ hearts; a powerhouse rebid that could lead to a slam if partner has support along with 12+ HCP)	

Strong five-, six-, or seven-card suits (suits headed by two of the top-three or three of the top-five honors), *demand* an upgrade: One extra point for a five-card suit, two for a six-card suit, and three for a seven-card suit. Such suits take extra tricks!

Limiting your hand by supporting partner's suit

Happiness is having an opening bid; true happiness is having an opening bid with four-card support for partner's major-suit response. I show you how to translate that happiness into winning contracts by raising your partner's suit to the proper level.

Opener (You)	Responder (Your Partner)
1♥	1♠ (6+ HCP, 4+ spades)
2♠ (Four-card support, 13–15 SP)	
3♠ (Four-card support, 16–18 SP, invitational)	
4♠ (Four-card support, 19–20 SP) Use one-three-five scale when supporting.	

Rebids by the opener after a one-level response

In response to your opening bid, your partner makes an unlimited response at the one level. The sky could be the limit, or your partner may have as few as six HCP. Other than a 1NT rebid showing 15 to 17 points, almost all other rebids are similar to those in Standard American (see Chapter 12).

Limited rebids by the opener after a two-over-one-response

When partner bids a new suit at the *two* level, your partner is still unlimited and has nine or more HCP with a five-card suit, or ten or more HCP with at least a four-card suit.

With a balanced hand, you can rebid 2NT, a game force, or 3NT. The following chart illustrates these two rebids.

Opener (You)	Responder (Your Partner)
1♥	2♣ (9+ HCP with a five-card suit or 10+ HCP with a four-card suit or longer)
2NT (15–17 HCP, forcing to game)	
3NT (18–19 HCP)	

Unlimited rebids by the opener after a two-over-one response

You can't always limit your hand by rebidding your suit, rebidding notrump, or raising your partner. You may have a second suit that is screaming to be mentioned. Bidding a second suit is considered an unlimited rebid. I show you in this table how it works.

Opener (You)	Responder (Your Partner)
1♥	2♣ (9+ HCP with a five-card suit or longer, 10+ HCP with a four-card suit or longer)
2♦ (A *lower*-ranking suit shows 12–18 HCP. It is a one-round force; partner cannot pass)	
2♠ (A *higher*-ranking suit shows 16+ HCP. It's called a *reverse* and is a game force.)	

Responder's Rebid, the Fourth Bid

Partner opens, you make an unlimited response, and your partner makes a minimum limited rebid showing 12 to 15 HCP. What should you do? Of course, your degree of fit with partner's suit as well as the strength of your long suit enters into this decision. Think of your hand in these terms:

✔ **6 to 9 HCP:** Minimum hand. Either pass or make a nonforcing rebid.

✔ **10 to 12 HCP:** Worth a second bid; make an invitational rebid.

✔ **13+ HCP:** Get thee to at least a game contract by either bidding a game contract or introducing a new suit, forcing partner to bid.

If partner's rebid shows an intermediate hand (16 to 18 HCP):

✔ 9+ HCP should be enough to make some game even without a fit.

✔ 8+ HCP is enough to bid game with a known eight-card major-suit fit. In any case, make an invitational bid.

If your partner's rebid shows a strong hand in the 19 to 20 HCP range, he has either jumped to game already or has made a game-forcing jump shift. Facing a jump shift, 13+ HCP is enough for slam in a suit if you have an eight-card fit or longer. Lacking a fit, try 6NT. Just do it! (Check out Chapter 13 for more details on responder's rebid.)

Wreaking Havoc with Preemptive Opening Bids

Opponents do not like to be preempted; all the more reason to make as many preemptive opening bids as you can.

✔ **Weak two bids:** Strong two-level opening bids have evolved in the United Kingdom in order to make room for more preemptive opening bids. While keeping the strong 2♣ opening bid, weak two opening bids in diamonds, hearts, and spades have become increasingly popular. For details on weak two opening bids as well as the strong 2♣ opening, head for Chapter 10.

✔ **Three-level opening bids:** These bids are identical to weak twos but require a seven-card suit.

✔ **The gambling 3NT opening bid:** Are you ready for this? It shows a solid (headed by the AKQ) seven- or eight-card minor with no outside stoppers! Your partner has to decide whether to pass holding outside stoppers or whether to escape to your long minor suit. If partner doesn't know which minor you have, he will bid 4♣, 5♣, or even 6♣! If your suit is clubs, pass. If your suit is diamonds, correct to the same number of diamonds. If partner *knows* your solid suit is diamonds (partner may have the ace, king, or queen of clubs and make a Sherlock Holmes deduction), he can bid four, five, or six diamonds directly.

✔ **Four-level opening bids:** These bids are similar to weak two- or three-level opening bids as to suit strength and point count. However, the bid shows an eight-card suit, or possibly a 7-4 pattern.

Making Strong Two-Level Opening Bids

In the following section, I show you how to deal with very strong opening bids, dealing with both balanced and unbalanced hands — hands you love to be looking at.

The Acol 2♣ opening bid

An opening bid of 2♣ is an artificial bid showing a powerful one- or two-suited hand with 19+ HCP. It describes a hand that can take nine to ten tricks facing nothing! The negative response is 2♦ showing zero to seven HCP. Any response other than 2♦ is a game force. After a 2♦ response, if opener rebids 2NT, showing 23 to 24 HCP, a rebid that can include a five-card suit, responder can pass.

Some Acol players still use *two* strong artificial opening bids:

- ✔ 2♦ (called *Benjamin*) is a super-strong game forcing opening bid. It almost always shows an unbalanced hand that can take at least ten tricks. However, if opener rebids 2NT with 23 to 24 HCP or 3NT with 25 to 26 HCP, he does show a balanced hand that can include a five-card suit.

- ✔ 2♣, the weaker Acol bid, shows 19+ HCP, is *always* unbalanced, and describes a hand that can take eight to nine tricks. It is not a game-forcing opening bid.

The 2NT opening bid

An opening bid of 2NT shows 20 to 22 HCP, balanced, and can contain a five-card major. The responder can use both Stayman and transfer responses.

Defensive Bidding

After they open the bidding, you and your partner need not take a vow of silence. You each have several ways of joining the fun and perhaps getting the bid, or pushing them too high! Your two main weapons are the overcall and the takeout double. You can also flex your muscles with a 1NT overcall.

The one-level overcall

One-level overcalls log in with 8 to 16 HCP and a minimum of five cards in the suit. With as few as 8 to 10 HCP, your suit *must* be strong (typically three of the top five honors), because it is often used as a lead directing bid.

Because Acol parallels Standard American in this regard, you can check out Chapter 14 for more information on the one-level overcall.

The preemptive jump overcall

A jump overcall is an overcall one level higher than necessary. For example, if the opening bid to your right is 1♦, a jump to 2♥, 2♠, or 3♣ would be a jump overcall. It describes a hand similar to a weak two opening bid, preemptive in nature. It is lead directing, with typically six to nine HCP. This weak or preemptive jump overcall takes away one level of bidding from the opponents, who probably have the majority of the high-card strength. See Chapter 14 for more info on this topic.

In some parts of the United Kingdom, the jump overcall is played as strong, some call it *intermediate,* with 12 to 16 HCP along with a good looking six- or seven-card suit. It shows a hand that can take close to eight tricks. It is not a forcing bid.

Some hedgers play weak jump overcalls, not vulnerable, and the stronger variety vulnerable, thinking they have the best of both worlds. See Chapter 20 for more on being vulnerable or not vulnerable.

The takeout double

The Acol and Standard American versions of the takeout double are virtually identical, including the responses. See Chapter 15 for details on when to make a takeout double and how to respond to one.

Index

Notes

Notes

Notes

Notes

Notes

Math & Science

Algebra I For Dummies,
2nd Edition
978-0-470-55964-2

Biology For Dummies,
2nd Edition
978-0-470-59875-7

Chemistry For Dummies,
2nd Edition
978-1-1180-0730-3

Geometry For Dummies,
2nd Edition
978-0-470-08946-0

Pre-Algebra Essentials
For Dummies
978-0-470-61838-7

Microsoft Office

Excel 2010 For Dummies
978-0-470-48953-6

Office 2010 All-in-One
For Dummies
978-0-470-49748-7

Office 2011 for Mac
For Dummies
978-0-470-87869-9

Word 2010
For Dummies
978-0-470-48772-3

Music

Guitar For Dummies,
2nd Edition
978-0-7645-9904-0

Clarinet For Dummies
978-0-470-58477-4

iPod & iTunes
For Dummies,
9th Edition
978-1-118-13060-5

Pets

Cats For Dummies,
2nd Edition
978-0-7645-5275-5

Dogs All-in One
For Dummies
978-0470-52978-2

Saltwater Aquariums
For Dummies
978-0-470-06805-2

Religion & Inspiration

The Bible For Dummies
978-0-7645-5296-0

Catholicism For Dummies,
2nd Edition
978-1-118-07778-8

Spirituality For Dummies,
2nd Edition
978-0-470-19142-2

Self-Help & Relationships

Happiness For Dummies
978-0-470-28171-0

Overcoming Anxiety
For Dummies,
2nd Edition
978-0-470-57441-6

Seniors

Crosswords For Seniors
For Dummies
978-0-470-49157-7

iPad 2 For Seniors
For Dummies, 3rd Edition
978-1-118-17678-8

Laptops & Tablets
For Seniors For Dummies,
2nd Edition
978-1-118-09596-6

Smartphones & Tablets

BlackBerry For Dummies,
5th Edition
978-1-118-10035-6

Droid X2 For Dummies
978-1-118-14864-8

HTC ThunderBolt
For Dummies
978-1-118-07601-9

MOTOROLA XOOM
For Dummies
978-1-118-08835-7

Sports

Basketball For Dummies,
3rd Edition
978-1-118-07374-2

Football For Dummies,
2nd Edition
978-1-118-01261-1

Golf For Dummies,
4th Edition
978-0-470-88279-5

Test Prep

ACT For Dummies,
5th Edition
978-1-118-01259-8

ASVAB For Dummies,
3rd Edition
978-0-470-63760-9

The GRE Test For
Dummies, 7th Edition
978-0-470-00919-2

Police Officer Exam
For Dummies
978-0-470-88724-0

Series 7 Exam
For Dummies
978-0-470-09932-2

Web Development

HTML, CSS, & XHTML
For Dummies, 7th Edition
978-0-470-91659-9

Drupal For Dummies,
2nd Edition
978-1-118-08348-2

Windows 7

Windows 7
For Dummies
978-0-470-49743-2

Windows 7
For Dummies,
Book + DVD Bundle
978-0-470-52398-8

Windows 7 All-in-One
For Dummies
978-0-470-48763-1